Anne Schröder (ed.)

Crossing Borders

Afrikanische Studien

Band 23

LIT

Anne Schröder (ed.)

CROSSING BORDERS

Interdisciplinary Approaches to Africa

LIT

Bibliographic information published by Die Deutsche Bibliothek
Die Deutsche Bibliothek lists this publication in the Deutsche
Nationalbibliografie; detailed bibliographic data are available in the
Internet at http://dnb.ddb.de.

ISBN 3-8258-7787-6

© LIT VERLAG Münster   2004
Grevener Str./Fresnostr. 2   48159 Münster
Tel. 0251-23 50 91   Fax 0251-23 19 72
e-Mail: lit@lit-verlag.de   http://www.lit-verlag.de

Distributed in North America by:

Transaction Publishers
New Brunswick (U.S.A.) and London (U.K.)

Transaction Publishers
Rutgers University
35 Berrue Circle
Piscataway, NJ 08854

Tel.: (732) 445 - 2280
Fax: (732) 445 - 3138
for orders (U. S. only):
toll free (888) 999 - 6778

Acknowledgments

The annual *Afrika in Chemnitz* series of events and activities, and thus this collection of articles, would have been impossible to realise without the help and support of numerous committed people. I would therefore like to take this opportunity to express my sincere thanks to everybody involved.

For the past four years, I have been supported by many colleagues from the various departments involved, especially by Sebastian Berg, Christoph Haase, Ulrike Brummert, Hans Kastendiek, and Josef Schmied, as well as by the University's 'Gleichstellungsbeauftragte' (equal opportunities officer) Karla Kebsch.

I am also grateful to the Studentenwerk Chemnitz-Zwickau, and most notably Dirk Hammer and Christiane Lorenz, for supporting us – not only financially – from the very beginnings. The same holds for Eva Auerbach und Martina Lorenz from the Internationales Universitätskolleg, and the Konrad-Adenauer Stiftung, Bildungswerk Leipzig.

In addition, the *Afrika in Chemnitz* series has been supported by many local firms and organisations, such as the 371 Stadtmagazin – most notably André Schenkel, the Frauenzentrum Lila Villa e.V. – especially Iris Tätzel-Machute, the Thalia Buchhandlung, the Verein Partnerschaft Chemnitz-Timbuktu e.V., Verein der Mosambikaner as well as societies and organisations at University level such as the StuRa, the PEB Studentenkeller, the Windkanal e.V. and many more.

But most of all, I would like to thank all those committed students and former students who – during the past four years – have spent much of their time and energy and without whose help *Afrika in Chemnitz* would neither have started nor would it have continued. My most heartfelt thanks thus go first of all to my co-organizer Tabea Putschli, but also to Andrea Vasas, Balbina Ebong, Bernadett Putschli, Bolang Butake, Brenda Gwanvoma, Chidi Cegwuom, Christian Friese, Franziska Tauber, Ines Brunner, Inga Riedemann, Inken Carstensens, Jean-Marie Kengne, Katharina Herda, Kati Brucksch, Katrin Höppner, Kay Strauss, Kristiane Dürich, Mark Schreiber, Martina Schäfer, Miguel Ziad, Rodolphe Fotsing, Sandra Otto, Shokri Alyaser, Simon Enumah, Soromo Haman, Susann Bunzel, Susanne Rantzsch, Sylvia Voigt, Thomas Pencs, to all the helpful members of the *Club der Kulturen* and to whomever I might have forgotten. To you all, I dedicate this book. I hope you'll like it!

Anne Schröder

Hello Tomorrow…

I stood there, a bundle of mixed feelings, looking at them all;
The people who had walked with me from the days I could not even remember
And there I was, walking away from them.

It felt like cutting away a part of me,
And words can't tell how bad it hurt
But I knew that the wounds heal eventually, and with time
I would put first things first.

I left my home behind, looking forward
To the adventure that lay ahead
I had heard a lot of things about going to face the unknown,
Yet I wanted to find that out on my own.

Each time I shut my eyes, I heard the voice in me say
"It won't be easy": that was a fact; still I had to take the chance
And the moment I stepped on foreign soil,
I knew that the journey had just begun.

A long winding road stretched out before me …
I took a deep breath and look up to the sky
"I'll be alright" I told myself …
A journey of a thousand miles begins with the first step …

BOLANG BUTAKE

Contents

Introduction 11

KERSTIN BOLZT
Cultural Manifestations of Collective Identity in Contemporary Zimbabwean
Literature 13

JOYCE A. ABUNAW
Writing Woman Writing Culture: The Scripting of *Potent Secrets* 43

BOLE BUTAKE
Kamerun – Reliving German Occupation through Theatre:
Zintgraff and the Battle of Mankon by Bole Butake & Gilbert Doho 53

VIRGINIA MUKWESHA AND FLORIAN HETZE
The Presence of the Past for the Future
Virginia Mukwesha: A Modern Approach to an Ancient Music 61

BIRGIT ENGLERT
Africa Raps Back: Reflections on HipHop from Tanzania and South Africa 77

JIGAL BEEZ
How Asterix Learnt Swahili:
The Tanzanian Appropriation of a French Comic 99

EVELYN WLADARSCH
Notions on Time in Burkina Faso 117

HANS-GEORG WOLF
Cultural Approaches to Second Language Varieties of English: A Call for New
Methodologies and a Review of Some Findings on (West) African English ... 133

ANNE SCHRÖDER
Deeper Insights through Triangulation:
Experiences from a Sociolinguistic Study on Pidgin English in Cameroon 151

SEBASTIAN BERG
Black Scousers: The Long Presence of British Africans in Liverpool 183

KATRIN FISCHER
Not just Making the Faces Black: The Representation of African Americans in
Contemporary Crime and Detective Fiction 197

EMELDA NGUFOR SAMBA AND SEBASTIAN BERG
African Popular Theatre in Diasporas: Racism and Identity 215

List of Contributors 233

Introduction

This collection of articles has been inspired by the great success of and lively discussions during the *Afrika in Chemnitz* series of events at the Chemnitz University of Technology. As we could see in the preparation of this series of events and during the lectures, there is a vast number of people both working on and being interested in a variety of issues concerning the African continent. However, we also discovered that many people have a very limited, superficial, or one-dimensional knowledge of this vast and varied part of the world.

The aim of this project has therefore been to show new approaches to the African continent and its various cultures, to explain different facets of African cultures as they exist and/or undergo changes and to illustrate how and where African and European cultures come or have come into contact, interact, and create something new.

The contributors are researchers from various disciplines who investigate topics in or on an African country and who use novel – often interdisciplinary – methods. These researchers are joined by colleagues who work on what might be referred to as 'transplanted Africanness', i.e. the cultural, historical and social conditions of African Europeans and African Americans in Western societies. But we are also very glad that some artists, who have come into contact with the other continent and who thus are capable of presenting their view on 'the other', have joined this project and have taken up the opportunity to present, explain and make known the cultural background of their work.

It goes without saying that such an eclectic collection of contributions may bear its problems as there is no single thread running through this volume, linking all the papers presented here. The overall approach of the contributors assembled in this volume, however, is their joined interest in contemporary African societies and cultures and their aiming at contributing to a better understanding of the multifaceted character of the African continent, which – more often than not – is still primarily depicted as a cultural monolith bearing primarily strong archaic, rural and underdeveloped traits.

Thus, the contributions by Birgit Englert, Jigal Beez, Kerstin Bolzt, and Joyce Abunaw show that in various African societies new forms of culture, such as Hip Hop music, comic strips, modern literature and film are thriving, that African themes and topics are reinterpreted, that European or Western forms of cultural thought and expression may be adapted to, and further developed by, African needs and may, in turn, inspire Western cultural endeavours. The same holds for the contributions by Bole Butake, Virginia Mukewsha and Florian Hetze, who – using different methods and approaches – illustrate how historical events, traditional means of expression and modern ways of life can be fruitfully combined to create new forms of original African cultures. These five contributions thus clearly illustrate that indigenous African cultures have gone a far way from the European conception of it, i.e. consisting primarily of oral story telling and rhythmic drum beating. Evelyn Wladarsch also invites the European readers to rethink their conception of some values which they might take for granted, i.e. of the way the notion of time can be conceived. Hans-Georg Wolf and Anne Schröder take a more technical approach and illustrate how research methods can and need to be adapted to investigate African forms of speech and how, through this adaptation, not only new insights into an African research topic but also into research in general may be gained. Their centre of interest, i.e. forms of language 'transplanted' from a European to an African context, is – in a very broad sense – reversed in the contributions by Katrin Fischer and Sebastian Berg, who approach the African continent from an entirely different perspective. Their articles aim at familiarising the reader with the effects of an African community's 'transplantation' into a European context in the case of the latter and with forms of literary expression of Africans transplanted to the US in the case of the former. Emelda Ngufor Samba and Sebastian Berg finally show how the methods of African Popular theatre, which are used to address communal problems in Africa, may also be used in a European context to explore the problem of racism.

As the contributors are social, cultural and literary scientists, linguists, and artists of various cultural backgrounds, the contributions necessarily reflect a wide range of personal and scientific styles. In editing, I restricted myself to the necessary minimum of suggesting some appropriate changes and to correcting some obvious errors. The views and opinions as well as the styles expressed in the papers of this volume thus remain the sole responsibility of their authors.

However, I hope to have produced a book that all people interested in the African continent, experts and lay-people alike, may enjoy.

Anne Schröder

Cultural Manifestations of Collective Identity in Contemporary Zimbabwean Literature

KERSTIN BOLZT
Bayreuth, Germany

Introduction

After the achievement of independence in 1980, Zimbabwe's new black majority government adopted a policy of reconciliation in an attempt to transform black-white relations.[1] The effect of this policy was further enhanced by the formation of a government of national unity which included in its cabinet some members of the white minority regime. Contemporary literature in Zimbabwe has been mainly a response to these policies of reconciliation, nation-building, and socialism.

Although "one cannot speak of a national literature of Zimbabwe" (Veit-Wild 1992: 2), several efforts have been made with regard to the idea of nationhood.[2] Literature since independence has been very flexible in experimenting with various constructions of collective identity.[3] In some novels, Zimbabwe and collective identity are constructed by referring to a common past and, in particular, the national myth of Nehanda. *Nehanda* is the title of Yvonne Vera's first novel, published in 1993. The female spirit medium also plays a role in Chenjerai Hove's *Bones* (1988, new edition in 1999).

---

[1] The policy of reconciliation has been revoked by now (*The Economist* 2000: 53).
[2] A useful definition of the concept of nation has been provided by Benedict Anderson. His cultural analysis of the nation as an "imagined community" (Anderson 1983: 31), however, ignores inequalities and politics of disenfranchisement stemming from race, class, gender, ethnicity, and other social discriminations. Timothy Brennen relates Anderson's definition of the nation to similar ideas in which nations are viewed as imaginary constructs, or in the case of Eric Hobsbawm and Terence Ranger, as inventions whose existence depends on "an apparatus of cultural fictions" (Brennen, quoted in Simatei 2001: 20).
[3] According to Assmann (1988: 132), collective identities are constructs that describe what people have in common. In addition, the mechanisms used to create a collective identity are central to this analysis. Crucial are the reasons for and elements of belonging to a collective basis. Essentially, the existence of a collective identity is marked by a reference to a common past, and, in particular, the existence of national myths is emphasised in this (Assmann 1994: 22).

Furthermore, people like to emphasise their group identity and psychological distinctiveness from others by language. Language is based on a collective sense of national and group consciousness which emphasises similarities. Collective identity is as strong or weak as it is alive in the thinking of the group members. Thus, it will be tried to show how Zimbabwean writers use the English language and alter it in order to give it a new identity.

This paper will be structured as follows: First of all, it will give an overview of the problems the authors were confronted with after independence and their attempts to find a new identity, including the process of 'Africanising' the English language. On the basis of a textual analysis, the next part will deal with the two chosen works. The sequence is chronologically by dates of publication, as well as contextually, marking the development from a nostalgic and old-fashioned to a modern and democratic picture of a Zimbabwean nation. To begin with, Chenjerai Hove's novel *Bones* will be looked into, followed by Yvonne Vera's *Nehanda*.

Challenges for the Writers

The Choice of Language

Colonialism led to bilingualism in the colonised countries, although the specific relationship between the indigenous and colonial languages varies greatly.[4] Bilingualism has always been an issue of consideration for the writer from a colony and it has been a controversial issue in the debates on African literature since the 1960s. In his essay "The African Writer and the English Language" (1965), for instance, the Nigerian novelist Chinua Achebe defends

---

[4] In Zimbabwe, English is an official language, in addition to the other two officially recognised languages, Shona and Ndebele, spoken by 80% and 15% of the population respectively. Although these three languages are officially recognised, Emmanuel Ngara (1982: 20) indicates that in terms of the status and function of each language, English is the dominant language, while Shona and Ndebele are subordinate languages. The hierarchy of language functions suggests that the English language exists in a diglossic relationship with the two other official languages in Zimbabwe. The concept of 'diglossia', developed by Charles Ferguson (1959), is used to describe a sociolinguistic situation in which there are two separate language varieties, each with its own specific functions within the society. The 'High' language variety is the language variety used in writing, in education, in government administrative and legal institutions, and generally in public and formal situations. The 'Low' variety is the one used by the mass of the population in the course of their everyday private and informal interaction, within the family, and in the various forms of popular culture. In the Zimbabwean situation, English could thus be seen as the High language and Shona and Ndebele as the Low languages.

the use of an 'Africanised' English, while Ngugi wa Thiong'o from Kenya is known for his resolution to write only in his mother tongue Gikuyu (see his work *Decolonising the Mind: The Politics and Language of African Literature*). While in these debates the vernacular has usually been considered the more authentic and a sign of the de-colonisation of the mind, this must be qualified in the Zimbabwe/Rhodesia context. There, the vernacular written discourse was appropriated by the hegemonic colonial power and so was not, or only in a limited way, suitable for authentic expression of thought. On the other hand the colonial language, English, served as a counter-discursive tool to break away from the restrictive "native policies" (Veit-Wild 1992: 229) of the Rhodesian government and the Literature Bureau, which aimed to keep the "native discourse" (Veit-Wild 1992: 230) apolitical and safe, and hence became an emancipatory force.

Vernacular writers express a strong affinity with their mother tongue. Writing in their native language enables them to explore and convey the richness of their cultural background. Kohn, in his analysis of Herder's *Essay on the Origin of Language* (1966), points out that "language, national language, became a sacred instrument; each man could be himself only by thinking and creating in his own language. With the respect for all other nationalities went a respect for their languages" (quoted in Appiah 1992: 50). When using English, this emotional component often gets lost. Moreover, the aspect of thinking in one's own language is important; when using English, the construction of a Zimbabwean identity is problematic.[5] Those, however, who have an equal command of both languages, due to the privilege of higher education, can benefit from bilingualism. They can choose either language according to a specific purpose or feeling:

> For me an experience expresses itself in its own language. I think I am reasonably fluent in both languages. The experience tells me that this would be well captured in Shona and sometimes the experience comes in English, and if I wrote it in Shona it wouldn't be the same (Hove, quoted in Veit- Wild 1988: 39).

Because of the colonial control over the use of their language, Zimbabwean writers started to develop subversive language strategies. They began to transform either language by incorporating elements of the other. The most prolific writer in two languages is Charles Mungoshi, who tried to counteract colonial discourse in both languages. Quite a few Zimbabwean writers have tried to 'Africanise' English. Especially in Zimbabwean poetry written in

---

[5]For more on the English language and the construction of identity in Zimbabwean literature, see Bamiro (2000).

English, much of the imagery of the Shona or Ndebele language has been retained. Since the advent of independence, this has developed into a conscious language policy practised by many writers, in particular by Chenjerai Hove in his novel *Bones*.

Chinua Achebe writes "I feel the English language will be able to carry the weight of my African experience. But it will have to be a new English, still in communion with its ancestral home but altered to suit new African surroundings" (Achebe 1975: 62). Here, Achebe alludes to the paradoxical situation in which African writers using European languages to express an African condition find themselves. They have to rework the language in such a way that, while remaining accessible to the outside world, it does justice to the African experience. This exercise is often referred to as indigenisation, that is, "when a writer attempts to convey African concepts, thought patterns and linguistic features via the European medium" (Zabus, quoted in Zhuwarara 1996: 42). Ashcroft et al. (1989: 38) assert that standard written English is turned into 'Englishes' and altered into radically new modes of apprehending reality. In *The Empire Writes Back* Ashcroft et al. (1989: 38) go on to explain that post-colonial writers can define themselves by seizing the language of the centre and replacing it into a discourse fully adopted to the colonised place.

In Zimbabwe, as is the case in the other English-speaking African countries, certain scholars have addressed the question of what form of English has emerged. In his foreword to Emmanuel Ngara's foundational study, *Bilingualism, Language Contact and Language Planning* (1982), D. Mutumbuka, Minister of Education and Culture of Zimbabwe, predicts that "[t]he English that we are going to have in this country is Zimbabwean English" (quoted in Ngara 1982: ix). The writer Yvonne Vera confirms that "the English language had become indigenous to Africa" (*Independent* 1997) and therefore she writes her novels in English. Finally, the writer "Hove strives to alter the colonial language in order not only to give it a new identity, but also to turn it into a new medium of artistic expression" (quoted in Bamiro 2000: 60). *Bones* is deliberately designed to reflect an African, or more precisely a Shona, rather than a European sensibility. Yet, as Bamiro (2000: 202) indicates, whatever the influence of the mother tongue, Hove is also drawing on specific registers of Standard English that signals identification with imperial culture.

Thinking about Nativism

Literature, as Anderson points out, "provides the technical means for 'representing' the kind of imagined community that is the nation" (1983: 25). Vera and Hove prove that not all writers who emerged after 1980 have condemned nativist strategies of writing; nativism here stands for "the claim that true African independence requires a literature of one's own" (Appiah 1992: 948).

Solomon Mutswairo, whose *Feso* (1957) is regarded as the first piece of Zimbabwean literature, appeals to what Appiah calls "the imaginative recreation of a common cultural past that is crafted into a shared tradition" (Appiah 1992: 149-150). But even after independence, Mutswairo carried on with his studies of the cultural and ethnological history of his people. With his novels, *Mapondera: Soldier of Zimbabwe* (1978, new editions in 1983 and 1994) and *Chaminuka: Prophet of Zimbabwe* (1983), he revived the mythical life stories of Shona heroes of the late nineteenth century. Vera's novel *Nehanda* shows parallels with the celebration of a Zimbabwean past found in Mutswairo's work (Imfeld 1994: 23). Likewise, Hove feels no need to abandon a glorification of African history (Gibbs 1997: 856).

Thus, in independent Zimbabwe, the rebirth of a black identity has been a prevalent topic as a title like that of George Kahari's assessment of the Zimbabwean novel in English, *The Search for Zimbabwean Identity* (1980), demonstrates. Kahari's aim was "a recovery of identity that will help in reminding both writers and their readers that they are not misfits in the land of their birth" (1980: 10). In 1988, the critic Emmanuel Ngara, who has always been in search of a national literature, praised Hove's *Bones* as a 'milestone' in Zimbabwe's literary development (Veit-Wild 1992: 319). In this novel, Hove tries to recreate a national history and a national identity. There are similarities between the ways in which writers like Mutswairo and Hove employ a discourse of the nation, something that Veit-Wild (1993) finds problematic. She points out that after independence many writers moved away from the idea of a national mythology, by emphasising that the nationalistic discourse of an African identity, which had a progressive function during the colonial era, has become not only outdated, but also extremely dangerous when used by the black elite as a means to justify their autocratic rule. Veit-Wild (1992: 319) now raises the question whether the term and concept of national literature has not become obsolete in postcolonial experience.

Important is, however, that Zimbabwean writers who maintain nativistic tendencies in their works are critical of the post-colonial condition. Although there is an obvious recognition of and a strong belief in the Zimbabwean nation in Hove's work, it has very little in common with the kind of rhetoric used by the political leadership. Rather, Hove's focus is on building an alternative solidarity by shifting the terms of the national debate to include issues the nationalists once championed, issues concerning the people of Zimbabwe, like women, land reform, education, and literacy.

Publication and Restrictions

With the onset of Zimbabwe's independence, the conditions for black writing changed dramatically. Several efforts have been made to establish national publishing houses. Existing literary associations such as the PEN Club of Rhodesia now allowed black writers, and new publishing houses like Baobab Books emerged. Baobab Books was formed in 1988 and one important working area is to publish books by Zimbabwean authors (Lewin, quoted in *Informationsdienst Südliches Afrika* 1988: 5).

New groups of writers emerged towards the end of the first decade, notably young Zimbabwean high school and university students, and underprivileged social groups, such as women. As they did not want to rely on slow moving publishing houses and restrictive government agencies (such as the Literature Bureau), they founded their own writers' organisations in 1990: the Budding Writers' Association of Zimbabwe (BWAZ) and the Zimbabwe Women Writers (ZWW). These organisations have involved a large number of people in writing workshops, readings and discussions and have attracted much public attention. They are affiliated with the Zimbabwe Writers' Union (ZIWU), founded in 1984, which provides forums for public presentations and discussions of literary ventures. All these measures aim at making Zimbabweans familiar with local authors and their versions of Zimbabwe and collective identity so that the people can identify with these ideas.

Access to the international book market and to international writers' conferences became possible. The Zimbabwe International Book Fair (ZIBF), established in 1983 and run by an independent trust of professionals, visits the Frankfurter Book Fair annually. ZIBF itself, is the most important book market in Sub-Saharan Africa and, together with Writers' Workshop, has made the Zimbabwean capital a centre for literary exchange and debate.

However, high costs of books and shortage of libraries prevents the majority of Zimbabweans from reading, says Trish Mbanga, the executive director of ZIPF (*The Herald* 1999). Also the high rate of illiteracy is an obstacle for the writers' efforts to bring their picture of a Zimbabwean nation to the people. As a result, the writers produce signs which often do not get to their real destinations. Poor and illiterate people will not read the books that deal with their history. The situation is hardly encouraging for young talented writers and Shimmer Chinodya notes that: "I am actually worried that some publishing houses may be forced to close and this will be a blow to our budding writers. It will be doubly difficult for them to enter the market" (quoted in *The Mirror* 2000).

The government does little to improve the situation. On the contrary, while political power changed in 1980, political restrictions remained. The new government did not change or abolish the censorship laws, and hence writers are still subject to the approval of the Censorship Board, only under different auspices. Vernacular writing is still to a large extent channelled by the Literature Bureau whose policies hardly changed. Thus, vernacular writers have found it hard to break away from the accustomed styles and themes, and so their literature "is still very poor [...] the themes tend to be almost the same all the time, like love, jealousy, polygamy, young people coming from the rural areas into the city etc." (Mungoshi, quoted in Veit-Wild 1988: 81).

Yet, new political areas have been tackled gradually, such as the experience of the war. The writer Tsitsi Dangarembga thinks that "recording this period of the country's history is a necessary part of forming a new national identity which Zimbabwe so badly needs" (quoted in Hove 1989: 45). On a linguistic level, a few younger writers have tried to break away from the conservative language policy of the Literature Bureau to liberalise styles in Shona writing. The struggle to build a Zimbabwean identity preoccupies the country's intellectuals. Hove believes the writers must see to it "that one day we shall dream like Zimbabweans, not like half-baked Europeans" (quoted in *The Economist* 1990).

Promotion of Women Writing

> Zimbabwean women played an active role in their liberation struggle. Given that role, Zimbabwe's women were determined to be included in the fruits of liberation. The new nationalist state complied, rhetorically, by recognising women's central role in development and the need to improve women's status. In practice, however,

the state has dragged its heels in enforcing laws that were designed to give women greater equality with men (Davidson 1997: 9).

Since the beginning of independence in 1980, the laws pertaining to women in Zimbabwe have been amended so that women are now equal under the law. The contradictions between traditional and modern practice, however, mean that women are still fighting discrimination in society. Compared to their male colleagues, women writers suffer from less education; they are often cut off from sources of information about writing and male society, including husbands, friends, employers, and publishers are heavily prejudiced against writing women:

> My first manuscript was complete when my husband burnt it saying I wasn't giving him due attention.
>
> Being a Shona woman writer, Shona men tend to regard women's ideas, writing or literary attempts as not worthwhile for public digestion (Muringaniza and Lwanda, quoted in Veit-Wild 1992: 239).

The ignored topic of women in Zimbabwe has finally been scooped by Tsitsi Dangarembga. Her *Nervous Conditions* was the first published novel in English by a black Zimbabwean woman. Submitted to a Zimbabwean publisher, the book was rejected. The pointedly feminist perspective was apparently off-putting to the editor concerned. Only after its publication by the Women's Press of London in 1988 was it also published in Harare.

To change these conditions and to break the isolation of women writers, the Zimbabwe Women Writers (ZWW) was founded.[6] It is a non-governmental organisation, with the following objectives:
- to promote women writing in Zimbabwe
- to develop women's writing skills
- to encourage the reading of women's writing
- to promote the publication of women's writing
- to promote literacy among women
- to promote positive images of women in writing (Kitson 1994: v).

The latter aspect, however, is controversial. Promoting only positive images of women can also be seen as discrimination and not useful for women's quest for identity. In 1994, ZWW already had over six hundred members, most of which were active in rural areas "because women there are simply

---

[6] About the structural problems of literary creation for women in Zimbabwe, see Schwarzer (1993: 112-120).

thirsty for anything to do in order to improve themselves" (Msengezi, quoted in Wittmann 1999: 23). For young talents, there is the Female Budding Writers' Association. A book team that was introduced to offer book-publishing skills to women and give women of rural communities the feeling of being part of Zimbabwe. Since the 1990s, there has been an enormous feeling of breaking new ground among the women in Zimbabwe (Vera, quoted in Imfeld 1994: 23). In 1994, ZWW published its first *English Anthology*. A *Shona and Ndebele Anthology* was set about. By putting together this collection of one hundred and five short stories and poems, the women of Zimbabwe joined others elsewhere in re-organising a society that has never given them any credit. Three writers have become symbols of change: Ama Ata Aidoo from Ghana, Tsitsi Dangarembga and Yvonne Vera. "Girls, let's tell them" (*Moto* 1994: 19) is the motto, and the women declare that the only way for women writers to strengthen themselves is through organising as women.

Women were the central focus of the Zimbabwe International Book Fair in Harare in 1999. The Indaba conference, the annual curtain raiser to the Book Fair, that year was entitled 'Women's Voices – Gender, Books and Development'. The organisers intended to use the theme "to highlight women's information needs in Africa and to support women to enter and to be effective within the information book and publishing sector" (*The Herald* 1999). Free entry for women functioned as a symbolical gesture for easier access in the education area.

All these efforts are aimed at helping women artists in the "process of reclaiming cultural space" (Chitauro et al. 1994: 113), which is constantly negotiated and contested. In Zimbabwe, women artists have been pushed out of areas of social space, a policy that has its roots in the culture of the empire and an indigenous African patriarchy. Anne McClintock, writing on gender and nationalism in South Africa states: "Excluded as national citizens, women are subsumed only symbolically into the body politic. Nationalism is thus constituted from the very beginning as a gendered discourse and cannot be understood without a theory of gender power" (1991). In an article on gender, nationalism and women's writing Elleke Boehmer argues that

> the idea of nationhood bears a masculine identity though national ideals may wear a feminine face [...]. Figures of mothers of the nation are everywhere emblazoned but the presence of women in the nation is officially marginalised and generally ignored" (1991: 6).

From Kumari Jayawardena's historical survey of *Feminism and Nationalism in the Third World* (1986) to more specific articles like the ones by Anne McClintock and Elleke Boehmer, nationalism and national liberation movements continue to be criticised for their failure to serve women's needs. Obviously, gender is an issue which is not only discussed in the Zimbabwean context but also in other cultures and literatures. In fact, all the topics debated in this paper such as the choice of language, the gender and the religion question are problems which are dealt with in other African and postcolonial literatures, too. In the following, however, I will focus on two Zimbabwean writers and discuss how they try to give more space to the female character.

Chenjerai Hove's *Bones*

Literary and Cultural Programme

Chenjerai Hove was born in south-western Zimbabwe on 9 February 1956. Around 1980, he emerged as a major poetic observer of the liberation war and in the mid-1980, Hove evolved from a literary observer into a cultural politician. He worked as literary editor at Mambo Press and the Zimbabwe Publishing House and served as chairperson of the Zimbabwe Writers' Union. In writing *Bones*, Hove aimed at a literary and cultural programme. Like Chinua Achebe, he imagines the African writer as teacher and conscience of his people who has the task to give voice to the voiceless and powerless: "Writers have this immense responsibility of persuading the world to listen to the many cries of Africa. As writers, we have as well to turn around and be publicist for the sake of the survival of our people" (Hove, quoted in Veit-Wild 1992: 314).

Regarding literary form, Hove considers it the duty of the African writer to re-examine and rediscover oral and traditional art forms:

> We owe the world the complex fusion of the arts so ably celebrated in our dances and rituals to which the dancer, the story-teller, the poet, the singer, the priest, the actor, the healer combined in a unique artistic harmony which makes fascinating reading today if rendered in a novel or poem or a theatrical piece (quoted in Veit-Wild 1992: 314).

As a consequence, Hove, in the tradition of Achebe, has consciously striven to 'Africanise' the English language. However, his outlook on language is still self-consciously counter-colonial. He conceives of the task of the Zimbabwean writer as cleansing the colonial languages to the extent of representing them to our former colonisers as languages which can also be used to depict human dignity, not human slavery and anger. This is a task which we can only achieve with the inspiration of the great masters of oral narrative to whom we are accountable (Hove, quoted in Veit-Wild 1993: 6).

Collective Memory – Collective Voice

With *Bones*, Hove finally fulfilled his literary programme. The novel is about Marita, a poor illiterate wife who lives in a peasant community and goes on a journey for the city to search for her son who left with the freedom fighters of the second *chimurenga* - Zimbabwe's war of liberation (1965 - 1980) - and never returned. Linked to her fate are two other women: Janifa, who as a young girl received a love letter from Marita's son; and the 'unknown woman' in the city, who travels with Marita on the bus.

To give voice to a defeated people, the author has chosen a narrative structure that combines aspects of traditional art with modern literary form. The story is told from the point of view of the characters and the protagonist Marita appears only through the memory of those who knew her. The interior monologue of each voice is lively because it moves back and forth in time and changes through the frequent use of second person narration in direct dialogue.

Hove achieves two aims with this structure: there is no omniscient authorial narrator, and the people can speak for themselves. He, therefore, blends the flexibility of the oral tale with the splitting of narrative voice in modern non-focalised narration and with modern techniques of flashback and foreshadowing. At the same time he escapes the limitations of linear time and arrives at what he calls "the collective memory" (Hove, quoted in Veit-Wild 1992: 315). In his article "Children of Memory" (1988), Hove remarks that he uses writing to remember the past and stresses the need for a national memory.

This collective memory brings the various narrative voices together into one collective voice. The linguistic and stylistic basis for this fusion is the communal idiom that holds everything together. Hove uses an Africanised English, alters the colonial language and gives it a new identity. His language, which all characters speak, carries the tradition, the wisdom, and the perception of their people and of their culture thereby creating one "communal and collective voice" (Veit-Wild 1992: 315) out of individual voices.

In *Bones*, Hove captures the rhythms of thought in a poetic language distinctly rooted in Shona vernacular expression. He tries to relate the experience of *Bones* in that language which would make it the voice of the Zimbabwean people. His language is concerned with evoking feelings. For instance, the anguish of Marita's disciple Janifa is depicted vividly when she is about to go insane:

> Tears are not water. They must not be seen everyday. They are not water. The well of tears is not visited by anyone. No one knows the colour and shape of the well of tears. If tears are seen everyday, things are bad inside, Marita. Things are bad. Dark things that eat you from inside until you grow as thin as me. They say there is a worm that wriggles inside the heart of trouble (*Bones* 1999: 94).

According to Veit-Wild (1992: 316), the novel reads like a long prose poem, a fairy tale that is lyrical and entrancing. She points out that "Hove's internationally acclaimed 'Africanised' English is a fairly literal translation of Shona sentence, proverbs, terminology, and imagery" (Veit-Wild 1993: 7). For example, in the following example, the cook Chisaga uses a series of metaphors and Shona imagery:

> But Marita did not know that words must be filled with trust. She has roasted me like a sweet potato so that I can see the power of her breast. Now I am like a feather that flies to nowhere. I am the hornbill whose journey was disturbed by the wind. I am like the hornbill whose feathers make it look like a lot of meat (*Bones* 1999: 87).

Moreover, Chisaga tries to justify his subservient role on the white farm by citing the traditional Shona proverb *Mwana washe muranda kumwe* which he translates, "A king's son is a nobody in other lands" (*Bones* 1999: 35). Hove counter-identifies with colonial discourse by employing figures which reterritorialise the English language in his Shona culture. He has the ability to convey feelings in ways that Zimbabwean readers can recognise as similar to their own.

Veit-Wild argues that the language used by Hove in *Bones* "recreates a world of sayings and proverbs and registers a sense of oneness with the land and with tradition. It celebrates a form of Africanness which does not exist anymore" (Veit-Wild 1992: 317). She goes on to accuse Hove of being a romantic, painting a "monolithic view of African society" (Veit-Wild 1993:10). Her critique is based on the assumption that Hove "does not pay tribute to the changes in society, the disruptions and contradictions which have taken hold of people's lives and are reflected in Zimbabwean speech" (Veit-Wild 1993: 8). Zhuwarara (1996: 43) admits that in a way most of these sayings are more exotic to international readers than to the Shona speaker; fascinating is, however, the manner in which Hove is either transliterating or modifying the original Shona expressions to suit his contextual purpose.

Zimbabwe's Past and Traditions

This communal and collective voice is especially obvious in the two chapters entitled "The Spirits Speak". The introduction of the national conscience through the spirits' voice is consistent with Hove's aim of constructing the collective history of his people through collective memory. The spirits' voice links the events of the present story to the national history of resistance and evokes the myth of the guiding force of the spirit mediums in the first and second *chimurenga*. Chapter seven alludes to the first *chimurenga* (1896/97) that was preceded by drought and locusts, personifying "white locusts" (*Bones* 1999: 47) as the symbol of white invaders.

Mbuya Nehanda is the woman who inspired African forces to fight against the white settlers during the 1896/97 uprisings. Just before the female spirit medium was executed by the settler forces, she is claimed to have said, 'my bones shall rise again'. It is from this prophecy, which has reverberated amongst generations of Africans, that Hove derived the title of his novel. As a writer, Hove portrays the liberation war of the 1960s and 1970s as having been partly inspired by the 1896/97 uprisings (Zhuwarara 1996: 39). Since the oppressed Africans have come to see Nehanda as a larger than life figure, a living legend often cited by freedom fighters, Hove can mark the existence of a collective identity by the reference to a common history. Hove's spirits try to evoke the national myth for the reader:

> Arise all the bones of the land. Arise all the bones of the dying cattle. Arise all the bones of the locusts. Wield the power of the many bones scattered across the land and fight so that the land of the ancestors is not defiled by strange feet and strange hands (*Bones* 1999: 51).

The cited passage, taken from an appeal for the first *chimurenga*, is well known to the people because the guerrillas used it to mobilise the peasants to fight to regain the land during the liberation war of the 1960s and 1970s (Engelke 1998: 5).

In the chapters in which "The Spirits Speak", Hove recalls the mystification of the spirit mediums. His claim to be in conversation with nature is reminiscent of David Lan's (1985) study of the ways in which Shona discourses of the people's relationship with the land were played out during the war. Mythology and a sense of being tied to the soil were at the centre of struggles over the politics of tradition. For the guerrillas, this sense of tradition was actively shaped by the spirit mediums who were helping them in the struggle. Hove's main character, Marita, is so close to nature that she "seems to be talking with the soil" (*Bones* 1999: 15). Thus, the theme of the novel is supported by the depiction of the main character, Marita. She has a certain warmth, strength and love. She is defined as the long-suffering mother Africa and the embodiment of the spirit that most of Zimbabweans unconsciously come to admire.

Hove is accused of celebrating an image of Africa, which recalls long ago phases of negritude and the rediscovery of an African identity.[7] Veit-Wild criticises that Hove's "romantic picture of the guerrillas and their affiliation with the people" (1992: 318) stands in contrast to the description of the severe conflicts between guerrillas and peasants in war novels like Shimmer Chinodya's *Harvest of Thorns* (Veit-Wild 1992: 321-323). According to Zhuwarara (1996: 399), Hove does not demystify the legend in order to show how Nehanda's progressive historical consciousness can be an integral part of the peasant and worker consciousness that could inform the outlook and activities of people such as Marita. Hove feels no need to abandon a glorification of Zimbabwean history. History is a construct and Hove paints a certain image of the past and the national myth. He mystifies tradition, culture, and history in order to construct an idea of Zimbabwe and collective identity with which people can identify.

The Depiction of Rural Zimbabwe

Bones has received positive reviews and has been translated into German, Dutch, Danish, Swedish, Norwegian, and Japanese. In 1989, Hove won the Noma Award for Publishing in Africa. In particular, the way his novels recreate a sense of oneness with the land has been praised, about which Hove has the following to say:

---

[7] Negritude was a literary and ideological movement led by francophone black intellectuals, writers, and politicians. The founders of negritude, known as the three fathers (Aimé Césaire, Léopold Sédar Senghor and Léon-Gontran Damas), were originally from three different French colonies in Africa and the Caribbean but met while living in Paris in the early 1930s. Although each of the fathers had different ideas about the purpose and styles of negritude, the movement is generally characterised by a reaction to colonisation (denunciation of Europe's lack of humanity and rejection of Western domination and ideas), an identity crisis (acceptance of and pride in being black and valorisation of African history, traditions, and beliefs), and Marxist ideas.

In my work there is a constant conversation between the earth, nature and sky. [...]
I will speak with the rivers, the soil, the boulders, and the mountains of my country
and hear the voices of my people coming through them (Hove 1994: 13).

Hove emphasises that the human being is part of nature. The association of his work with the land, nature, and the sky are a hallmark of nativism. His is an imagined country where once "the earth breathed" (*Bones* 1999: 18) and "the trees, the rocks, the soil [...] talked like people" (*Bones* 1999: 18). He is convinced that Zimbabweans can find their identity in the countryside where people smile "at the cowdung smoking fresh near the cows [...] and [their] eyes glitter in answer to the singing of the birds running after each other in the sky" (*Bones* 1999: 18). In the rural area, there is still harmony of humans in a balanced life situation. Moreover, the nature of rural Zimbabwe is not an artificial one: "But the leaves of the new trees of the city do not shake as wildly as the trees of the forests in the country-side" (*Bones* 1999: 82).

Nature gives strength and "[e]ven the birds which jump up and down from the nests of their little ones, they are my friends. They give me the power to go on" (*Bones* 1999: 96). Hove puts nature in the front and praises rural life. In a natural and peaceful environment people can try to see who they are. Hove stresses the moments of an isolated individual: "Rest. Go up a tree or a boulder. The leaves of the tree will share their secrecy with you for the remainder of the night" (*Bones* 1999: 100).

Hove's idea of a Zimbabwean nation is a romanticised one. He makes clear that identity can only be found in nature through immediate contact with nature. The author praises the advantages of rural life while the city is perceived as a frightening entity where people lose their identity.

The Zimbabwean City

In *Bones*, the city is described as a place where people "change their names until their own mothers cannot recognise the seeds of their own wombs" (*Bones* 1999: 17). Visitors to the capital Harare, for instance, fear to lose their identities. They have a feeling of isolation and estranging: Janifa says that "when we got to the city, Marita fell dumb" (*Bones* 1999: 76).

Hove refers to the past and the war of liberation in order to create a collective identity. However, only people who live in the countryside can identify with this version of a Zimbabwean nation because "people of the city do not know what war was all about" (*Bones* 1999: 75). He continues:

People of the city are spoilt with soft foods so they think that life is soft. People of the city look at their watches and then leave work without finishing any task. [...] For people of the villages, to eat is to look for life, but for people of the towns, to eat is to look for something to do. The city is a wild place where many things lose their purpose (*Bones* 1999: 75).

Obviously, it is only in rural Zimbabwe, where people can find a true identity while it is almost impossible that people in the city can identify with Hove's image of Zimbabwe: "People of the city are strange. A lot has gone into their heads that to clean them is very difficult. Very difficult for anybody to do" (*Bones* 1999: 76).

Hove's characters, however, use familiar images to describe the city: "The city is like the throat of a crocodile; it swallows both the dirty and the clean" (*Bones* 1999: 17) and it is "full of lions" (*Bones* 1999: 19). They use these images to make the city comparable to nature and to find nature in the city. The city is full of images of nature but these images are alarming: "The city is so frightening [...].What is bad will remain bad even if people say many good things about it" (*Bones* 1999: 24).

The city can also be seen as the nation. That the city is full of lions indicates that the lions, the owners of the land, own the land while the Zimbabwean people have not received land yet. Members of the government, who used the *mhondoro* ('mediated spirits of royal ancestry' and meaning 'lion') to legitimate their rule, are new potential conquerors; they are the forces of neo-colonialism. The crocodile, too, a dangerous and greedy animal, stands for Zimbabwe's autocratic political leadership. It is noticeable that a division of the country's society into poor and rich is felt. While president Robert Mugabe and his party lead a luxurious life, Hove sees the "people wearing rags in our streets" (*Bones* 1999: 81).

"Romanticised Image of the African Woman"[8]

Bones is one of the first novels in Zimbabwean literature to focus on a Zimbabwean reaction to colonialism from the point of view of gender. Hove desired to create more space for the female character whose actual historical significance had either been neglected or distorted (Zhuwarara 1996: 31). In creating a phalanx of female figures in Nehanda, Marita, Janifa and the unknown woman, Hove attempts to reassert the centrality of the woman character in the Zimbabwean experience.

---

[8] The term is borrowed from Veit-Wild (1992: 317).

It can be argued, however, that the roles assigned to women characters hardly break new ground in the context of the Zimbabwean literary discourse. What *Bones* successfully depicts is the extent to which the African woman suffered in the hands of the coloniser, as well as in the hands of their men folk. The text also captures the energy of Marita, her passion for life, her love of her fellow sufferers and her yearning for justice and a fulfilling existence. Nonetheless, Hove shows an "outdated and over-simplified image of the poor, illiterate, "native woman" (Veit-Wild 1992: 317) with her "cracked knees" (*Bones* 1999: 7), "coarse finger" (*Bones* 1999: 7) and torn and soiled cloth around her head. In a sense Marita remains the victim especially when her vision of the future does not extend beyond the return of her son. Marita remarks: "I am waiting for my son, that is all" (*Bones* 1999: 110). Her horizon is limited when, in fact, "[i]t was the rural women, the ordinary uneducated women, who took the lead in the 1960s" (Weiss 1985: 12).

Hove presents a "romanticised image of the African woman" (Veit-Wild 1992: 317), who meets with her fellow friends behind the anthill where they share secrets about their husbands. Womanhood is described by Hove as follows: "What is this I hear about Marita running away last night? They tell me she has left all the things of her womanhood with you. The pots, the baskets, everything that makes a woman feel a woman" (*Bones* 1999: 84). Veit-Wild sees Hove's work as mystifyingly romantic, so much that she equates it – as the title of her article "'Dances with Bones': Hove's Romanticised Africa" (1993) suggests – with Kevin Costner's movie "Dances with Wolves." Like this film epic, *Bones* has become "something of a cult book" (Veit-Wild 1993: 5) for Europeans.

Bones, therefore, achieved a controversial success, which will probably satisfy more the romantic longing of the western woman literature researcher than the expectations of feminist writers and thinkers in Zimbabwe. Yet, Zhuwarara (1996: 43) stresses that Hove should be given credit for experimenting with language in a way that captures the modes of perception and expression associated with the rich oral tradition of the Shona. It remains to be discussed, if Hove's language experiment is helping to revitalise the language of the colonial master or the Shona literary discourse.

Yvonne Vera's *Nehanda*

The Author and Her Accounts

Vera, a youth-full looking young woman, was born in 1964 in Bulawayo where she is now the Director of the National Gallery of Zimbabwe in Bulawayo. She holds a doctoral degree in English literature from York University, Toronto, and it was in Canada that she wrote her first novel, *Nehanda*. The novel was published by Baobab Books, Harare, in 1993, and short-listed in the Commonwealth Writer's Prize for 1993.

In writing about Nehanda, Yvonne Vera "celebrates women' s courage, dignity, integrity, enterprise, prowess, intellect and appeal" (Musandireve 1995: 20). Nehanda is a woman who engages in activities that will help to shape a future nation. Yvonne Vera announces the end of women's silence. She is a woman who writes against the quietness that had been put on her by society, tradition, and family. With courage and rage, she writes about "the people who were ignored" (Vera, quoted in Gray 1997) and about taboos like incest. Her books are about women speaking out. The writer is convinced that language has both the power to "heal old wounds" (Vera, quoted in Gray 1997) and to allow those who have once been victims to transform themselves and their future.

In August 1993, Yvonne Vera returned to Zimbabwe for the launch of *Nehanda* at the Zimbabwe International Book Fair. Her decision to have the book debut in her home country was deliberate: "When I wrote *Nehanda*, I said that I had to find a home for her in Zimbabwe. I wanted to give Nehanda back to Zimbabweans" (Vera, quoted in Hill 1993: 19).

Reconstructing a National Myth

The day Vera realised that no one else had tackled the legend of Nehanda in fictional form she started writing. Vera points out that "[t]here are all kinds of possibilities for a book [about Mbuya Nehanda]. She's an inspiration for women, someone who can strengthen and empower us. That's what makes the novel contemporary" (quoted in Hill 1993: 19). She continues: "That mother image is more embracing than a male image. She is the leading figure in Zimbabwe's history" (Vera, quoted in Hill 1993: 19). In *Nehanda*, Yvonne Vera reconstructs the national myth and tries to re-introduce the female part of the national liberation myth that had been lost. Although women played an important and active role during the struggle, they were forced back into their traditional position after the introduction of independence.

It is a basic tenor of traditional Zimbabwean religion that after people die, their spirits continue to affect the lives of their descendants. When an ancestor wants to communicate with its descendants it chooses a man or a woman and uses him or her to speak. Nehanda had been a princess in the ancient Munhumutapa (or Monomatapa) empire in the fifteenth century and her spirit is referred to as *mhondoro* (meaning 'mediated spirits of royal ancestry'). Yvonne Vera explains in an interview with *The Northern News*: "I would not have written *Nehanda* if she hadn't presented herself [to me]" (quoted in Hill 1993: 19). She continues: "And when I finished writing this novel I felt extremely old and tired. I felt I'd been in touch with her, and the intensity of the experience aged me" (quoted in Hill 1993: 19). The author did no historical research on her central character, and so *Nehanda* emerges out of Vera's own sense of mysticism and intuition. It is imbued with a "sense of passionate intimacy, a love of her country and her people that gives her language a lyric intensity" (Bose 1995: 213). The writing is lyrical and almost hallucinatory as the mythic female fighter faces struggle and death:

> She has heard the drums, and now she will dance the histories of her people. She dances against Mr. Browning and his God, against these strangers who have taken the land. She dances the faces of her people, the betrayal of time, the growth of wisdom, the glory of their survival – a shadow, moving on the wall. She dances in harmony with the departed who protect the soil from the feet of strangers. Thorns dig deep beneath her feet and she bursts into song (*Nehanda* 1993: 116).

Vera portrays Nehanda's death as a bridge (Musandireve 1995: 20), melting the boundaries between the two worlds of the living and the dead. Symbolically, the melting pot is the calabash, "which holds memories of the future, and carries signs of lasting beauty. Forgetting is not easy for those who travel in both directions of time" (*Nehanda* 1993: 3). Time is thus a continuum, which makes the schism between the dead and the living apparent.

The entire novel reverberates with Nehanda's messages from the spirits, rituals performed to appease the spirits, and the power the spirits hold in the life of the individual and the village:

> The dead are not dead. They are always around us, protecting us. There is no living person who is stronger than the departed. When the whole village prays together, they pray to the ancestral mudzimu of their clan. When we pray to mhondoro for rain, we are praying to the guardian that unites the whole clan. This is one of the strongest spirits of the land (*Nehanda* 1993: 27).

Vera emphasises the ability of the *mhondoro* to unite people and the strength traditional religion may bring to the Zimbabwean people: "We can become stronger and whole if we believe in our traditions" (*Nehanda* 1993: 79). Faith, here, implies a belief that the ancestors control fate and that praying to the ancestral spirits represents a way of looking for guidance, knowledge, and the answers to life's questions.

Vera is recreating a myth by addressing the issues of tribalism and nationhood. She is like the "wind [...] that covers the earth with joyful celebration" (*Nehanda* 1993: 118). "Hope for the nation is born out of the intensity of newly created memory" (*Nehanda* 1993: 111), creating a story behind which to unify, a heroine for several cultures whereby she uses language and story to reorganise perspectives on colonialism in new myths. The story of Nehanda has a mythic quality that carries a powerful conviction of faith in the rightfulness of hindering the colonialist endeavour: "'My people will not rest in bondage. The day has ceased too quickly.' Her telling awakens the dead part of the living" (*Nehanda* 1993: 117).

Nehanda versus Colonial Oppressor

In *Nehanda*, Vera defines the essential differences between the native and colonising race, by "deliberately juxtaposing vibrant and rich historical/cultural tradition with the dullness of a strait-laced idiom of ruling" (Bose 1995: 212-213). The latter is epitomised in the characters of two English government officials, Mr. Browning and Mr. Smith who represent the typical colonial oppressor ignorant of the struggle and the plight of the Zimbabwean people. Vera does not mention the officials' first names, but refers to them by their Western classifications as 'misters'. Mr. Browning grows tired of listening to his colleague Mr. Smith talk about Africa for he is not able to appreciate the verbal nature of humanity, a trait embedded within the indigenous culture, and therefore, misunderstands the nature of the Zimbabwean people completely:

> I mean the knowledge of the world that we have. We have drawn maps, and know how to locate ourselves on the globe. The native only knows where he is standing. I have been collecting maps since I was a boy. This is what we should teach at the new school, a knowledge of the earth (*Nehanda* 1993: 52).

Mr. Browning speaks from the typical colonial perspective and maintains an openly superior attitude. He views the natives as ignorant and uneducated beasts who must be taught Western subjects such as geography so that they may 'know where they are' in the world. The colonial intentions of the

British, both to "civilize a barbarous" (*Nehanda* 1993: 31) nation and to introduce the Christian faith, are sketched by Vera, from the misguided missionary schools to the renaming of Browning's native servant Mashoko to Moses.

Vera paints native Zimbabwean life in rich, bold strokes against this backdrop of colonialism: The significance of ancient wisdom evoked in colourful rituals and the overriding sense of community and kinship (which, for instance, is keenly felt among the women in Nehanda's birthday scene in chapter five) are all symbolically contained in the figure of Nehanda. Vera depicts her as a resistance figure, a unique woman who is granted special powers to help her Zimbabwean people fight the colonist's oppression. Her visions give hope and energy to the beleaguered revolutionaries.

Nehanda represents a resistance figure because her "special powers and her gift do not involve or relate to any Western or colonial institution" (Yang 1999). Her gift to inspire revolutionaries does not stem from a superior Western education or intellect, an ability to speak the coloniser's language, or a belief in Western religion. Instead, Nehanda's visions originate purely within indigenous culture and religion. Vera constructs Nehanda as a special character free of any colonial influence, politically, culturally and socially. She is the rallying cry of the revolutionaries:

> Spread yourselves through the forest and fight till the stranger decides to leave. Let us fight till the battle is decided. Is death not better than this submission? There is no future till we have regained our lands and our birth. There is only this moment, and we have to fight till we have redeemed ourselves. What is today's work on this land if tomorrow we have to move to a new land? (*Nehanda* 1993: 66).

Nehanda's visions are supernatural, and she communicates orally to her indigenous people ideas diametrically opposed to Western and colonial social and cultural norms. If Vera's novel *Nehanda* serves as an anthem for resistance against colonial oppression, then her title character and Mr. Browning function as cultural and political foils of one another.

A Clash of Religions

In the section of *Nehanda* in which a priest tries to convert Kaguvi to Christianity, Vera shows a clash of cultures in which two sincere, believing individuals misconceive each other's positions. Kaguvi, whom Vera presents as the personification of oral culture, finds the notion that a printed book could contain divinity deeply problematic, in part because writing to him separates the words of the speaker from his or her presence. Since Kaguvi does not come from a printed culture, the multiple implication and functions of a book puzzle him; and as he points out to the Christian, his is a "strange [god who] is inside your book, but also in many books" (*Nehanda* 1993: 105). Kaguvi's god stands in utter contrast to this book-bound divinity:

> My god lives up above. He is a pool of water in the sky. My god is a rain-giver. I approach my god through my ancestors and my mudzimu. I brew beer for my god to praise him, and I dance. My mudzimu is always with me, and I pay tribute to my protective spirit (*Nehanda* 1993: 105).

The priest explains that his god also "is in the sky" (*Nehanda* 1993: 105), but then makes a theological claim that appears completely bizarre and inappropriate from a Shona point of view: He tells Kaguvi whom he wishes to convert because "my God is the true God. He is the way to eternal happiness" (*Nehanda* 1993: 105). Two aspects of Christian belief here puzzle Kaguvi: First, that happiness is eternal and, second, that hard work is bad and that any form of happiness involves freedom from what Kaguvi takes to be a crucial and pleasurable human activity:

> Kaguvi [...] has never entertained such an improbable idea as eternal happiness. If a man harvests his crops, that is happiness. If a man marries and has children, that is happiness. If a man talks to his neighbours and they respect him, that too is happiness. [...] Work is not suffering, even though the priest insists that work has come into the world as a punishment on one man. What kind of god is this that will not be appeased with beer poured on the ground? It is not punishment for a man to do all he can for a good harvest. For a man not to labour is laziness. "Shall we go to heaven to be lazy?" (*Nehanda* 1993: 105).

Another idea that is nonsensical to the Shona community is that all "shall be kings in heaven" [...] "We shall all be kings?" Kaguvi repeats incredulously. To him, this would be a chaotic world indeed. He makes impatient sounds through his cheeks. This was a matter for a man to consider with his kin" (*Nehanda* 1993: 106). The individualism implicit in this presentation of Christianity conflicts with a worldview based upon community – something that Vera reveals through Kaguvi's thought that this strange idea is something a man does not consider by himself, but discuss with those closest to him. When the priest then tells Kaguvi, "Your god is an evil god" (*Nehanda* 1993: 106), explaining that he has come to save him from "eternal flames" (*Nehanda* 1993: 106), Kaguvi finds the priest's arrogance shocking. Looking for common ground, Kaguvi agrees that "there is life after death" (*Nehanda* 1993: 106), meaning, of course, a "life as a spirit, to help protect those who are living" (*Nehanda* 1993: 106) while the priest insists on an afterlife "in which men will rise from their graves in their former bodies" (*Nehanda* 1993: 106).

Vera illustrates that the two approaches to spirituality are fundamentally different. Neither man is truly able to reconcile his vision of God and worship with that of the other. But it is Kaguvi who consistently makes the effort to interrogate the other man's belief system and practices; he "is not one to close his mind to a mystery. It is better to know what governs the stranger's world, and what secret fears he holds" (*Nehanda* 1993: 104). The priest, however, does not seek more information in order to reach an understanding or reconciliation between the two men and their cultures, but instead tries to convert, teach, and save his ignorant audience. It can be argued that this scene suggests a kind of a moral and humanistic superiority on the part of Kaguvi and his people that is echoed throughout Vera's text.

Oral Culture versus the Written World

While the colonisers revere the spoken word, the native people do not understand the potential power of written language: "How can words be still, without turning into silence?" (*Nehanda* 1993: 43). Language is an inherent part of the life and souls of the Zimbabwean people. In fact, the concept of language is central to acquiring an understanding of the true losses incurred as result of colonisation. Vera's prose is redolent with references to the power of words:

> Our people know the power of words. It is because of this that they desire to have words continuously spoken and kept alive. We do not believe that words can become independent of the speech that bore them, of the humans who controlled and gave birth to them. [...] The paper is the stranger's own peculiar custom. Among ourselves, speech is not like rock. Words cannot be taken from the people who create them. People are their words (*Nehanda* 1993: 39-40).

In a speech at the Royal Palace in Amsterdam on 19 December 1997, Vera pointed out that "much importance is placed, and should be placed, on oral culture – folk tales, narratives, proverbs and inherited wisdom and values" (Vera 1997: 16). Consequently, "there is importance in developing permanent information systems and 'memory banks' that are more easily accessed" (Vera 1997: 15). Vera (1997: 16) refers to Chinua Achebe's *Things Fall Apart*, one of the most crucial books in the development of African identity, which responds to Joseph Conrad's *Heart of Darkness*. Achebe's novel demonstrates that the natural idiom of a language, and the defence of a culture and an identity, can all be accomplished through writing.

Writing gathers the laughter of generations and collects it to satisfy hunger. Writing, and in particular women writing, unites in a way that goes beyond every other unity. It makes the richness of the oral world visible and helps in the effort at recovery. Silence would mean death, and so writing has rescued the Zimbabweans from the death of their words by keeping them alive. In an article for the *AZ*, Vera concludes that writing has become freer than speaking (*AZ* 1997: 51). Hence, she supports that books are made much more accessible in Zimbabwe, for instance by mobile libraries (Vera 1997: 16).

Change has already occurred, and new values have been integrated: "In the valley [...] the beginning of a new language and a new speech [is heard]" (*Nehanda* 1993: 112). Vera's use of the book format – like the use of the guns by the freedom fighters – to protect the pre-colonials from change signals that change is bound to occur. Instead of denying its propensities, Vera emphasises the inevitability of change and victory. In fact, the more exerted the struggle, the more signs of change are likely to occur: to fire guns is more powerful than to throw stones, and to publish a book is a more effective way of speaking to a wide audience than to give a series of speeches. According to Vera, resisting change gains effectiveness if knowledge of its inevitability is addressed. This implies that liberation grows out of change, especially when the liberation of women is concerned.

Postcolonial Feminism in *Nehanda*

One of the fundamental tenets of recent postcolonial theory is that among the first necessary steps in the newly found colonial independence is the reclamation of the previously disparaged and disrespected culture. This project, called the cultural nationalist phase by Frantz Fanon (1967: 145), carries with it some dubious baggage. An apparently necessary result of the glorification of pre-colonial culture is the acceptance of, or the refusal, to deal with inherent issues of gender inequality or abuse within society. With the passage of time since independence, authors have begun to turn their eyes to the harsher realities of the present, and in doing so, attempt to initiate a dialogue about the issue of women in African society. Looking at Vera's novel with an eye towards trends in postcolonial theory, Greenwald (1999) suggests that one could assume that it was written with an awareness of this need for a new, more consistent and realistic vision of women in Africa. Vera comments: "In cheerful voices the women celebrate their shelter-giving selves, and see new existences come out of the dreaming air. [...] They clap their hands and create new songs to help clear the path into new lives" (*Nehanda* 1993: 113).

That Nehanda is introduced first as a daughter (the description of her birth, difficult and intriguing) and then as a woman with near-supernatural powers of inspiration and eyes "filled with prophecies" (*Nehanda* 1993: 80) is indicative of the novel's feminist overtones and challenges the essentially masculine ethics of colonialism. Nehanda is a woman praised by her community for her uniqueness, rather than solely for her fulfilment of a traditionally prescribed role. If Nehanda represents the spirit of Zimbabwe, as Vera seems to imply, then the nation, born under pain and difficulty and possessing a rich and unique vision, must struggle to maintain its independence against the overpowering strength of British imperialism, "microcosmically pitting female against male in a cataclysmic battle of forces that will determine the history of both peoples" (Bose 1995: 212). Nehanda is transformed into a spiritual leader, the guide and heart of the resistance. She seems to possess a true vision of the future when she tells her people that "the tradition of the white man will destroy us" (*Nehanda* 1993: 81). Yet, what immediately follows is troubling: "Nehanda speaks as she gives guns to the people" (*Nehanda* 1993: 81). Instead of seeking to avoid the future, Nehanda appears to fulfil it by instructing her people to take up guns in the technological tradition of the white man. This scene from the novel hints at a genuine ability or realisation of the need to adapt to the future.

So what is it that the "Zimbabwean Jean of Arc" (Patsanza 1993: 2) wants to tell her folk? In a review of the book, Brinda Bose talks enthusiastically about *Nehanda*, stating that the "poetic novel [...] speaks to both postcolonialism and feminism in the historical context of Zimbabwe" (1995: 212). *Nehanda* is a novel that seeks to restore women in African society. Vera's book could be read as an attempt to legitimise a ravaged culture. However, in a published interview, Vera (quoted in Hill 1993: 19) states that there is no exact historical accuracy in her frequent examples of culture and cultural ritual – she made up most of it. Vera was more interested in writing about Nehanda out of her own experience and instinct. So her issue, then, is one of feminism. Yet, Nehanda's role in this remains unclear. Is she a mistaken vision of women, a woman so respected that she is ushered out of relevance? Or is she a bold example of the inextricable bond that exists between the African feminist battle for equality and the African battle against colonialism? No answers for this are provided within the text; however, as the book ends, the "chasm between the living and the dead is broken" (*Nehanda* 1993: 118). The gender issues that exist within Africa, like the issues of colonialism, clearly cannot be solved with the old solutions. Without new things, the cycle of failure is bound to repeat itself.

Conclusion

After independence, writers were confronted with several dilemmas, in particular the use of language. Hove has tried to Africanise the English language in order to give it a new identity. To him the colonial language had become indigenous to Africa and appropriate to express his Zimbabwean experience. Identification with the country takes place through a poetic language rich in Shona idiom. Vera, too, uses English but in a lyrical way that shows a love for her country. Both writers finally prove that "Zimbabwean literature can be read as a quest for [...] identity ("Who are we?")" (Bamiro 2000: 203).

Hove's novel tries to create unity and identification with national greatness by referring to Zimbabwe's national heritage. Vera' *Nehanda* also refers to Zimbabwe's history of resistance and the myth of Nehanda and stresses the need for traditions. Yet, whereas Hove only focuses on Zimbabwe's past and the cultural heritage, Vera expresses an interest in the reality of Zimbabwe as well. The picture she paints does not allow the construction of a single version of Zimbabwe, but rather shows its diversity. By diversity, the young writer means especially gender diversity. In *Bones*, Hove's identification with Zimbabwe primarily crystallises through the country's cultural heritage and rural Zimbabwe's self-image. His is an imagined country and a countryside described along romanticised tradition. He constructs a specific idea of Zimbabwe with a sense of unity rooted in the past and traditions, thereby excluding economic and social realities.

Moreover, the characters in the novels are presented as typically Zimbabwean, embodying essential Zimbabwean values. They can therefore be taken as representatives of the different ideas of Zimbabwe. In *Bones*, especially the Zimbabwean country people are portrayed as representatives of Zimbabwe. Hove depicts rural women who define themselves as women in the traditional sense. Vera takes the spirit medium Nehanda as the epitome of the unique and quintessential Zimbabwean woman. Hers is a picture of the true Zimbabwean people and, in particular, Zimbabwean women who actively shape their lives.

The largely rural and traditional Zimbabwe, with which Hove and, partly, Vera identify, disappeared with the onset of colonisation and modernisation, yet their novels show that this self-image of the nation still persists today. Moreover, a conflict between the city and the country becomes visible in Hove's idea of contemporary Zimbabwe. Urban Zimbabwe is shown from a negative perspective and explained as an outcome of Robert Mugabe's autocratic rule. The merit is clearly given to the countryside which embodies the traditions and values inherent in and crucial for a healthy nation.

Hove also feels a division between the rich and the poor growing within Zimbabwe. While the country's leadership take as much as they can, people in the streets can only afford to wear rags. Both his and Vera's novel depict Zimbabwe as a society dominated by class differences. With the help of Nehanda, Vera attempts to convince the whites of the virtues of diversity. To her, a future collective identity is not possible without the inclusion of new things, like the book format and, in particular, a new perception of womanhood. At the 1993 Book Fair in Harare, Vera was wearing clothes made out of differently shaped and coloured pieces. The outfit bears something magical for her, and she stated that only fundamentalists believe that theirs is something pure (Imfeld 1994: 23). Ultimately, her central message was the promotion of diversity in race, ethnicity, religion, and gender. It seems that Vera, unlike the political leadership, is in favour of a deliberate process of building a collective identity. In her opinion, the process of nation-building itself should take into account the cultural and linguistic differences, which will finally enrich the nation.

References

ACHEBE, CHINUA
    (1962). *Things Fall Apart*. London: Heinemann.
    (1965). "The African Writer and the English Language." *Transition*. Also published in Patrick Williams and Laura Chrisman, eds. *Colonial Discourse and Post-Colonial Theory: A Reader*. London: Harvester Wheatsheaf, 428-434.
    (1975). *Morning Yet on Creation Day*. London: Heinemann.
ANDERSON, BENEDICT
    (1983). *Imagined Communities: Reflections on the Origin and Spread of Nationalism*. London: Verso.
APPIAH, KWAME ANTHONY
    (1992). *In My Father's House. Africa in the Philosophy of Culture*. Oxford: Oxford University Press.
ASHCROFT, BILL, GARETH GRIFFITH, AND HELEN TIFFIN
    (1989). *The Empire Writes Back. Theory and Practice in Post-Colonial Literatures*. London: Routledge.

ASSMANN, ALEIDA
  (1988). "Kollektives Gedächtnis und kulturelle Identität." In Jan Assmann and
  Tonio Hölscher, eds. *Kultur und Gedächtnis*. Frankfurt: Suhrkamp, 9-19.
  (1994). "Zum Problem der Identität aus kulturwissenschaftlicher Sicht." In Rolf
  Lindner, ed. *Die Wiederkehr des Regionalen. Über neue Formen kultureller
  Identität*. Frankfurt: Campus-Verlag, 13-15.
AZ
  (1997). "Gegen das Schweigen. Die Autorin Yvonne Vera über afrikanische
  Literatur." *AZ*, 19/20 April, 51.
BAMIRO, EDMUND OLUSHINA
  (2000). *The English Language and the Construction of Cultural and Social Identity
  in Zimbabwean and Trinbagonian Literature*. New York: Peter Lang.
BOEHMER, ELLEKE
  (1991). "Stories of Women and Mothers: Gender and Nationalism in the Early
  Fiction of Flora Nwapa." In Susheila Nasta, ed. *Motherlands: Black Women's
  Writing from Africa, the Caribbean and South Asia*. London: Women's Press, 6-25.
BOSE, BRINDA
  (1995). "Review of 'Nehanda'." *World Literature Today* Winter, 212-213.
CHITAURO, MOREBLESSING, CALEB DUBE, AND LIZ GUNNER
  (1994). "Song, Story and Nation: Women as Singers and Actresses in Zimbabwe."
  In Liz Gunner, ed. *Politics and Performance: Theatre, Poetry and Song in
  Southern Africa*. Johannesburg: Witwatersrand University Press, 111-138. (Also
  published in Eckhard Breitinger, ed. *Theatre and Performance in Africa*. Bayreuth:
  Bayreuth African Studies 31, 1994, 169-198).
CONRAD, JOSEPH
  (1994). *Heart of Darkness*. London: Penguin Books.
DANGAREMBGA, TSITSI
  (1988). *Nervous Conditions*. Harare: ZPH.
DAVIDSON, JEAN
  (1997). *Gender, Lineage and Ethnicity in Southern Africa*. Colorado: Westview
  Press.
ENGELKE, MATTHEW
  (1998). "Thinking about Nativism in Chenjerai Hove's Work." *Research in
  African Literatures* 29: 2, 1-23.
FANON, FRANTZ
  (1967). *The Wretched of the Earth*. Harmondsworth: Penguin.
FERGUSON, CHARLES
  (1959). "Diglossia." *Word* 15, 325-340.
GIBBS, JAMES
  (1997). "Review of 'Ancestors'." *World Literature Today* 71: 4, 856.
GRAY, STEPHEN
  (1997). "The Unsayable Word." *Mail & Guardian*, 20-26 March, 6.
GREENWALD, ANDY
  (1999). "Postcolonial Feminism in Nehanda."
  www.landow.stg.brown.edu/post/zimabwe/vera/greenwald1.html. 19.03.01

HERDER, JOHANN GOTTFRIED
    (1966). *Essay on the Origin of Language*. New York: Ungar.
HILL, HEATHER
    (1993). "Writer Sends Spirit Medium from Canada with Love." *Northern News*: October, 19.
HOVE, CHENJERAI
    (1988). "Children of Memory: Reflections on the Southern African Novel." *The Guardian*: 15 August, 17.
    (1989). "View from Two Worlds. A Writer's Thoughts on Art, Women, and Life." *Africa South*: September/October, 44-45.
    (1995). "Nation under Siege." *Financial Gazette*: 21 December.
    (1999). *Bones*. Harare: Baobab Books (first published in 1988).
IMFELD, AL
    (1994). "Schriftstellerinnenfrühling in Zimbabwe. Nadelstiche und Bewusstseinsübungen." *WoZ* 42: 21 October, 23.
INDEPENDENT ZIMBABWE
    (1989). *Independent Zimbabwe*. Harare: Government Printers.
INFORMATIONSDIENST SÜDLICHES AFRIKA
    (1988). "Schritte zu einem nationalen Verlagswesen." *Informationsdienst Südliches Afrika* 8, 5.
JAYAWARDENA, KUMARI
    (1982). *Feminism and Nationalism in the Third World*. The Hague: Institute of Social Studies.
KAHARI, GEROGE P.
    (1980). *The Search for Zimbabwean Identity*. Gweru: Mambo Press.
KITSON, NORMA, ed.
    (1994). *English Anthology*, no.1. Harare: Zimbabwe Women Writers.
LAN, DAVID
    (1985). *Guns & Rain. Guerillas & Spirit Mediums in Zimbabwe*. Berkeley, Los Angeles: University of California Press; London: James Currey.
MCCLINTOCK, ANNE
    (1991). "No Longer in a Future Heaven: Women and Nationalism in South Africa." *Transition* 51, 104-123.
MOTO
    (1994). "'Girls, Let's Tell Them!'" *Moto*, June, 19.
MUTSWAIRO, SOLOMON
    (1957). *Feso*. Oxford: Oxford University Press.
    (1978). *Mapondera: Soldier of Zimbabwe*. Washington DC: Three Continents Press.
    (1983). *Chaminuka: Prophet of Zimbabwe*. Washington DC: Three Continents Press.
MUSANDIREVE, CHIGANGO
    (1995). "Great Expectations. Ladies and Gentlemen – Yvonne Vera has Arrived!" *Moto* February, 20.
NGARA, EMMANUEL
    (1982). *Bilingualism, Language Contact, and Language Planning: Proposals for Language Use and Language Teaching in Zimbabwe*. Gwelo: Mambo Press.

NGUGI WA THIONG'O
(1987). *Decolonising the Mind: The Politics and Language of African Literature.* Harare: Zimbabwe Publishing House.
PATSANZA, JIMMY
(1993). "Zimbabwe's Joan of Arc. Nehanda by Yvonne Vera." *The Herald*, 2 August, 2.
SCHWARZER, PETRA
(1993). "Schreibende Frauen in Zimbabwe." In Liselotte Glage and Martina Michel, eds. *Postkoloniale Literaturen: Peripherien oder neue Zentren?* Gulliver Deutsch-Englische Jahrbücher, vol.33, Hamburg: Argument-Verlag, 112-120.
SIMATEI, TIROP PETER
(2001). *The Novel and the Politics of Nation Building in East Africa.* Bayreuth: Bayreuth African Studies 55.
THE ECONOMIST
(1990). "Zimbabwe's Literary Voice. Talking to the Soil." *The Economist*, 28 April, 117.
(2000). "Zimbabwe's Tighter Belts, and Shorter Tempers. How Long Can Robert Mugabe Hold On?" *The Economist*, 28 October, 53.
THE HERALD
(1999). "ZIBF." *The Herald*, 25 February.
VEIT-WILD, FLORA
(1988). *Patterns of Poetry in Zimbabwe.* Gweru: Mambo Press.
(1992). *Teachers, Preachers, Non-Believers. A Social History of Zimbabwean Literature.* London: Hans Zell Publishers.
(1993). "'Dances with Bones': Hove's Romanticised Africa." *Research in African Literatures*, 24: 3., 2-9.
VERA, YVONNE
(1993). *Nehanda.* Harare: Baobab Books.
(1997). "Zimbabwean Lives: the Visual Arts, Books and National Development." *Prince Claus Fund Journal* .1, 12-16.
WEISS, RUTH
(1985). *The Women of Zimbabwe.* Harare: Nehanda Publishers.
WITTMANN, VERONIKA
(1999). *Nehandas widerspenstige Töchter. Eine Analyse zimbabweanischer Frauenorganisationen.* Linz: Universitätsverlag Rudolf Trauner.
YANG, JOHN
(1999). "The Dilemma of 'Progress'."
www.landow.st.brown.edu/post/zimbabwe/vera/yang.html
ZHUWARARA, RINO
(1996). "Gender & Liberation. Chenjerai Hove's Bones." In Emmanuel Ngara, ed. *New Writing from Southern Africa. Authors Who Have Become Prominent Since 1980.* London: James Currey, 29-44.

Writing Woman Writing Culture: The Scripting of *Potent Secrets*

JOYCE A. ABUNAW
Storrs, USA

"Potent Secrets" directed by Ako Abunaw, is a video film shot in Yaounde, Cameroon in 2001. Potent Secrets tells the story of Philip Nso. Philip gets married to Laura and for five years they have no children. It doesn't bother him until his mother, Ma Nso starts complaining about the quietness of the house. She insinuates that the problem must be with Laura who had a secret child before marriage and therefore must be cursed by the gods for hiding this child. Philip, who was unaware of this secret child, gets angry and throws Laura out because she tells him that the answer to their infertility may be a medical check-up for both of them. With the help of his mother and sister, Philip marries a new wife, Matilda, who gives birth to a baby boy, Anakin, exactly nine months after their marriage. All is well for five years until Matilda's ex-boyfriend Kevin lays claim to Anakin. With circumstantial evidence pointing towards Philip's infertility, he decides to consult a medical doctor and...

The story ends here ... It was written as part of a series and was just packaged into one film as a marketing alternative while we shopped TV markets for buyers. Thinking about scripting *Potent Secrets* took some months but the actual writing was done in five fitful days. The polishing and fine-tuning followed.

To write about one's writing process is confronting at once the writer as subject and object. Interrogating this writing process then conjures up certain questions. Why did I want to write? What assumptions and influences did I bring to the script? How did I package my message so it could be best understood?

There are as many different reasons for writing as there are writers. What underlies every writing, however, is the need to communicate. *Potent Secrets* is my response to a number of Nigerian video films I have watched. I returned to Cameroon from the United States in 1999 and found many Cameroonians, especially Anglophones (since the films are in English), devouring video films pouring into Cameroon from neighboring Nigeria. These films were replete with diverse themes, but the representation of women was almost always the same. "Woman" was constructed within a patriarchal ideology reinforcing society's dominant values. With Cameroonians watching these films avidly, the films were agents of socialization, transmitting stereotyped images of sex-roles, particularly to young people. I immediately became fed up watching the stereotyped scenarios: a woman marries a man, sacrifices all she can for the man and has children. When the man dies earlier than expected, she is blamed for his death and is made to undergo untold suffering. Another scenario: When a young girl gets pregnant, she is abandoned by her boyfriend and abandoned by her own family, and this girl may die in the process of abortion. If she got married and could not conceive, the girl was blamed for having had an abortion while her boyfriend suffered no stigma. The scenarios are countless. Nevertheless, one of the themes that kept popping up was infertility. Problems faced by childless couples were heavily dramatized, and the woman always carried the blame suffering both physical and psychological anguish. The childlessness was always blamed on the woman's "rough" past or witchcraft practiced usually by another woman, and the men were never in the picture.

There is a common saying, "when you want something and can't find it already made, it may be time to create your own." I knew I had to write a film script that would present these same familial issues from a woman's perspective. My women characters were not going to be saints but justified sinners, women with logic to their actions. As Joan Didion, an American writer, asserts "in many ways, writing is the act of saying I, of imposing oneself upon other people, of saying listen to me, see it my way, change your mind [...] (qtd. in Kennedy, Kennedy and Aaron 149). Like Sue Thornham, I believe that "film is particularly an effective carrier of ideology because its textual systems are based on the moving photographic image" (216). I had to get Cameroonians and the rest of the world to see it from my perspective.

Two years ago when I began writing *Potent Secrets*, I had no experience in scriptwriting, although I had acted in many TV and stage dramas in Cameroon and had even taken Theater Arts as a minor as an undergraduate. I did not have any woman scriptwriter as a model to follow. However, I was aware of the general assumptions of feminist theories, which have three major tenets:

> [That] gender is a social construction, which oppresses women more than men; that patriarchy shapes this construction; and that women's experiential knowledge is a basis for a future non sexist society. These assumptions inform feminism's double agenda: the task of critique (attacking gender stereotypes)[...] and the task of construction. (Maggie Humm, 194).

But I had to situate these feminist perceptions within the women's tradition in African Literature that I am familiar with. So, although I was scripting for a film, my influences were from African literary texts, particularly Flora Nwapa's *Efuru*, Buchi Emecheta's *Joys of Motherhood*, Nawal El Sadawi's *Woman at Point Zero* and Mariama Ba's *So long a letter*. These novels all illuminate women's spaces in African societies. Interestingly enough, *Efuru* and *Joys of Motherhood* deal with the problems of infertility and the impact they have on women. In fact Susan Andrade, in "Rewriting History, Motherhood and Rebellion: Naming a Women's Literary tradition," has pointed out the intertextuality between these two novels. In terms of style, however, Emecheta's *Joys of Motherhood* has always tickled my creativity. Emecheta tells the story and leaves the reader to figure out its implication. Nnu Ego, the central character, is presented as innocently as in the title *Joys of Motherhood*. She fulfils the cultural expectations of marriage by having many children including boys. She sacrifices her own life to take care of her children, but her life becomes one long story of suffering, and she dies without experiencing the 'joys of motherhood', or does she? The final passage from the text reads:

> After such wandering on one night, Nnu Ego lay down by the roadside, thinking that she had arrived home. She died quietly there, with no child to hold her hand and no friend to talk to her. She had never made friends, so busy had she been building up her joys as a mother...
>
> Stories afterwards, however, said that Nnu Ego was a wicked woman even in death because, however many people appealed to her to make women fertile, she never did...Still many agreed that she had given all to her children. The joy of being a mother was the joy of giving all to your children, they said...And her reward? Did she not have the greatest funeral Ibuza had ever seen [...]
>
> Nnu Ego had it all, yet still did not answer prayers for children (224).

The way she dies and her refusal to grant fertility to women who beseech her is Emecheta's punch line. It doesn't take a sophisticated reader to see that Nnu Ego's failure results in her total fulfillment of cultural expectations. The reader comes to this conclusion through the way Emecheta constructs meaning. There's no browbeating, only logical chaining of events. This is what I intended to do with my script so that in the film "representations are not merely reflections of reality whether 'true' or 'distorted' but are rather the product of an active process of selecting and presenting, of structuring and shaping, of making things mean" (Sue Thornham, 215).

Chinua Achebe reports that in reading Conrad, Cary, Rider Haggard and other colonial writers, he realized that "Stories are not innocent; that they can be used to put you in the wrong crowd, in the party of the man who has come to dispossess you" (7). While reading the works of these writers, Achebe admits that he initially was on the side of the hero who was usually white. He did not see himself as one the black savages presented as docile and primitive. It is with this innocence that many women enjoy Nigerian movies in Cameroon. While women characters are abused and victimized in the films, the women viewers sympathize with the male heroes who have to endure these "bitches" and "witches." Having seen how African women writers like Nwapa, Emecheta, Ba, and Sadawi enter into dialogue with African male writers by writing women-centered texts, I entered into dialogue with these male dominated video films.

However, not only did I lack an African woman filmmaker as a model, in Cameroon the video film industry was still at zero. Working therefore as a pioneer carried a big challenge and a whole lot of responsibility. As Humm posits, "to centralize women's experiences of sexuality, work and the family inevitably challenges traditional frameworks of knowledge" (194). Now for me, the challenge posed itself even before I started writing. The director was not just male; he was my husband; and his vision of the script was supposed to influence the final product. I was aware that our interpretation of the script could be different and this could generate a power struggle at different levels. Thus, winning the director to my side was a metonymy for overcoming male myopia.

Adeola James once asked Ama Ata Aidoo, the veteran African writer, "Do you see any distinction in the way male and female African writers dramatize their themes and select significant events?" Aidoo's response is worth quoting at length:

> That is a question I have always been a bit nervous about. People have asked and I have heard other women writers say that because they are women, they relate to things or select their themes or treat things in a certain way. I have not actually gone into that question in relation to myself and I don't know. I think as a woman writer, you approach issues from your position in life, in society in history as a woman. Now, as to whether the result of that position is saying things different from how a man would say or select them, that is a question critics ought to answer [...] I hope that in operating as a woman, that doesn't mean anything silly, in the way people think women are silly" (qtd. in Adeola James, 12).

What underlines Aidoo's response here is not the fear of sounding "woman." Rather, it is the societal construction of the term "woman." It is this same fear that made Flora Nwapa refuse the label of "feminist" and Buchi Emecheta to claim, she is a feminist with a small "f". Writing *Potent Secrets* also generated such doubts and questions. What does writing from a woman's perspective mean? How significant are these issues I want to raise? Do they disturb the general peace? What if the director finds my concerns trivial? These doubts are real, and they will confront any serious-minded African woman who has been made to look at the realities of womanhood as trivial and too parochial to be of "national" interest. Thus confronted with writing 'woman', there is always this anxiety laced with the fear of rejection in the African cultural market place. Despite the growing number of African women writers, writing one's self as subject is still like standing naked in front of the mirror with others watching. What you see, they see. Writing thus becomes an interpretation of one's self, a presentation of one's reflection from the self.

Therefore, in negotiating this space between "I" and "We," I found my vehicle of communication — comedy of errors involving humor, dramatic irony, innocence and the alignment of the "I" and "We" viewpoint. I was not going to impose any new theories or ideas on the characters. I was just going to let them speak and act the way they do in real life and let the viewers (we) decide from the writer's privileged point of view (I). I refrained from giving high-sounding feminist jargons to my women characters to regurgitate. All they had to do was maintain their African woman sensibilities and the truth was going to prevail. I also wrote the script with our African participatory audience in mind and in the mode of popular theater. I wrote lines, which induced certain reactions and I expected them. If I did not get those reactions then I must have failed. With this in mind I created the characters and the story.

Philip: A sensible man with the capacity to think, but he has been brought up in a society which has led him to believe that only women are responsible for conception. So he asks his wife questions like, "Am I the one unable to get pregnant?" This question underlies some of the cultural assumptions that underlie conception. Since it is a woman who carries the baby for nine months, she must be the one in charge of conception. The reaction of the viewers at different screenings has been quite revealing. The viewers scorn his seemingly intelligent question. One of the high points for viewers is when Philip goes to the hospital to consult a doctor on his situation. After telling the doctor his experiences with his two wives, he adds, "And I used to make love to them very well." This always draws hysterical laughter from the audience and in several of the screenings the viewers shout: "That's not the point." Indeed, that's not the point, but I made sure that the logic is presented in a way that will make the viewers come to that conclusion. This has led Fusi Martin to assert that "Abunaw uses humor as a technique to ridicule dominant cultural assumptions, for there is no mistaking the serious undertones belying the humor in the film [...] the film is a bold attempt at facing harsh realities that are unspoken of in Cameroonian society" (Unpublished Review). At the end Philip is as much a victim as the women. He is a victim of a society that has nurtured his false sense of self. Thus, when he comes to suspect the truth, he takes the logical step of seeking expert opinion. The viewers empathize with him and applaud his courage. Some members of the all-male technical crew appealed to me to take out the ending where Philip consults a doctor. They claimed "We understand what you are trying to say but don't punish the man too much. That's too much for an African man to endure," but I insisted to the director on keeping it since that was precisely the reason why that scene was created. I made a half joke, saying I was even kind to Philip because I did not make him strip before the doctor and I did not make the doctor female. Indeed the all-male crew gave me the kind of vibes I expected from the viewers. I want the viewers to get a sense of what it entails for countless women to go stripping in front of countless doctors during countless medical examinations for the sole purpose of having children, while the men sit at home and absolve themselves of any biological problem.

Ma Nso (Philip's Mother): As the oldest character in the story, she embodies traditional African assumptions. She comes in with her own cultural stereotypes: a woman who has had a baby before marriage is not good enough for her son. Such a woman is a "second hand" article. Although she herself is a woman, Ma Nso also believes that conception is the sole responsibility of a woman. Hence, although her daughter in-law has already conceived a child before marriage, she is blinded to her fertility and still pins the problem on her. She argues that her daughter-in-law has been cursed because she has kept her child secret. When Philip's second wife, Matilda, gives birth to Anakin, Ma Nso is beyond herself with excitement. Matilda is scared that the child's features will expose her secret, but her friend, Claire, calms her using a cultural jibe, "Have you seen a child that does not resemble the father especially a male child? Relax, anyone who comes here will see some form of resemblance." Just as she finishes saying this, Ma Nso enters and exclaims, "This child looks exactly like Philip when he was a baby." The viewers go wild with laughter because they know the truth. Claire, Matilda's friend, knows that in Ma Nso's cultural blindness she would not notice the absence of Philip's features on the new baby's face. Ma Nso's reasoning is clear: All men are potent. Philip is a man. Therefore, the child is Philip's.

When it is revealed at the end that Philip's "child" with Matilda is not biologically his, the viewers can't wait for Philip's mother to reappear. They want to hear what she has to say now. The viewers actually murmur "finally" when Ma Nso starts to suggest to her son that he may be the problem. Fortunately he has come to that conclusion too. But the big question remains one of custody. Philip is bent on keeping the boy and gives his reasons methodically. He tries to negotiate for custody with Matilda. He tells Matilda:

> This is the time for action, we are going to stick together and face Kevin. I am not going to let Anakin go without a fight. We will win if you remain on my side. Kevin wanted an abortion. I have raised the child for five years. He gave up any rights toward the child when he asked for an abortion. We will win. The court cannot ruin the child's life like that (*Potent Secrets*, "The Script" 38).

At all the screenings where I have been present, the viewers shouted "correct" following all these assertions. However, perhaps in an overzealous attempt to balance out my arguments, I get Ma Nso back in the picture to give a counter argument. In response to Philip's desire to go to court to get custody of Anakin she retorts:

> My son, are you out of your mind? You want to go to court to fight to get another man's child? Even if you are impotent, do you have to go in front of the whole world to show it? My son we hear things like that happening in the white man's land not here in Cameroon. A full-blooded African man will be fighting for another man's child. (Sighs)[...] Don't get emotional. When Anakin gets old enough to know his real father, he will go to him. How will you stop him? Let him go now. I speak with the wisdom of years (*Potent Secrets*, 'The Script" 41).

After the three screenings launching the film in Cameroon, this issue on child custody was hotly debated outside, with tempers flaring. Two lawyers offered to write out the legal arguments for me, for and against, in event that I create a scene where Philip actually goes to court to fight for custody of Anakin.

Laura and Matilda: They are guilty of keeping "Potent Secrets," but their reasons for keeping these secrets are lodged in society's cultural expectations of them as women. Hence, instead of simply seeing their secrets as baseless acts of wickedness, there's an exploration of where things went wrong. Laura is raped at fourteen and she has a baby. Her mother knows that society stigmatizes women who have children out of wedlock, even if it is through rape. She is thus forced to hide the fact that she has a child in order to be "good material" for marriage. Her mother is proven right because once her husband finds out about the child, he sends her away. Matilda, on the other hand, is abandoned by a selfish boyfriend who only thinks of his own future.

Depressed and lonely, with the prospect of having a "bastard" child, she capitalizes on the African society's high premium on children by planting the baby on Philip. This works since Philip is quite willing to be culturally declared "a man."

In *Potent Secrets*, the issue of infertility serves as a launching pad for varied discussions on contemporary African problems exacerbated by African cultural assumptions. I initially titled the Script "Facing Myself" because the main character, Philip, confronts his infertility and because, perhaps subconsciously in writing *Potent Secrets*, I faced "me" as a woman.

Potent Secrets has had a hearty welcome wherever it has been screened. In the US it has been publicly screened four times: in 2002 at the Festival of Arts, University of Southern California, Los Angeles; as part of the 2002 women's History Month celebration in Lehman College, City University of New York; at the 28th annual African Literature Association Conference in San Diego; and as a Postcolonial Studies event at the Graduate School and University Center, City University of New York. In Cameroon, *Potent Secrets* launched the new wave of African films on video spearheaded by Nigeria and it is hoped that this film will open the floodgates of video film production in Cameroon. Especially since video films are more accessible to the community than films on celluloid.

References

ACHEBE, CHINUA
    (1990). "African Literature as a Restoration of Celebration." *Kunapipi* 12:2, 1-10.
ANRADE, SUSAN
    (1990). "Rewriting a History, Motherhood and Rebellion: Naming a Women's Literary Tradition." *Research in African Literatures*, 91-110.
EMECHETA; BUCHI
    (1979). *Joys of Motherhood*. New York: George Braziller, INC.
HUMM, MAGGIE
    (1998). "Feminist Literary Theory." In Stevi Jackson and Jackie Jones, eds. *Contemporary Feminist Theories*. New York: New York University Press, 194-208.
JAMES, ADEOLA
    (1990). "Interview with Ama Ata Aidoo." In *In Their Own Voice: African Women Writers Talk*. London: Heinemann, 1990, 8-27.
KENNEDY, X.J., DOROTHY KENNEDY, AND JANE AARON
    (2003). *The Brief Bedford Reader*. New York: Bedford/St Martins.

THORNHAM, SUE
(1998). "Feminist Media and Film Theory." In Stevi Jackson and Jackie Jones, eds. *Contemporary Feminist Theories*. New York: New York University Press, 213-208.

Kamerun – Reliving German Occupation through Theatre: *Zintgraff and the Battle of Mankon* by Bole Butake & Gilbert Doho

BOLE BUTAKE
Yaounde, Cameroon

Introduction

How many Germans remember that their country was a leading colonial power like Great Britain and France until after the First World War (1914-1918) when the colonies were seized and placed under the trusteeship of the League of Nations that would later transform itself into the United Nations Organization after another World War (1939-1945)? The German Empire played a leading role in the scramble for Africa especially in the organisation of the Berlin Conference (1884-1885) when the African continent was partitioned among a handful of European nations over chunks of pork, dumplings and wine: the United Kingdom, France, Belgium, Spain, Italy and Portugal. Germany grabbed Kamerun, Togo, Tanganyika (Tanzania) and Namibia in what historians would later describe as the partition of Africa. In effect, the Berlin Conference was a way of formalising spheres of influence previously created by the work of missionaries, traders and explorers from the various European nations in different parts of the African continent. In the case of Cameroon, it was a very close struggle between Germany and the United Kingdom of Great Britain, which already had effective control of what was later known as Nigeria. In the end Germany succeeded because its envoys persuaded the chiefs of Duala to sign treaties with them ahead of the sluggish British. German occupation was more along the coast where they established a military base at Duala but were forced to move the capital to Buea, on the foot of Mount Fako, which had a temperate climate and hardly any mosquitoes, the bane of the white man. In order to ensure effective occupation of the territory, expeditions were despatched to explore the interior northwards and eastwards. Dr. Eugen Zintgraff and four other German soldiers, Huwe, Nehber, Tiedt and Von Spagenberg, explored northwards from Duala passing through Mundame and on to Bali which was ruled by Fon Galega, a very powerful king, anxious to expand his kingdom through conquest of neighbouring Fons and their kingdoms. Galega was not alone in his ambitious territorial expansionism in the Grassfields; the Sultan of the Bamouns, the Fon of Nso and even Bafut and Mankon also had their eyes on other peoples' lands thereby throwing the entire region in turmoil resulting in the formation of alliances in order to contain such expansionism. When Galega heard about Zintgraff and his expeditionary force, he saw this as a golden opportunity to fulfil his ambitions by allying with him instead of standing shoulder to shoulder with the Fons of Bafut and Mankon to stop the ongoing occupation of the territory by Germany. But, of course, neither Galega nor the other warring Fons could at the time fathom the colonising intentions of Zintgraff and his fellow country-men.

Dr. Eugen Zintgraff is on record as the first ever European to explore the Grassfields between 1889 and 1891. His personal account of this journey was published in 1895 under the title, *Nord Kamerun,* in which he describes his visit to Yola through Gashaka and Takum; and on his way back was misled to Bafum instead of Bafut. Chilver (1966) gives the following historical account:

> The German explorer, Dr. Eugen Zintgraff, visited Bafut in 1889. He had earlier stopped in Bali Nyonga where he had received a warm welcome from Galega, the Bali Nyonga Fon. However, Abumbi, the Bafut Fon, received him with circumspection since Bafut was not on good terms with Bali Nyonga. Zintgraff is said to have committed two breaches of etiquette. He seized the drinking cup from the Fon's hand and drank from it and he insisted on calling Abumbi by his princely name 'Gualem'. This open display of disrespect was interpreted in Bafut as a deliberate attempt to belittle the Fon and it was assumed that Galega of Bali Nyonga was behind this.
>
> Relations between Bafut and the Germans subsequently deteriorated to the point of armed conflict. In 1891 Bafut went to the aid of its neighbour and ally Mankon which had been attacked by a German-led Bali Nyonga force en route to Bafut. This force had been sent to avenge the death of two of Zintgraff's messengers sent to Bafut to demand ivory. On the 31st of January 1891 it attacked Mankon and burnt the town. As the attacking force retired Mankon warriors, assisted now by their allies from Bafut, counter-attacked and inflicted heavy losses on their enemies. Ten years later the Germans, under Pavel, returned in full force.[1]

This then is the historical background in which the play, *Zintgraff and the Battle of Mankon,* is set.

---

[1] Cf.: http://lucy.ukc.ac.uk/Chilver/Paide.

Summary of the play

The dramatic action takes place in or around Bali Nyonga: the Fon's palace, Zintgraff's residence, etc. The story is dramatized in the African story-telling tradition with a Narrator who gives background information, comments freely on the events in the story and links them with contemporary experiences, and also interacts freely with the characters in the story as well as the spectators. The story opens with the Gweis, Bali Nyonga spies coming to report to Fon Galega that they have gathered information to the effect that there are ghosts (meaning white men) in a neighbouring kingdom. They also report that these white men are causing a lot of havoc, killing and maiming people. Fon Galega immediately sees this as an opportunity for him to form an alliance with these strange people in order to expand his own kingdom through the conquest of Bafut and Mankon, his nearest and most recalcitrant neighbours. This strategy immediately generates opposition from one of his sons, Titanji, who would prefer an alliance with Bafut and Mankon rather than with the white man. The heir to the throne is thus pitted against his father the reigning monarch. It is this conflict between the two that subsequently determines the development of events, culminating in the battle of Mankon and the deaths of all four of Zintgraff's German compatriots. So Titanji, because of his anti-colonial stance, is regarded by his father and the rest of Bali as a traitor; and in the end he suffers the fate of such people: ignominious death. Apart from this highly diplomatic conflict in the play, there is also the development of the love story between Kassa, the Bali princess, and Zintgraff to which Titanji is again vehemently opposed. At the end of the day German colonisation is established with the active assistance of the Fondom of Bali thus signalling the founding of Kamerun.

Although German occupation of Cameroon lasted hardly more than a quarter century, their renown as no-nonsense people is still legendary in Cameroon today among people who were born in the early 1900s. This apart, there are still some very remarkable German landmarks to be found scattered all over the country especially in Buea with its imposing *Schloss*, the Bismark Fountain which was only recently restored, some bridges (such as Idenau) and the Bamenda Fort which is today occupied by services of the North-West Governor's Office.

It was in this background that in 1994 Gilbert Doho and myself wrote and produced *Zintgraff and the Battle of Mankon*, in collaboration with the Goethe Institut (whose country director at the time was Claudia Volmer-Clark) where it premiered. The grandeur and sheer spectacle and, above all, the message, which came at a time of increasing restlessness among the peoples of Cameroon in the wake of the reintroduction of multi-party politics were very deep. *Zintgraff and the Battle of Mankon* was our resounding response to the nonchalant and amateurish manner in which the so-called politicians were playing around with a nation that had been crafted through sweat, tears and blood. But how did the idea of the project come about?

Genesis of *Zintgraff and the Battle of Mankon*

My colleague, friend and co-author of the play, Gilbert Doho, discovered during his research for the Doctorat de 3ème cycle, 1980-1983, the richness of the Bali Chamba culture, as he attended the Lala festival every year. He was made welcome by the late Fon Nyonga and Tita Kunang as well as many other enlightened nobles narrated to him all the historical figures that made the exciting history of the Chambas. He was seduced by the personality of Gawolbe and Galega and read the little book by Chilvers about the fascinating warrior and his cunning alliance with the German colonizer, Zintgraff. It was then that a trilogy came into his head (Gilbert Doho, personal communication).

The first section finished was a novel entitled *Désastre à Bafu-fodong*. In this literary piece, Gilbert Doho depicts the first drastic defeat of a warrior people in the Grassfields. The Chambas were not only defeated, they were humiliated. The bed and skull of their king were captured and taken away by the Fodong people. The second part, *Crusade for Relics* is yet to be written, as Doho states (personal communication). In this part, Doho intends to show the power of manipulation of the Bali people. In history as well as in fiction, Galega will use Zintgraff to go to war against the Fodong in order to recuperate the cherished relics, the bed and skull. One then understands that, beyond the nationalistic chord, there were also the selfish and vengeful desires of the Chambas. Zintgraff did come back. He helped in constructing the great kingdom of Galega and the nation, Kamerun. He also helped the Chambas to regain possession of their relics. The last part of the above mentioned trilogy, *Zintgraff and the Battle of Mankon*, came at a very crucial historical moment of our country. The lesson of this co-writing experience between Gilbert Doho and myself is the combat against the French and Franco-French 'divide-and-rule'-tactics. At a moment when Francophones and Anglophones were tearing at each other, we proved that we can build a solid Cameroon with all our diverse heritage and cultures.

Zintgraff and the Battle of Mankon is then a manner of deconstructing ethno-centricism that the French laid as the foundation stone of governance in our country. In addition, *Zintgraff and the Battle of Mankon* is also a cultural crusade against those who would like to see our cultures annihilated.

The actual writing of the play was done in Germany in the summer of 1993 when I spent three months at the Universität Bayreuth working on the first book on Anglophone Literature in Cameroon with Eckhard Breitinger and Nalova Lyonga. This project resulted in the publication of *Anglophone Cameroon Writing* in the same year.

Collaboration between Doho and myself however had already started in the late 1980s when we were called upon to constitute the nucleus of the teaching staff of 'Arts du Spectacle' (Performing Arts) in the process of creation at the University of Yaounde, the only University in Cameroon at the time, which in 1990/1991 had a student population of 40.000 and was thus the hotbed of political scheming at a time when multi-party politics was re-introduced on the political landscape of the country. He came from the Département de Francais and I from the Department of African Literature and, ever since, we have collaborated in the realisation of a number of projects, especially theatre productions, which transformed the Ngoaekelle (University) campus into a veritable cultural centre for the inhabitants of Yaounde, the capital of Cameroon. This did not please many people, especially the Chancellor of the University at the time, Peter Agbor Tabi, who saw in our theatre work nothing other than subversion against the CPDM (Cameroon People's Democratic Movement) government and so banned all theatre performances on campus and cut off all funding. Ten years later, the situation has not changed.

Producing *Zintgraff and the Battle of Mankon*

Given the above circumstances in which it was impossible to do a production at the University of Yaounde I (the Government had proceeded to create five other Universities in Yaounde, Douala, Buea, Dschang and Ngaoundéré in order to decongest Yaounde) we turned to the Goethe Institute and its director, Claudia Volmer-Clark, all the co-operation which we needed to realise our dreams of a very elaborate and spectacular production that needed very rich costuming, properties, sets, lighting, etc. She also gave us the space for our rehearsals and put all her logistics at our disposal for the opening night which took place in the gardens of the Goethe Institute's premises in down-town Yaounde.

Even before the raising of the curtain, all seats in the garden had been taken and more than one-half of the spectators watched the performance on their feet. The play was full of spectacle, choreographed movement, dialogues spiced with rich idioms, proverbs and riddles, music, song and intricate dance steps; and, above all, history, humour, satire and tragic moments. The standing ovation which the playwrights/directors, actors and the entire production team received during the curtain call was ample proof that the play had struck home, deep at the hearts of the spectators, at the hearts of Cameroonians. Unfortunately, there was no way of continuing with a series of performances because the garden of the Goethe Institute was not suitably fitted for repeat performances. A few months later, there was another performance at the Centre Culturel Français in down-town Yaounde which was patronised mostly by the diplomatic corps and other important personalities in the capital city. Some time later, there was yet another performance at the Centre Culturel Français this time for international medical researchers attending a conference on diabetes in Yaounde. So the play has had its successes; but not without problems. A leading university professor at the University of Buea tried to bring a legal injunction against further performances with the excuse that the play was tarnishing the good image of his late grandfather. We managed to persuade him that such action would only result in ridicule for his high professorial rank seeing that the character in question had not only been fictionalized like practically all the characters in the story but more so, because his grandfather was in fact, as portrayed in the play, the first nationalist to resist colonisation. In fact the play was so successful that the government stole (they did not ask our permission) some of the dance sequences to incorporate into a publicity stunt on Cameroon's participation of the World Cup of 1994 in the United States of America.

Casting

Our casting procedure was based on acting capabilities rather than on their ability to express themselves well in English. This resulted in a fulfilment of one of our desires, namely, making our students capable of expressing themselves in both English and French which is at the base of our curriculum in the Performing Arts Section. So Flaubert Ngassam (francophone) played the lead role of Fon Galega whose two rival sons, Titanji (heir to the throne and anti-Zintgraff) and Titambo (the obedient one) were played by Anderson Funfe and Tita Tabi (both anglophones). Zintgraff was played by a British citizen, Peter Riddlesby, who was at the time a teacher of English at the

British Council, Yaounde, while his girl-friend and princess Kassa was played by Judith Bi Suh. The play has a large cast of noble men, queens, courtiers, soldiers, etc. and the divide between anglophones and francophones was about half and half.

Zintgraff and the Battle of Mankon has just been published by Patron Publishing House, Bamenda (2003), in a bilingual edition (English/French) because the first publisher with whom we had signed a contract more than five years ago defaulted. It will be interesting to see what Germans make of this very fascinating semi-historical play about early German occupation of the Grassfields of Kamerun through the enterprising Dr. Zintgraff.

The Presence of the Past for the Future
Virginia Mukwesha: A Modern Approach to an Ancient Music

VIRGINIA MUKWESHA
Berlin, Germany
FLORIAN HETZE
Berlin, Germany

1 Introduction

We would like to start our contribution to this volume with a provocation: There is no African music. There is no African art, as there is no African dance nor philosophy nor religion. Because, if one speaks of phenomena, which within the European context are referred to by these concepts, one must be aware of the fact that in an African culture, these phenomena are not perceived as autonomous entities. All aspects of African culture can only be understood in a holistic dimension. Thus, if African music is only heard or analysed as a musical or an acoustic phenomenon, then its understanding always remains limited within Western conceptions. It is only in its connection with religion, dance, language, work, daily life, mythology, rituals, applied rhythmic mathematics that African music may be properly understood. The acoustic dimension of the music is only one of its functions in a variety of social and cultural contexts.

In most African languages, there is no word which corresponds in a one to one fashion to the European concept of music. As Gelfand correctly points out:

> In the Shona language, no word precisely translates the Western concept of "music". The Shona have separate words for singing (kuimba) and for playing an instrument (kuridza).[1] Since dancing includes both instruments and songs, the word for dancing (kutamba 'play') implies the combination of these three elements." (Gelfand 1977/1982: 28)

Music, as other artistic forms of expression, is not perceived as an art but as a technique which exists only because it fulfils a particular function. Music is

---

[1] The author is mistaken here as the right word is *kurira* and not *kuridza* ('cause to cry out'). Mbira, however, the instrument of which we will talk in the following, is not 'played' but 'scratched'.

never simply "listened" to but it is used for a particular purpose. For what follows in this article, it is therefore necessary to keep in mind that the use of the term "music" in a European sense does not correspond to its use in an African context.

It is equally important to realise that we do not talk of the past or of tradition as something which is finished, as something which is dying out. To the contrary, we know that traditions are alive and 'kicking'. Tradition in Africa still continues because it has changed and because it keeps constantly changing. This will become clear through our discussion of some cultural implications of the artistic work of the female African musician Virginia Mukwesha.

Virginia Mukwesha is a 'modern traditional' musician from the Shona population of Zimbabwe in southern Africa. As singer and instrumentalist she works both as traditional and as pop musician. She plays the mbira, a lamellophone or so called 'thumb piano', as well as ngoma and hosho, drums and percussion respectively. She has released five albums, made European tours with her band and she has played for years on possession ceremonies, where dead people reappear to possess mediums, as well as working in the field of traditional healing.

However, in order to fully understand her impact and intentions, we need to give some background information on the relevant part of the country of Zimbabwe and its people.

2.1   The history

The area in which the Shona live today is mainly a high plateau with natural borders consisting of rivers and mountains, i.e. the Zambezi river in the west and north, the Limpopo river in the south and the Eastern Highlands. Before the arrival of its present inhabitants, this area had been used by other human cultures of Khoisan or Pygmy origin as testified by many thousands of rock paintings, which have been dated to approximately 20.000 years BC.

Around 3000 years ago, Bantu populations started several migration waves from the region of Cameroon. There had been a route of migrating eastwards and then southwards, and another route which first went south and then eastwards. These Bantu people arrived in southern Africa ca. 300 years AC establishing an early Iron Age culture. Probably, they first settled in the south of the Zimbabwean plateau. After 400 years of a warm and moist epoch they moved to the centre and north of the plateau.

A second wave of immigrants arrived around 900 AC. These people are the direct ancestors of the Shona. They absorbed the original population of Khoisan people by assimilating them.

2.2. Shona states, economy, trade, society

The Shona states may well be understood as empires which were no less systematically and regularly administered than the classic Holy Roman, Persian and Turkish empires. Typical evidence of the Shona settlements are the ruins of the stone enclosures "dzimba dzemabwe" (lit: "houses of stone"), of which there are more than 300. These enclosures surrounded the compounds of the villages or cities. Their location seems to correspond to a system of cattle pastoralism based on the distribution of the tsetse fly and the availability of water and grazing grounds. The economy of the Shona as of many Bantu people was centred on a dual system of agriculture and cattle meat. From the archaeological evidence it seems as if there had been some kind of ruling elite which consumed the prime cattle beef.

The Shona empires had a pre-colonial industry of iron, pottery and cotton fabrics whose products were the exchange goods of internal local and regional networks. Hoes for farming were the overall commodity. But there was also an international connection of long distance trade, which may be dated back as long as the Arab and Swahili coastal traders were operating: 2000 to 3000 years. Long distance trade was in luxury goods for the elite. Already from the thirteenth century onwards, i.e. long before the trade with Europe and especially Portugal started in the sixteenth century, imported goods like glass beads, materials and cloth but also porcelain, came from Persia, China and India. Long distance export goods were gold, ivory and cattle. There is evidence that gold was exported to Arabia as early as in the 4th century.

The children of the Shona emperors used to be educated on Goa in India. Ancestral lineages formed (and still form today) the social organization of patrilineal, totemic, and exogamic clans giving existence to ruling dynasties but serving also as a base for the religion.

The oldest and largest of the stone house complexes mentioned above is the famous Great Zimbabwe on the southern end of the plateau, which dates from the twelfth century. Its extensions make it the largest prehistoric structure in southern Africa. It was the capital of an empire which existed from 1250 to 1450 and which at its peak period counted about 20000 inhabitants.

At a certain point in time, the exploitation of the natural resources was no longer possible and thus Great Zimbabwe declined, eventually collapsed and satellite Zimbabwe states appeared in the centre and west of the plateau: Mutapa 1450-1880 and Torwa 1450-1650, the latter of which became part of the Rozvi empire (1680-1840). Gold production reached its peak with the rise of these two satellite states.

The arrival of the Portuguese did not bring any substantial changes to this state of affairs. From the middle of the 19th century onwards, however, the establishment of a colonial settler regime by the British oppressed the native population and changed its culture dramatically through the forceful introduction of a cash economy.

2.3. Spirituality

Contrary to Western perceptions of life, in the Shona culture the community of people consists of three types of human beings: the dead, the living and the unborn (grandparents, parents and children). They all have an immortal soul and no qualitative distinction is made between the living and the dead or the future living. Both dead and living people are referred to as grandfather or grandmother. The souls of the dead are part of the living community as ancestral spirits. For a soul to become an ancestral spirit, it is necessary that the living relatives fulfil certain rites. The ancestors can only be worshipped if they are not just remembered but also known by their names.

As elder people are more experienced, they are the natural leaders of the community. The older they are the more experience they have and so it is natural for the Shona that the oldest spirits alive, i.e. those of the dead ancestors have the most authority in guiding the community in all its matters. So the closest dead relatives act as what in Western terms could be called 'guardian angels', guiding and protecting the family. These guardians are treated like living people who have needs and wishes, which in turn should be satisfied. If they are not satisfied, accepted, honoured and respected by the living, the guardians – just as anybody else would – might get angry and aggrieved and may punish the family.

As in the world of the living, in the reign of the spirits there also exists a strict hierarchy, ranging from the simple to the high and influential people, from the spirits of the direct ancestors of the family to the clan heroes, from the regional to the national spirits. Most important is the overall communication among the spirits. Thus, for reaching the highest spirit it is also possible to charge the immediate ancestors to pass on matters to the higher and more powerful levels of the spirits' hierarchy until reaching even the creative principle of all and everything. Besides the ancestral spirits, there are also other spirits who avenge (ngozi) or give special talents to a person (shavi or njuzu).

As wealth is traditionally owned by the family and as the ancestors are still part of the family, the country is also owned by the ancestors or their spirits or the spirits of the founders of the family's lineage. Therefore, any political authority is only the living representative of the ancestors' rights administering territory and community on their behalf. So it is also the spirits' right to name the successor of a king or any other ruler. Spirits also mediate in conflicts, give advice in war, guide individuals, etc.

The presence of the spirits is achieved through the phenomenon of the spirit possession. The spirit appears in the body of a person in trance and then can be talked to like any other ordinary person. Westerners often confuse the medium and the spirit. The spirits use the person, who is the medium, only as a material to incorporate themselves. In Shona, the medium is therefore called the "pocket" of the spirit. When possessed, the medium's personality disappears. Afterwards the medium does not remember anything. Anybody of the Shona community can become a medium.

2.4. Shona healers

Most of the traditional medicine is handled by healers who are guided by spirits or who are mediums of spirits.

> [...] in addition to being a medical practitioner, the traditional healer was a religious consultant, a legal and political adviser, a marriage counsellor, a police detective and a social worker. Traditional healers also played an important part in the field of public health. Within each chiefdom, traditional healers, in cooperation with chiefs and headmen, controlled a wide range of basic health conditions: they advised, for example on the choice of village sites and cemeteries. [...] traditional healers of Zimbabwe normally selected defensible locations on high mountain ridges near clean water sources. [...] The society also depended on the skills of certain traditional healers in other arenas of social life such as rain-making, the making of war charms, the treatment of widespread epidemics and the control of locusts. Traditional healers were also expected to find answers to all kinds of personal problems. They were consulted, for example, about the future. (Chavunka 1994: 1)

Apart from their medical work these persons normally live the life of ordinary people. Most of the healers do not charge fees. If a patient wants he or she is free to give some offerings after the successful healing. As in any religion, among the Shona there also are impostors and quacks. The majority of healers were and are women. In Zimbabwe there are today over 40000 registered traditional healers in a country of about 11 million people.

2.5. Shona music and possession ceremonies

It is more than normal in Zimbabwe that you gather your family to hold a ceremony of ancestral spirit possession. Among other possible elements and in the right cultural context, the sound of mbira music attracts the spirit to take possession of the body of the medium which then becomes host of the soul of the dead ancestor.

The living family members consult the wisdom and advice of their dead elder. In such a culture people continue to be part of the community even after their death and the present community is guided into its future by the presence of human experience from the past. Strict rules must be observed for the success of such a ritual. Only then the music will have the desired effect.

A mbira song is a melodic and rhythmic theme, which in performance is coupled with improvised variations. As mbira music probably dates back at least several thousand of years, there are about fifty mbira themes, which are handed down from generation to generation and which are known to have supernatural effects on the listener, i.e. are instrumental in calling a spirit to possess a medium. This classical mbira repertoire is among the deepest musical styles of the planet. Mbira's most important function is to preserve the religious foundation of the culture: the communication with the living spirits of dead ancestors.

Let us have a close look at the music which has such power: mbira music is made of "equi-durational lines": tones are played in lines of equal duration. Special groupings or leaps of intervals make a song. Two or more of these lines are interlocked so that the pulses of one line fall into the intervals of the other line(s). Mbira is mostly played by two people together so that normally four equi-durational lines are interlocked.

The patterns consist of 48 beats subdivided into 4 phrases of 12 beats each. They are constantly repeated so that time starts to take the form of a circle which then expands into kaleidoscopic inner spaces, shifting melodies and criss-cross rhythms beyond your senses. The effect is not only the increased speed of tone production but also the melting of the lines into unstructured sound material. The crucial point comes here: The music is made of more tones than the human ear can perceive in the given time. The ear starts to select only a certain amount of tones to be heard and groups them into melo-rhythmic motives which constantly circulate around each other in a kaleidoscopic manner. This mechanism has an effect on all people who listen to it, irrespective of their cultural background. The resulting patterns may vary from person to person, but also the same person may hear the same mbira song in different ways. The music which is heard is never played as such but it is the ear of the listener which selects tones to form melodies... So it is actually the listener herself or himself who produces the music by playing it inside themselves. This mechanism is the basis for the otherworldly effects generated by mbira music.

So mbira music is basically the interwoven, cyclical interplay of two tone patterns which are interlocking each other so as to reach a certain speed of tone production. By shifting accents or emphasis the musicians can create new sound material for the resulting process which transforms the resultant patterns constantly without playing any new tones.

This way of music with resulting patterns is the essential Central African musical style. The best term to describe the music is "interactive music". Because it differs from 'normal' music in the same way as cinema differs from photography. Just as many images shown per second make the photos join into a movement, so do the tones when played in such a high speed as in mbira interactive music. As mbira music is very soothing it is also used for healing certain illnesses.

The music is more or less fixed but the lyrics are the domain of freedom and improvisation.

A very special feature of Shona music is that it has incorporated structural elements of Khoisan music. The music-ethnologists (special mention to Gerhard Kubik) have discovered that the harmonies of mbira music correspond to those of the Khoisan mouth bow music and also that the Shona have a solo singing style which is probably adopted from the Khoisan, because it is without the usual Bantu call-and-response-structure.

2.6. Shona mbira and lamellophones

'Mbira' literally just means 'key'. Mbira thus is a musical instrument, but also the single key as well as the music played on it. It is also a family of instruments. This plugged instrument is wider spread in Bantu Africa than the drum. No parallels of lamellophones can be found in musical cultures outside Africa – lamellophones are *the* original African musical instrument. The version of the Shona people of Zimbabwe figures among the most perfect and sophisticated of lamellophones based on a highly developed iron processing culture. There are several types of mbira in Zimbabwe just as there are different Shona people. Mbira is not the only instrument of Zimbabwe. Some people play drums and some only sing and dance. The Shona have developed the largest instrument, and use them most frequently in rituals.

The Zezuru mbira or 'mbira huru' – also called 'Dza vaDzimu'[2]- is made of 22 tuned metal sticks, flattened at one end and pinned with the other end on to a flat wooden sound board, which is then wedged into a calabash gourd or fibreglass resonator. Pieces of metal, bottle tops or shells are attached to the soundboard and buzz when the mbira is struck. The players hold the board between the palms of their hands with the free end of the keys pointing towards them. The keys are plucked with thumbs and right index finger and are grouped in three manuals. Hosho – rattles made of dried gourds and filled with seeds - keep time with simultaneity of duple and triple beat.

The oldest archaeological evidence for the existence of iron lamellophones dates back to the fifth century. But there may have been lamellophones and their music before this date, because the keys can also be made of raffia grass or bamboo wood. Musical ethnologists like Gerhard Kubik think that lamellophones date back at least three thousand years. The Bantu probably have invented them even before migrating away from Cameroon, thus spreading the knowledge of the instrument throughout Africa. On their way they learned to manufacture iron lamellae. The mbira playing technique of interlocking tones is the reason for the unique creativity of African music. The harmonies of mbira music derive directly from the 30000 years of Khoisan ("bushman") culture of Southern Africa. The story is that the first mbira ever to appear was found under water. Somebody was crossing a river and stepped on something hard; he picked it up and it was mbira.

2.7. Shona musicians in tradition

Anybody who is to become a professional mbira player – "gwenyambira" or "maridzambira" – must be a strong person, not necessarily only in a physical

---

[2] 'Mbira dzaVadzimu' is actually a wrong use, because the instrument can be referred to by this term only if it is used in ceremonies, otherwise it is just called 'mbira'.

sense but also spiritually speaking. They are invited by people from different parts of the country. Mbira players have rules to follow. They play for the whole night and the payment is low.[3] Even if they are tired, they have to play on. If blisters grow they burst whilst they continue playing. It is one of the most difficult jobs in the Shona society.[4]

To be a mbira musician requires not only the capacity to play several days and nights in a row but also a particular lifestyle. A gwenyambira is obliged to play for the spirits if asked by anybody. A gwenyambira has to follow the traditional rules for daily life. Gwenyambira spend most of their time playing the instrument. Not to follow the rules of handling the instrument weakens the music and the strength of playing. There are rules to keep the mbiras if they are used for spiritual purposes.

In Europe, people say that it is a talent when somebody plays an instrument, but the Shona people say that it is a deceived spirit which makes people play the mbira. The deceased spirit is a spirit of an unknown person who just chooses a person for possession. A person can live for years not knowing that she or he is a medium. One may even die without ever knowing it. Most mbira players dream the tunes they are supposed to play. If they have the mbira next to them, they just wake up and play it. Any person may be capable of dreaming tunes.

For a long time, the mbira had been played only by men, because mbira music was said to be a male domain. None of the men today can give a satisfactory answer as to why women should not play it (cf. footnote 4). Some people were probably afraid that the women would not be able to fulfil their roles as housewives and mothers, since they would always be travelling to play on ceremonies. It was therefore impossible for women, who were interested, to learn to play the instrument because men did not tolerate anybody to teach them. This really affected the role of women as mbira players and therefore we find only a handful of female mbira players in Zimbabwe today.

In pre-colonial times there were families specialised in the making of mbira music. Shona kings used to maintain large groups of mbira players. Mbira songs are still passed on from one generation to the next.

---

[3] If it was high then ordinary people from the rural areas would not be able to afford it.
[4] Maybe this is why men thought that women were not suited to do it. However, by now they have been proven wrong and it has been documented that female mbira players are just as strong as male ones.

3.1. Childhood and Maridzambira

Despite a first guerrilla rebellion in 1896, European settlers imposed a redistribution of the land on the culture of Zimbabwe. The indigenous owners of the land were forcefully settled in homelands which were characterised by infertile soil and a scarcity of rains. The European settlers occupied the best land for "commercial farming" but also founded cities modelled on European standards. Taxes, which had to be paid in cash, were imposed on the indigenous population and they were thus forced to look for work at the farms and industries owned by Europeans. The African workers were segregated in townships far away from the city centres – surprisingly thus anticipating the Western suburbs of the sixties in Europe.

The colonial regime and the Christian missionaries not only despised traditional Shona culture but even fought against it, declaring traditional healers and their patients as worshippers of the devil.

Because of its spiritual power, even the instrument mbira had been banned by the Rhodesian settler regime. It constituted a major crime to possess it. Later, during the liberation war, when the African population fought for its freedom, its possession was defined as an act of terrorism. It was not the music as such but the purpose it serves, which made the colonial regime to forbid it. Therefore the mbira was only played privately and people had to hide it. This was indeed a terrible time for mbira players. The missionaries also tried by all means to make people stop to play it and to pray to their spirits. They called the ancestral spirits demons and looked at mbira music as the work of Satan. The missionaries' attitude had a tremendous affect on the culture of Zimbabwe because people naively followed the Christian religion, stopped praying to their spirits and became Christians.

Virginia Mukwesha is linked to these developments as she was born into a family of female Maridzambira, herbalists, midwives and mediums of famous spirits like Sekuru Kaguvi. Gumboreshumba, the great grandfather of Virginia Mukwesha, was the acting medium of Kaguvi, the ancestral spirit who advises in matters of war and also did so during the first uprising of the Shona against colonial occupation of the country (1895-97). The Rhodesians hanged the medium together with that of the spirit Ambuya Nehanda because they feared the mediums' amazing power. Virginia Mukwesha's mother is Stella Rambisai Chiweshe, who was the first known woman in Zimbabwe to learn and play the mbira in the traditional way, i.e. in fulfilling the duties of a maridzambira.

Following a prophecy of one of their ancestors about a precise number of mbira players in the family Virginia Mukwesha succeeded her mother to break into the formerly male domain of mbira playing and worked as traditional maridzambiras playing ceremonies and rituals each weekend for more than ten years.

> The first music I ever listened to – still in the womb – was mbira music. The only music I knew the first eleven years of my life was mbira and I loved it. My mother always played in the evening when we were sitting by the fire. I always wanted to learn but I never told my mother. One day I just took her mbira and plucked the keys very strongly just trying to express my feelings of wanting to learn. My mother asked me if I could sit beside her and learn one tune. I learned so fast that my mother was really astonished. (Virginia Mukwesha)

Still a young girl, Virginia Mukwesha learned to play mbira and started to accompany her mother to ceremonies where she was called to play. This meant to start to play at 7.30 p.m. until 6.30 a.m. "I could sleep with open eyes while marking the time and speed of the mbira with my hoshos." Virginia Mukwesha also worked as an assistant for her grandmother, who was a traditional healer.

3.2. Tradition and innovation in Virginia Mukwesha

The rural rock and roll of Zimbabwe is called "jiti". In the countryside during the night of the full moon, the young generations have held monthly parties from time immemorial. The unmarried or young people meet to feel free from social and cultural restrictions while dancing, drumming and singing.

In the nineteen sixties, these parties were overrun by a new rhythm and style introduced by migrant workers coming back from working in the mines of South Africa. The original kwela rhythm of South Africa was speeded up to form "jiti", the unique and special rhythm of Zimbabwe. It is a mystery why the Zimbabwean rural folk accelerated the speed of kwela, because – as a general rule – rhythms accelerate only if they are transplanted from the countryside into the city but with kwela to jiti it was the other way round! But after kwela music had spread via radio and record to the so-called "African reserves" of the apartheid-like country of the then 'Rhodesia', it was received enthusiastically by the rural youth. From the initial copying of urban pop music soon an original style emerged whose name differed from one region to the next, i.e. from jiti to chinungu, to pfonda or chibhanduru, but whose rhythm was and is the same and one and only everywhere. Kwela had transported the message of freedom and adventure into the closed stiff rural way of life of Zimbabwe and had turned into the musical raw material of so-called "konziratis" (concert-parties). The pennywhistle- or saxophone-part of kwela was substituted by a lead singer. The other kwela-instruments (guitar and bass fiddle) were imitated by drums, handclapping and a four-part-harmony answering-choir.

But the most important element of the jitis is not the music but the dancing and the lyrics. Dancing took the form of terrible contest between men and women for the best dancer of the night and obviously the women always won. The highly erotic element of jiti also found its way into the lyrics which may be called pornographic. This results from the fact that jiti was a social occasion outside the official society and therefore it offered the nearly exclusive opportunity of total freedom of speech. Just like the dancing, the singing also takes the form of a contest. The lyrics are 'hot' not only because of their sexual meanings but also from their overall provocative character: All the gossip, all the scandals, all the intrigues, all hypocrisies and all the jokes are exposed by the jiti singers to achieve maximum provocation of the persons involved. These people then feel 'tickled' to answer in the same way, and thus fun and excitement increase. So jiti is a dance, a rhythm, a musical style and a social occasion. Today the term is also often used to refer to any sort of non-traditional Zimbabwean pop music which, however, does not include the jiti meanings described above.

Jiti as music can also be played during an official social ceremony. This happens mostly on funerals when the adults play mbira music inside the houses while the youth outside plays and sings some jiti in mourning and honour of the dead person. But here the lyrics are without any sexual or provocative character. It is only used for dancing and passing time during the ceremony.

The gender distribution in jiti is very unusual. Unlike most African music jiti does not make any distinction between the sexes. Girls and women have the same rights as men. They may sing and even drum, apart from dancing. So jiti is a unique possibility for women to express themselves freely in traditional (rural) society.

As a teenager Virginia Mukwesha participated in many jiti concert parties as singer, dancer and drummer. She continued when jiti was adapted by the freedom fighters during the chimurenga liberation war where it became the only musical style actively involved in the struggle. Virginia Mukwesha played on many such jiti-pungwe events thus acting as chimbwido (female logistic supporter of the guerrillas).

African women initially had been excluded from the emerging new culture of the Western city introduced to Africa. Their economic arrival in the cities is now leading to the emergence of a generation of openly independent and autonomous women who look out to combine the good values of rural traditions with urban freedom for new positive cultural structures.

Therefore Mukwesha has created a new style of jiti translating the rural raw material – its original rhythm, the sound of ngoma drums and hosho shakers, loud, loud female and male voices, call and response singing in a group, emotional outburst – into an urban dimension by adding marimba, electric guitars, bass and drum kit to the rural line-up to metropolitise the sound. Mukwesha's lyrics present a new consciousness of women: to speak out from their hearts to express new and modern behaviour like talking openly and in public about women's' emotions and desires. In true jiti style this is not performed in an ideological way as a claim for women's rights but is done straight away by just doing it. To give a voice to women Virginia Mukwesha chose another musical style than mbira.

Virginia Mukwesha has started the new, urban age of jiti music. Contrary to the usual coolness of African music Virginia Mukwesha on her debut album *Farai* (lit: "Be Happy!") delivers hot dance music. "You can dance yourself to death". Also *Farai* is the first album ever to exclusively feature the true jiti rhythm as it is known throughout the countryside of Zimbabwe.

The jiti rhythm itself is played mostly with hands or sticks on long, standing drums. Add hand-clapping, whistling, a call & response choir of 13 elements and – above all – the lead singer who, because of the sheer volume of her voice, had to sing in a distance of two meters from her mike. On *Farai* Virginia Mukwesha has created the city-jiti. Virginia Mukwesha's very fast rattle playing speeds the beat up to the time of the city. The space between the jiti pulses is filled with interlocking, chorus like marimba patterns which melt the jiti beat into melodies. Mukwesha was the first artist ever to record albums with the original jiti rhythm. Following the success of "Farai" Virginia Mukwesha recorded a second jiti album named *Chamu* using the Black Spirits band of Oliver Mutukudzi. It was no surprise that Mukwesha's jiti at first was refused release in Zimbabwe because the lyrics were considered 'too modern' ...

The third jiti-album named *Tsika* – lit: "good behaviour"- marked the fusion of jiti with mbira beats. After *Farai* and *Chamu* Mukwesha has recorded the album *Matare*. On this album there is no jiti-music at all but seven mbiras play non stop for one hour. There are also no vocals. All other records with mbira music feature the old, classical songs, normally also with the traditional singing. But for Mukwesha these records are only quotations of the music, because in reality a song lasts around two or more hours whereas on the normal mbira records they last about ten minutes only and thus cannot fulfil the function of the music: to purify and feed the soul, not to talk of trance or possession. So the concept of *Matare* was to reproduce the functional aspect of mbira music on a sound carrier so as to make the benefit of the music available to people who cannot participate in the ceremonies. The same music of *Matare* is played when the spirits of dead ancestors talk during the possession ceremonies: music for meditation, healing and trance. As for a recording no specific spirit has to be called so no specific mbira song had to be recorded exclusively, but Mukwesha composed a kind of universal mbira song which she however based on the mother of all mbira songs "Nyamaropa".

Matare was composed by Virginia Mukwesha out of "variations", i.e. improvised patterns of traditional mbira songs. Seven mbiras play *Matare*, each with different variations, of which one works as lead part. As the whole song consists of five different lead themes about 35 variations have been combined. When Mukwesha's lead mbira changes to a new lead variation the other players use individual bridges to switch also to a new variation. Variations make melodies come out of the song. The idea to record an album like *Matare* with over sixty minutes of music non-stop was born because mbira music unfolds its psychic power only in time. So with *Matare* people may experience the power of mbira for the first time on a sound carrier.

The next recording project of Virginia Mukwesha was a – hitherto unreleased – double album with pure healing music as on *Matare* for Universal.

Then Virginia Mukwesha proceeded to record her debut mbira solo album. It is called *Nzira* literally "The Way". Its idea was born from the fact that female mbira players suffer certain restrictions because of their bodies. The concept of *Nzira* is Virginia Mukwesha's answer to the spiritual rule that breastfeeding women or those having their days should not participate in anything spiritual, be it a ceremony or an object which comes into contact with the spirits or even just a song used for spiritual functions.

So Virginia Mukwesha found several ways out of this dilemma: First of all she has composed entirely new songs during her off-days as a spiritual mbira player thus avoiding to use the spiritual tunes when in spiritually adverse conditions. Also the instruments used for the recording of *Nzira* were never used for spiritual functions. So also there Mukwesha is sure not to offend the spirits.

So *Nzira* is not only the first mbira music album on which the songs have been composed by a woman but also with *Nzira* women may listen to mbira music now 365 days a year without breaking a spiritual taboo. As Mukwesha can play her instrument now each and every day. In this surprising way Mukwesha has remodelled the tradition in order not to break it. On *Nzira* for the first time ever mbira and chipendan are played on one recording not only creating otherworldly sounds but also proving that Khoisan and Shona music really match.

As the classical mbira repertoire of the spirits evokes certain fixed moods in the listener, Virginia Mukwesha's new songs offer emotions which are open to many "ways". Whereas nearly all songs played by men talk of poverty, war and suffering, Virginia Mukwesha sings also of happiness, fun and joy. Her style is called "Sunungukai": "Music to relieve your heart".

Between performances and recordings Virginia Mukwesha teaches mbira music and dance. As traditional Maridzambira (mbira musician) she works for the constant change of traditional music according to the actual needs of her culture.

Being raised both in the countryside and in the capital of Zimbabwe in Southern Africa she has a sense of balance between tradition and change. She is a member of the "Zimbabwe National Traditional Healers Association".

Virginia Mukwesha's understands her work as a service to the society's musical needs to allow people to form their identity through music and dance. "You must not only be able to play your instrument and to sing, but you also have to respect the functional role of music and to develop into new directions if times are changing to serve the society as before".

A new, surprising mbira record is in preparation: *Haundizive*: "You don't know me!", embedding many musical styles into mbira music, in a truly interactive style.

Discography

VIRGINIA MUKWESHA
    Farai: SHAVACD006-2, released 1993.
    Chamu: SHAVACD003-2, released 1995.
    Matare: SHAVACD004-2, released 1996.

Tsika: SHAVACD009-2 & L4SHAVA009-2, released 1999.
Nzira: SHAVACD012-2 & L4SHAVA012-2, released 2001.
Unobvepi/Muchembere: SHAVACD013-2, released 2002.

References

BRENNER, KLAUS-PETER
    (1997). *Chipendani und Mbira, Musikinstrumente, nicht-begriffliche Mathematik und die Evolution der harmonischen Progressionen in der Musik der Shona in Zimbabwe*. Göttingen: Vandenhoeck & Ruprecht.
BRUSILA, JOHANNES
    (2002). "'Modern Traditional' Music from Zimbabwe. Virginia Mukwesha's Mbira Record 'Matare.'" In Mai Palmberg and Annemette Kirkegaard, eds. *Playing with Identities in Contemporary Music in Africa*. Uppsala: Nordiska Afrikainstitutet, 35-45.
CHAVUNDUKA, GORDON L.
    (1994). *Traditional Medicine in Modern Zimbabwe*. Harare: University of Zimbabwe Publications.
ELLERT, H:
    (1984). *The Material Culture of Zimbabwe*. Harare: Longman Zimbabwe.
GELFAND, S. MICHAEL
    (1977/1982). *The Spiritual Beliefs of the Shona*. Harare: Mambo Press.
HODZA, AARON AND GEORGE FORTUNE
    (1979). *Shona Praise Poetry*. Oxford: Oxford University Press.
KUBIK, GERHARD
    (1983). "Kognitive Grundlagen afrikanischer Musik." In Artur Simon, ed. *Musik in Afrika*. Berlin: Museum für Völkerkunde, 327-400.
    (1988). *Zum Verstehen afrikanischer Musik. Ausgewählte Aufsätze*. Leipzig: Philipp Reclam jun.
    (1994). *Theory of African Music Volume 1*. Wilhelmshaven: Florian Noetzel Verlag.
    (1998a). *Kalimba, Nsansi, Mbira - Lamellophone in Afrika*. Berlin: Museum für Völkerkunde/Staatliche Museen zu Berlin.
    (1998b). "Intra-African Streams of Influence." In Ruth M. Stone, ed. *Africa. The Garland Encyclopedia Of World Music Volume 1*. New York/London: Garland Publishing, 293-326.
NOVITSKI, PAUL
    (1996). "Embracing Mbira Rhythm." *Music*: August, 18-22
READER, JOHN
    (1997). *Africa. A Biography of the Continent*. London: Penguin Books.
TRACEY, ANDREW
    (1963)."Three Tunes for 'Mbira Dza Vadzimu'." *Journal of the African Music Society* 3:2, 23-26.

Africa Raps Back: Reflections on HipHop from Tanzania and South Africa

BIRGIT ENGLERT
Vienna, Austria

"actually african HipHop is growing and becoming stronger and stronger. i have this feeling that in eight months from now no one from this continent will even want to listen to HipHop from US cause we have all the artist we need in africa you name them we have them here so why give much attention to the western while we can do the same thing and our world would be much more good and presentable then them. we should do something in order to boost our HipHop crew."[1]
(guestbook entry by a Tanzanian HipHop fan on the homepage of africanhiphop.com)

"Here in South Africa, all of a sudden them record companies are taking interest in rap, not hip-hop cos they don't give a f*uck about our culture, they just thinkin' str8 record sales and as a result commercialising da music. [...] African MC's should not fall in the same trap as a lotta MC's in da US, where corporations dictate to us what to talk about and all. Hip-Hop is a revolutionary culture here to challenge the status quo in this white man's world. Our continent is fallin' apart, lets use Hip-Hop as a tool to free the mindz of our pepl, feel me..."
(guestbook entry by a South African HipHop fan on the homepage of africanhiphop.com)[2]

Introduction

Over the last decade the popularity of HipHop on the African continent has grown enormously. In this article I will discuss HipHop in Africa, which has taken quite different forms in different countries, with regard to its history, content and function. For this purpose I will focus on Tanzania while South Africa will serve as a contrasting example in many ways. Tanzania has one of the biggest HipHop scenes in Africa, comparable in its dimension only with South Africa in the South and Senegal in the West (and to a lesser extent also

---

[1] Posted at http://www.africanhiphop.com/core2/index.php?module=postguestbook on December 30, 2003, original spelling.
[2] Posted at
http://www.africanhiphop.com/phpbb/viewtopic.php?t=1585postdays=0postorder=ascstart=30 on February 25, 2004, original spelling.

Ghana and Nigeria).[3] Within Eastern Africa however, Tanzania is definitely the leading HipHop-Nation. The region has for long been dominated by dance-music from the Congo – now it seems to be Tanzanian musicians' turn to "rule the scene".

The beginnings – HipHop in the USA

HipHop culture actually consists of different components: graffiti art, breakdancing, deejaying (cutting and scratching) and emceeing (rapping), not to forget fashion. But as rap, which is commonly defined as "spoken words with an underlying rhythm section of bass, drums and keyboard sounds", has evolved as the most prominent aspect, the terms HipHop and rap are often used interchangeably (http://www.daveyd.com/raphist1.html).

HipHop is a youth culture, which was started by young African Americans in the decayed urban areas of the USA. As early as 1974 forms of rapping featured at neighbourhood parties in New York, the centre of early HipHop. At that time rap was essentially a party music with lyrics full of boasting directed at other rappers. (Klein/Friedrich 2003: 25) Grandmaster Flash and the Furious Five were the first to include a political message in their rap song "The Message" – thereby starting the era of using rap music to communicate strong believes – of which Public Enemy later became the great icons.

With the appearance of the Californian group N.W.A. (Niggaz with Attitude) in 1987, HipHop took again a new direction. Their style of talking straight about drugs and gang life became known as "gangsta" rap and the centre of HipHop shifted to Los Angeles. After their split in 1992 it was especially former N.W.A. member Dr. Dre, who made a successful solo career, later as the producer of some of the rap-heroes of the 1990s, such as Tupac Shakur and Snoop Doggy Dog. Increasingly rap music also attracted young "white"[4] people, mostly from the middle-class. Rebensdorf (n.d.: Part 1: 1) comments:

> Unlike many other black musical mediums that were watered down for white consumption, gangsta rap proved that blacker could sell better to those youth who seemed anxious for something powerful, something real, something raw.

---

[3] A good indicator in this respect is also the number of links and articles on the various countries on the largest and most prominent Internet portal to African HipHop: africanhiphop.com.
[4] The terms "white", "coloured" and "black" are in quotation marks throughout the text in order to underline the superficiality of such designations.

But it did not stop with consumption. With the emergence of "white" rappers such as Vanilla Ice or the Beastie Boys in the early 1990s, HipHop was no longer an exclusively "black" phenomenon and Eminem, a young "white" man from Detroit, who was discovered and produced by Dr. Dre, became the commercially most successful rapper.

As many US-rappers literally made their way out of the "ghetto", they were increasingly rapping about material wealth and their possession of status symbols like expensive cars or watches. At least from the 1990s on these lyrics could no longer be interpreted as caricatures of consumerism. (Rebensdorf n.d.: Part 3: 3)

HipHop, especially US-American, has been an academic research topic for long. An impressive number of courses on HipHop and related phenomena are taught in American Universities and the list of published literature on the topic is long. Much less has been written about HipHop outside the USA yet.[5]

HipHop outside the USA - the examples of Tanzania and South Africa

In countries as diverse as Germany and Greenland or Senegal and Sweden, young people are not only consuming HipHop from the USA but have also adapted it to their own cultural background and use it as their own means of expression. Many use rap to voice their opinion on all kinds of issues, ranging from corruption to HIV/AIDS. But also outside the USA HipHop has many dimensions and far from all rappers write politically or socially committed lyrics. The different forms and functions of HipHop in different African countries can mainly be related to the socio-political context in which HipHop took roots, but also to the language situation in the respective country.

---

[5] One exception is the volume edited by Tony Mitchell in 2001. Its aim, as expressed on the back of the book, is to "[counter] the prevailing colonialist view that global hip-hop is an exotic and derivative outgrowth of an African-American-owned idiom subject to assessment in terms of American norms and standards." However, the single contributions focus on European countries, Canada, Australia, Japan and Korea only; rap in Latin America and Africa is only referred to briefly in the introduction. The first CD compilation of African Rap distributed by a Western label is "The Rough Guide to African Rap. Rappers, Rebels and Ragamuffins" which was released in February 2004 by the British World Music Label at www.worldmusic.net. Its booklet offers a short but very useful introduction into African Rap and the CD features artists from Nigeria, South Africa, Cameroon, Senegal, Tanzania, Ghana, Mozambique, Kenya, Angola, Congo and Mali.

Language

In many countries it is the use of a language other than English, which distinguishes HipHop in other parts of the world from its US-version. Whereas in most countries rappers started by rhyming in English, success only came along after they had decided to use their own language. (comp. Beith/Spencer 2002: 79)

This observation also holds true for Tanzania where rap lyrics in English had limited appeal as they were not understood by the majority of the population and lacked authenticity to those who did. Since the early 1990s, Tanzania rappers rhyme almost exclusively in the national language Swahili, which is also the main language of the media and the main medium of communication for people of all ages. There may be borrowings from English or, though less frequent, other languages spoken in Tanzania, as well as some degree of code-switching, but Swahili definitely is the language of expression in Bongo Flava[6], as Tanzanian HipHop has come to be called.

The status of Swahili as the lingua-franca of the East African region gives Tanzanian rappers an ample opportunity on the East African market in general and the Kenyan market in particular. Tanzanian artists can be found in the leading ranks of the Kenyan charts and the success of Bongo Flava in Kenya has already stirred up heated discussion displaying nationalistic emotions within Kenya.[7]

In South Africa rappers are facing a very different language situation. South African HipHop has its roots in Cape Town or more precisely in the Cape Flats, an area which "might fit very well into the stereotypes of a ghetto" (Faber n.d.: 1) and which is mainly inhabited by people who were, according to Apartheid-ideology, categorised as "coloureds" and whose main medium of communication was Afrikaans, a language closely associated with the history of Apartheid. It was the Soweto uprising of 1977 in opposition to the introduction of Afrikaans as a medium of instruction in schools, which marked the beginning of a new dimension of protest that eventually led to the arrival of democracy in South Africa. English on the other hand, was the language used by the Anti-Apartheid political leadership and thus became

---

[6] Bongo, literally meaning "brain", "intelligence" in Swahili, is a common slang expression for the country's largest city Dar-es-Salaam from where Tanzanian rap started to conquer the country but can also refer to the country Tanzania in general. "Bongo Flava" as Tanzanian HipHop is called, thus refers to the sound (flavour) from Dar-es-Salaam or Tanzania.

[7] Sentences like "So they aren't Kenyan, after all, but they sound just as good, and they make the fans just as crazy as if they had been born and raised here" can be found in newspaper articles like the one by Philip Mwaniki for the Daily Nation September 13, 2003.

seen as the language of unity and liberation. (Mesthrie 2002: 22) Against this background it becomes obvious that rap in Afrikaans has a limited appeal within South Africa which now has eleven official languages in total.

While crews from Cape Town such as Prophets of Da City (POC), Brasse Vannie Kaap (BVK), Black Noise or Godessa, an all female crew, are widely known, their commercial success does not really follow suit.[8] Faber (n.d.: 5) blames this on the US-orientation of the HipHop audience who rather buy material from overseas than music produced locally.

The use of the cross-regional language Swahili with its generally positive image puts Tanzanian rappers in a totally different position than their South African, or more precisely Capetonian, counterparts who, by using to a large extent their first language Afrikaans, rap in a far less spread language with a burdened history.

History

In Tanzania the first ones who listened to rap music from the US and who started rhyming themselves were rather privileged youths who grew up in the rich neighbourhoods in the country's biggest city Dar-es-Salaam. Many of them had come into contact with HipHop while studying abroad or through relatives in overseas who sent them the latest tapes or CDs which were by then either not available in Tanzania or incredibly expensive.[9] HipHop music was played at parties, which took place in the big hotels of Dar-es-Salaam and the surrounding beaches. (De Rycker 2002: 3) Saleh Jabir, a Tanzanian of partly Arab origin, is usually cited as the first Tanzanian who started rapping in Swahili in the early 1990s. However, he did not write his own lyrics but translated lyrics by US-HipHoppers – such as "Ice Ice Baby" by Vanilla Ice – into Swahili.

It was Mr. II who first had success with his own verses in Swahili and who came to dominate the Tanzanian HipHop scene throughout the 1990s. His lyrics also appealed to the less privileged youth who could identify with

---

[8] These crews do not rap exclusively in Afrikaans but also in English and other South African languages and language varieties. See Watkins, Lee Williams. 1999. Tracking the Narrative: The Politics of Identity in Rap Music and HipHop Culture in Cape Town. MA. University of Natal, South Africa, cited in Mitchell 2001: 8.

[9] This holds also true for neighbouring Kenya as Rebensdorf (n.d.) asserts in her interesting study about the perceptions of HipHop by young Kenyans in the mid-1990s, when CDs, videos and fashion imported from the States were incredibly expensive, even in real prices much more expensive than in the US.

them – and got inspired to try rhyming and rapping themselves. While Tupac Shakur, the American rapper who got shot in 1996, was the biggest role model for the first generation of Tanzanian rappers, Mr II already fulfilled this function for the second generation of Tanzanian rappers.

Rap music was first spread among friends and later mainly pirated copies of American rap hits became available on the market. (De Rycker 2002: 5) A defining moment in the spread of HipHop music in Tanzania was the introduction of television in Tanzania in 1994 and the liberalisation of the radio sector. Before that there was only one radio station, which played mainly traditional forms of music such as Taarab[10]. Since the mid-1990s Bongo Flava has gained enormously in popularity. It is getting airplay on the now many Tanzanian radio channels and artists feature prominently in television programmes, newspapers and journals. In 2001 HipHop was recognised as an official genre within Tanzania's pop culture by the Tanzanian Arts Council BASATA and it also became one of the categories at the first national music awards which were held in 2002. The number of producers has grown rapidly and quite some informative websites emerged.[11]

The acceptance of Bongo Flava music – which is also referred to as "muziki wa kizazi kipya" ("music of the new generation") – by the Tanzanian society is constantly increasing and especially the music of those "with a message" seems to attract people of all age groups. Rap is no longer regarded as 'uhuni' which can be translated as hooliganism and was a frequently used term in relation to Bongo Flava – not so much because of any explicitness of its language, which has never been a characteristic of Tanzanian HipHop, but rather because of the fact that it was young people who started to question their society.[12]

While HipHop can be said to have become an almost inclusive medium of expression for young Tanzanians, in South Africa HipHop is still more

---

[10] "Taarab is a style of popular music widely spread at the East African Coast stretching from Somalia in the north to Mozambique in the South. *Taarab* blends Africa, Indian, Arab, and Western styles of singing, composition, and instrumentation. It is a musical genre that combines singing of Swahili *mashairi* (poetry) with instrumental accompaniment." (Beez/Kolbusa 2003: 51)
[11] While www.africanhiphop.com has been the portal for HipHop from all African countries since 1997, www.mzibo.net and "BongoExplosions" on www.darhotwire.com are exclusively dedicated to Bongo Flava and in Swahili, the latter being at the moment the only major website dedicated to Bongo Flava maintained from Tanzania.
[12] The negative attitude of elder Tanzanians towards Bongo Flava is referred to sarcastically in a dialogue between a fictive "mzee" (respected elder man) and the young artist on the tape "Machozi, Jasho na Damu" (2002) by Prof. Jay.

associated with one fraction of the nations young people – thereby reflecting the splits in South African society which were brought about by decades of segregation and which influenced the way HipHop developed in this country.

In South Africa HipHop culture started much earlier than in Tanzania. Already in the early 1980s – so even before the emergence of gangsta rap in the USA and before its commercial breakthrough – a HipHop scene developed in Cape Town.

While the first generation of rappers in South Africa were "coloureds" from the Cape Flats, later many "white" middle-class youth turned to HipHop – a development with obvious parallels to the one in the USA. The "white" second-generation rappers attribute to the first generation of HipHop artists their awareness "of the impact of racism on the lives of other young South Africans" and "the state's ongoing role in marginalizing already disempowered youths." (Klopper 2000: 185) They see themselves affected by the profound changes taking place in South African society:

> Although some of these skateboarders are still in school, they cite recent changes in South Africa as a reason for their involvement in hip-hop: no longer able to rely on the idea that the job market privileges white males, they have become increasingly sensitive to the marginalization experienced by other sectors of the community during the Apartheid era. (Klopper 2000: 185)

"Black" youth do not identify with HipHop but rather turn to Kwaito[13] whose language is Tsotsitaal, a township argot mainly used by male Africans in urban centres. Stephens defines it as

> ... a contemporary black dance-music genre that has emerged over the past decade and become intensively popular in South Africa. Even though the origin of its musical elements may be traced further afield, it is an evolution of music known as ,bubblegum' or South African disco, with elements of American hip-hop, European house music, and other international sounds thrown in. (Stephens 2000: 257)[14]

Klopper (2000: 183) sees the "slowness with which electricity has been introduced into South Africa's black townships" and which has "prevented

---

[13] As to the origins of the word there are two explanations: the first in reference to the township gangsters Amakwaitos, the other pointing at the slang word 'kwai' meaning 'great' or 'excellent'. (Stephens 2000: 257)

[14] Kwaito music is produced by DJs with the help of synthesisers and computers and live performances are backed by CD tracks. Rappers are exclusively male, supported by female background singers. As Stephens (2000: 257) asserts, Kwaito is a party music with "live performances [which] are renowned for the sexual explicitness of the dancing".

black youths from becoming active consumers of videos, which are (and always have been) the main source of information for South Africa's self-taught hip-hop artists and break-dancers" as an important factor which accounts for the dominance of "coloured" rappers in South African HipHop.

Godessa, the female HipHop act from Cape Town, comment in an interview with the South African youth magazine YMAG on the split between the music scenes of "coloured" and "black" youths:

> Coloureds and blacks are separated; it is bullshit but we do not know why that is. When there are events that are organised in Cape Town by a black person and all the blacks attend that event (sic), and it works exactly the same in the coloured community. Unless of course there is a big concert or events like Boogie Down Knights where coloureds and blacks are together. Those gatherings are beautiful. (YMAG Feb/March 2003, 43: 56)

Topics

The range of topics covered in Bongo Flava lyrics is broad and ranges from politics and corruption to social problems, from HIV/AIDS to love topics, career and party life. To some extent the emphasis on "serious" topics on the one side and "fun" topics on the other reflects the split of the Bongo Flava scene into two camps: "TMK" and "East Coast". In between are the so-called "solo artists", in the sense of "independent" artists, who do not let themselves be associated with either of the two camps. Prof. Jay and the now retired Mr II, both known for their very socially committed texts, are good examples. "TMK" stands for Temeke, one of the poor neighbourhoods in Dar-es-Salaam where some of the more radical and committed crews like Gangwe Mobb and Juma Nature come from. "East Coast" rappers on the other hand are from a middle- or upper class background and many of them reside in Upanga, a rather posh neighbourhood close to the city centre. Rappers like TID (which stands for "Top in Dar"), Crazy GK, or female superstar Lady Jay Dee, who represent this fraction of Bongo Flava, sing more about the "sunny side of life" or "commercial" as Tanzanians term it. Female rappers are still a minority, a growing one though, and women like above-mentioned Lady Jay Dee, Zay Bi or Sister P have made themselves a name in Bongo Flava.

The split into two competing fractions of rappers and especially the chosen names "East Coast" (Upanga) and TMK, which is also referred to as "West Coast", is an obvious allusion to the US rap-scene and its competition between East Coast (New York rappers) and West Coast (Los Angeles rappers). However, the competition between rappers is not violent as in the

USA but rather displayed in heated discussions among rappers themselves and their fans. An example is the Swahili language film "Girlfriend", the first Tanzanian movie to be situated in the HipHop milieu and a big success in 2003, which was starring a number of the most popular rappers from the "East Coast" camp. This provoked many angry reactions among the fans of those who are regarded as "TMK", as letters to the editors of various newspapers demonstrated.

As with US-HipHop, fashion also plays an important role in Tanzania – across the camps. In Tanzania's most popular youth magazine FEMINA,[15] stars like Prof. Jay, Mwanafalsafa and Sista P show the readers how to dress as real HipHoppers, their pictures being accompanied by slogans such as "Wear that over-sized T-shirt, add an earring and you are in the game!" or "Big gold or silver jewellery (they can be fake!) is also part of the game. That's cool in the Hip Hop world." (Femina 33, August/October 2003)

As the number of Tanzanian rap stars has risen, so has the number of "underground" rappers – not only in Dar-es-Salaam but all over the country. They show their rap-skills in contests, so-called "talent shows", which are taking place in many regional towns. Many of the rappers are very young, even below the age of ten.[16] In this article, however, the underground scene is not further discussed.[17]

Lyrics

As it is common within HipHop in general, transcriptions of Tanzanian rap-lyrics are not easily accessible. Some lyrics are being printed in newspapers and increasingly they can be found on the Internet at sites like Bongo Explosions, Mzibo Net and africanhiphop.com. But in most cases people other than the artists are doing the transliteration. Although lyrics are "written" in a fixed form they can be interpreted flexibly and, especially for the underground rappers, it is common to interchange verses from various songs or to add lines spontaneously.

---

[15] FEMINA is mainly dedicated to educating the Tanzanian young people (who can afford its high price of 1200 Tsh, equivalent to 1.2 Euro in 2003) about topics revolving around sexuality and HIV/AIDS. Its main sponsor is the Swedish Development Agency SIDA.

[16] The youngest rappers who became known nationwide are the girl and boy who form the Fortune Tellers. They already accompanied their elder brothers of the crew X Plastaz on their tour in Europe when they were only 12 and 9 years old. Compare "Dineh (Fortune Tellers, Tanzania) on http://www.africanhiphop.com

[17] For a discussion of the "underground" scene with special emphasis on Morogoro see my article "Bongo Flava (Still) Hidden. "Underground" Rap in Morogoro, Tanzania".

I would like to give two examples of lyrics – one from the "committed" and one from the "commercial" fraction of Tanzanian rappers. Both songs were major hits in 2003. The exclusive focus on Tanzanian lyrics is due to the fact that my knowledge of Swahili enables me to understand these lyrics to an extent, which would not be possible with lyrics in Afrikaans or other South African languages.

"Kikao cha Dharua"[18] *("Emergency Meeting") by Prof. Jay*

The song "Kikao cha Dharua" ("Emergency Meeting") is the follow-up to "Ndio Mzee"[19] ("Yes, Sir"), from Prof. Jay's first album "Machozi, Jasho na Damu" ("Tears, Sweat and Blood"). While "Ndio Mzee" caricaturised the way in which politicians make promises before elections, its criticism was mainly directed at the average Tanzanian who Prof. Jay blames to be too passive and to put too much trust in politicians.

The title of his second album "Mapinduzi Halisi" ("The Real Revolution") is programme: in "Kikao cha Dharua" the elected politician, the "mzee" who got unlimited approval from his audience during his election campaign reflected in "Ndio Mzee", is now being confronted with uncomfortable questions concerning the realisation of the promises he made.

Prof. Jay employs the means of cynicism by choosing very exaggerated pictures and examples such as promises of a helicopter to each policeman. The lyrics are in dialogue form in which the "mzee" first addresses his audience and sets the context in which this song is set. He is then confronted with questions posed by representatives from his constituency:

Question:
Naitwa sajent Byemero kwa niaba ya jeshi la polisi
I am called sergeant Byemero, on behalf of the police forces
Nilikuwa nauliza zile helikopta zetu vipi?
I wanted to ask what about our helicopters?

Answer:
Nafikiria kwanza kuanzisha chuo cha marubani
I think about opening a flying school first,

---

[18] Transcription of lyrics from http://www.mzibo.net/muziki/lyrics/kikao_cha_dharura.html (19.01.2004), compare also http://darhotwire.com/v2/go/tafuta/muziki/explosions/lyrics/pr.../kikao_cha_dharura.htm (23.9.2003). English translation mine.
[19] "Ndio Mzee" won the BASATA music awards 2002 in the category best HipHop single.

Vinginevyo mtapata ajali nyingi sana angani.
otherwise you are going to get a lot of accidents in the sky.
Baskeli hamjui kuendesha helikopta mtaendeshaje
You do not know how to ride a bicycle properly, so how do you want to ride a helicopter then?
Kila mtu aendeshe yake huko angani itakuwaje?
If everyone is going to ride his own, how is the sky going to be then?

Question:
Mheshimiwa sisi wakulima ulituahidi matrekta
Honoured, you promised tractors to us peasants
Na siku zinayoyoma tu mbona haujayaleta?
And the days are passing by like this, why haven't you brought them yet?

Answer:
Wakulima mngeendelea tu kutumia jembe la mkono
Peasants, just carry on to use the hand-hoe
Serikali haina hela bajeti imefika kikomo
the government does not have money, the budget has reached the limit
Naona kilimo cha mkono kiniendelea vizuri
I see that the manual agriculture is continuing fine
Jamani kazeni mikono endeleeni kukaza misuli
Guys, speed up your arms and continue to tighten your muscles

Chorus:
Wananchi tupo pamoja hapo.
People, we are together!?
  (siyo mzeeeeeee / no, mzee!)
Watanzania tunaerewana kule,
Tanzanians, we are understanding each other on this!?
  (siyo mzeeeeeee /no, mzee!)
Washika dau na wapiga kura pale,
The leaders and the voters there!?
  (siyo mzeeeeeee /no, mzee!)
Wakulima tupo pamoja pale,
Peasants, we are together!?
  (siyo mzeeeeeee /no, mzee!)
Wanafunzi tunaelewana kule,
Pupils, we understand each other on this!?
  (siyo mzeeeeeee /no, mzee!)
Mabahamedi na mapolisi pale
Seamen and policemen there!?
  (siyo mzeeeeeee /no, mzee!)

The song continues with verses, which address problems such as bad roads, lack of water and the poor condition of the educational system. In the end the constituency asks the politician for a share of his private property. He answers:

Eeehh? kugawana vya kwangu hilo swala litakuwa gumu
Eeehh? To share my things is going to be a difficult task.
Familia itanitazama ebo? nina majukumu
How is my family going to look at me? I have responsibility!
Imeandikwa kila mtu atabeba msalaba wake
It has been written that each man should carry his own cross
Kila mbuzi ale kwa urefu wa kamba yake
each goat eats at the length of its rope
Mbona mnaniuliza maswali mengi kunikomoa
Why are you asking me many questions, depriving me of my rights?
Jamani watanzania tunajenga tunabomoa
You Tanzanians, we are building and destroying.

"Niko Bize"[20] by Jahffarai Feat. Daz Mwalim

The song "Niko Bize" ("I am busy") from the soundtrack to the film "Girlfriend" is a good contrast to the highly political lyrics of "Kikao cha Dharua".

It is about a young man who explains to his girlfriend that he does not have time for her while he is pursuing his career as a rapper. As already evident in the title, the song contains a rather high amount of English words or Swahili words derived from English.

niko bize mpenzi tuonane labda week end
I am busy darling, we will see each other perhaps on the weekend
ipo siku moja tu kwa wiki tutaspend
we are going to spend only one day per week (together)
nakupenda sana honey najua hiyo hupendi
I love you very much honey, I know that you do not like this
lakini hakuna jinsi sababu na mambo mengi
but there is no reason whatsoever and there are so many things (to be done)
usinitafute kwenye simu huwa inarusha stim
do not look for me at the telephone, this is just going to throw up sparks
nafanya vocal studio nashindwa pokea simu
I am singing the vocals in the studio, I will not be able to pick up the phone
nakukumbuka bado mpenzi usione kama sikupendi

---

[20] Transcription of lyrics from http://www.darhotwire.com/v2/go/tafuta/muziki/explosions/lyrics/jahffarai/niko_busy.html (19.01.2004). English translation mine. On the tape of the Girlfriend soundtrack the name of this song is spelled as given above; in the transcription of the lyrics on the Internet the title was spelled "Niko Busy".

I still remember you darling, do not take it as if I do not love you
nakumiss kuliko vyote usione nafanya ushenzi
I miss you more than anything, do not think that I am doing something stupid
niko bize sana shortly ndio maana nakupa sorry
I am very busy for some time, that is why I am telling you sorry
nitakucall kila night ili tupige story
I am going to phone you every night so that we can chat

Chorus:
ndugu zangu msinitafute mpenzi wangu usinitafute
my friends, do not look for me, my darling, do not look for me
mi mwenzenu nipo bize[nipo bize] ndugu zangu nipo bize x2
me, my friends, I am busy, my colleagues, I am busy x2

What about Black Consciousness?

One of the major topics of US-American HipHop, Black Consciousness, does not really play a role in Bongo Flava – the most obvious explanation being the lack of discriminatory experiences on the grounds of their skin colour by Tanzanian youth. In South Africa however Black Consciousness plays a role, although partly in quite an ambivalent sense which is due to the "in-between position" which people classified as "coloureds" took in Apartheid society, and which is far from resolved with the end of institutionalised racial segregation. The first generation of Cape Town rappers was faced with resistance from two sides. While people from their own "coloured" communities considered Hip-Hop music as 'daai kaffir musik' (that kaffir music), Xhosa speakers from Cape Towns "black" townships designated them as 'half breeds' and other discriminating terms. (Klopper 2000: 193) Klopper writes:

> According to Black Noise[21] leader Emile Jansen, the sense of displacement experienced due to this rejection by blacks, on the one hand, and a denial of one's own African heritage after decades of Apartheid education, on the other, is crucial to his own sense of identity, and it is certainly important to an understanding of the ways in which hip-hop cultural forms have been embraced by Western Cape youths looking for a political home in recent years. (ibid.)

The fact that Apartheid and its aftermath became one of the dominant topics of HipHop in South Africa is not surprising. Township life, gangs, drug-abuse and unemployment are other major themes and like in the USA "gangsta

---

[21] As mentioned before, Black Noise is one of the most popular HipHop crews from Cape Town.

rappers" who glorified a violent lifestyle dominated the South African HipHop scene in the 1990s. In Tanzania this facet of HipHop was never of much importance.

Kwaito lyrics are again another case. While male consumers of Kwaito claim them to be meaningless, many women think that men actually like the sexual explicit lyrics which they find highly offending – to the extent that they refuse to listen to Kwaito music (Stephens 2000: 268). Stephens (2000: 270) elaborates:

> The female respondents feel that the contestations over the body in Kwaito are solely over the female body. The metaphorical use of the language was seen by some male respondents as a 'traditional' element of artistic merit and therefore excused from accusations of sexism. I have shown, however, that female respondents take offence to the sexist subject matter, whatever the linguistic devices used to convey it. They link the objectification of the female body on stage to the objectification in the verbal text, as both, as perceived by these women, are intended deliberately to appease male desires. The sexism in Kwaito is seen by these women as a reflection of contemporary South Africa.

What is African about HipHop? – How African does it have to be?

A question that is often brought up in discussions about African HipHop concerns the African origin of HipHop as such. The claim that with its establishment in the music scene of many African countries HipHop just returned to its roots is widespread.

Some, such as Reddy D., lead singer of the group Brasse Vannie Kaap (BVK), who is quoted in a BBC article, put it more generally:

> Hip hop and rap originated here on this continent – we were always out there telling stories in rhyme form. [...] It just took a 360 degree turn and came back home.... (in BBC News, November 20, 2000).[22]

Others again come up with more specific claims, referring for example to Tassu, a Senegalese music-style practised by women, as the roots of rap. (Maraszto 2003: 99) Senegalese rappers tend to see the origin of rap in the traditions of their country, and so do their South African counterparts. Emile Jansen from Black Noise even extends the claim to the other elements of HipHop when he sees the roots of break-dancing in Africa and graffiti art as

---

[22] A similar statement made by Tokollo Tshabalala from TKZee, one of the leading Kwaito bands from South Africa, is quoted in CNN WorldBeat Spotlight June 9, 1999.

the modern form of the rock paintings produced by South Africa's San ancestors. (Klopper 2000: 194)

Rap stands in the tradition of the characteristic way to treat rhymes and tone languages of West African cultures (Klein and Friedrich 2003: 15) but all aspects, which make up HipHop culture have their roots in the urban areas of the United States. They are more specifically the creative achievement of the African-American youth of New York City who certainly drew from African culture or rather from what they perceived as such – their ideas being based mainly on popularised pictures about Africa available in the USA. Afrika Bambaataa for example, one of the great and influential US-rappers of the first generation, formed his crew Universal Zulu Nation after he had watched the movie "Zulu" starring Michael Caine. (Klopper 2000: 195)

So while claims about the African roots of HipHop do not have any real foundation, they fulfil an important function in the assertion of identity for some artists but also their audience.

Another interesting question is how "African" HipHop from Africa needs to be in order to be accepted on the international market? In an article in the *East African* (September 08-14, 2003, Part 2, II) Doug Paterson a US producer who hosts a website on East African music is quoted to comment on the trend of local HipHop with strong American influence as follows: "this may work in the region but American music with local languages does not interest the international music market, where the preference is more for 'roots' music." The international audience does not yet look to Africa to find globalised sound but rather what they define as "African music". And in this respect the sound and not the lyrics, which are written in African languages, seems to be the defining characteristic. Likenkeng Thokoa who searched in vain for Kwaito in Berlin's music stores and reflected about it in the South African music magazine Rage, comments:

> The results, in short, are that there is no industry here for music from Afrika (sic) which doesn't live up to the idea of exotic, boogie Afrika (sic). This is a disadvantage for South Africans who produce music there in SA which sounds like music made here – which can be said about some SA rock acts. But on the other hand, there is space to take full advantage for South Africans who do the homebrew, local is lekker stuff. People want to hear this! (http://www.rage.co.za/issue43/)

Increasingly though, musicians aim to sound more "African". In Tanzania crews like Mambo Jambo became known for using various Tanzanian instruments like *ngoma* and *malimba* to create their sound. X Plastaz from

Arusha integrated Maasai horns and also Maasai singing into their songs and Zanzibari MC Cool Para combines rap with Taarab, making it "Taarap". In other African countries local music traditions are incorporated into their songs by rappers in similar ways (compare "Rough Guide to African Rap" 2004).

Also South African Kwaito with its synthetically produced *malimba* sounds, sounds increasingly African. (Stephens 2000: 264) On the other hand it has appropriated the ragga vocal style and aspects of modern European dance music, which Stephen's sees as "a direct result of black South African exposure to these. The presence of international musical dimensions in kwaito has resulted from producers recognizing what consumers are listening to." (Stephens 2000: 257)

Things are of course not that simple, but it seems that demands for the "internationalisation" of music from the side of the African audience are met by demands for its "africanisation" from the international audience. The "africanisation" of rap music is of course nothing bad, to the contrary – it is a creative and exciting endeavour, which is also appreciated by the local audience. Nevertheless, the questions remains when music from Africa, which does not live up to the idea of "African music" held outside the continent will have a chance on the international music market?

Does African HipHop still fulfil its "original function"? – What was it anyway?

Another much discussed question in the debate about African HipHop concerns its function. In the United States HipHop was created by young African-Americans who, through their music, could express their anger about the situation in the ghettos and the failure of politicians to improve their lives. In Tanzania HipHop became a channel to express criticism that had not existed in this way before. Although other forms of music also spread messages, they did not comment on contemporary issues to such an extent.

The days when rap was regarded as hooliganism ("uhuni") in Tanzania seem to have vanished, and increasingly the question is coming up whether the days when Bongo Flava promised social consciousness and asked uneasy questions have also vanished? While this is certainly a valid question, one should be more careful in defining the "original function" of HipHop in Tanzania.

The study by Rebensdorf, though in reference to Kenya, is of particular interest in this regard. In the mid-1990s when she did her fieldwork in Nairobi, HipHop was still the domain of the upper-class kids whereas the less-privileged Kenyan youth was rather into reggae, which was available at much lower prices. Another reason – as HipHop-kids explained to her – was that reggae and raggamuffin music was about the ghetto and reggae musicians appealed to the Nairobi "ghetto-kids" because they were "ruff" and "did not dress up" (TED 6/16 cited in Rebensdorf). Rebensdorf concluded:

> Hence the fact that American rappers were speaking from ghettos and about the oppression associated with such a marginalized position was either not heard or not related to any locally comparable phenomena. The idea of an authenticity rooted in American rapper's social and cultural oppression is unappropriated and connections between reggae's similarly counter-hegemonic lyrics are muted. (Rebensdorf 3: 5)

Therefore in Kenya and also in Tanzania the question as to the "original function" of HipHop has to be asked differently. In these two countries HipHop first served to foster the identification of the upper-class youth through consumption of status symbols like US-American music and clothing and was not perceived as a medium to express criticism.

The other, socially committed side of HipHop, emerged later and in Tanzania the current vibrant Bongo Flava scene comprises both.[23] Interpreters from both sides have been discovered by various interest groups as a means to transport their messages to the youth who constitute the majority of the African population.

In Tanzania as well as in South Africa, HipHop is taking on new functions as it is increasingly being used by NGOs, companies and political parties who sponsor emcees to translate their messages to the youth. Mr II was hired by *Population Services International* for an advertisement and UNICEF Tanzania uses rappers in their HIV/AIDS-awareness campaign, to name only two out of many examples. In Cape Town the community based radio station Bush Radio ran a project called HIV HOP, which combined rap music with weekly features of themes concerning HIV/AIDS and sexuality. This project was developed and supported by the Dutch NGO Madunia,[24] which has also

---

[23] And both have their following: in an online poll which asked after the favourite Bongo Flava musician Prof. Jay gained the pole position with 24 per cent, followed by one of the interpreters of the "commercial" side TID with 18 per cent. www.mzibo.net/images/vote01.jpg (19.01.2004)
[24] The mastermind behind Madunia (www.madunia.nl) is the same as behind the website africanhiphop.com: Thomas Geesthuizen who also contributed much to the "Rough Guide to African Rap" compilation.

been active in the support of Tanzanian rappers, producing discs, cds and videos and organising rap-performances in Europe.

When it comes to involvement in politics, rappers also take ambiguous positions to say the least. One good example is the new song by Mr. Ebbo who became famous with the single "Mimi Mmasai", a positive confirmation of his Maasai identity. In 2003 he collaborated with the Presidential Parastatal Sector Reform Commission (PSRC) in the production of a song whose main objective "is to show the people how privatisation helps the economic development of a poor country like Tanzania." (Mr. Ebbo quoted in The Guardian, January 16, 2003: 7)

Also in South Africa reasons for involvement in Hip-Hop have changed. Klopper (2000: 193) puts it as follows: Originally "a means through which to express a vaguely articulated identification with other organisations and movements struggling to undermine the apartheid state in the early 1980s", HipHop can now "be used to develop a new sense of belonging for those who question the racist values and beliefs of the large number of older-generation coloured who still refuse to embrace the idea of a truly democratic South Africa." As the political mainstream is controlled by "black" South Africans, "coloured" people remain in a rather marginalized position where they are joined by "white" youth who are also asking new questions concerning their identity.

Conclusion

In this article I have tried to show how differently HipHop developed in two African countries, Tanzania and South Africa, and that the respective socio-historical context and the language are the determining factors.

In Tanzania HipHop spread from urban privileged youth to the underprivileged youth and also into the rural areas. Bongo Flava has become the sound of the new generation of Tanzanians, which, due to the use of the regional lingua-franca Swahili, is also spreading successfully over the regional borders.

In South Africa on the other hand, HipHop, initially the domain of the Afrikaans-speaking youth from Cape Town's "coloured" townships, does not play the same unifying role among young South Africans. "Black" South Africans identify more with Kwaito music, which, although it incorporates also elements from HipHop, uses a different language and transports different messages.

However, for many young people in Tanzania as well as in South Africa, HipHop serves as a medium of expression that helps them negotiate and define their identities. It is the increase in communication and discussion about their own situation as well as of problematic issues affecting their societies in general, which accounts for what could be termed socio-political changes. In small quantities though: the "real revolution", as (not too seriously) proclaimed on Prof. Jay's second album, is not in sight yet.

References

BEITH, MALCOM AND KATY SPENCER
    (2002). "HipHop's Message Now Spans the World." *Newsweek, Special Issues 2003 Edition,* December 2002 - February 2003, 78-81.
BEEZ, JIGAL AND STEFANIE KOLBUSA
    (2003). "Kibiriti Ngoma. Gender Relations in Swahili Comics and Taarab-Music." *Stichproben. Wiener Zeitschrift für kritische Afrikastudien* 5, 49-71
BUYANZA, ERIC
    (2002). "DoT."*Historia ya HipHop ya Bongo.*
    http://www.darhotwire.com/v2/go/burudani/bongoexplosion.html (31.1.2003)
DE RYCKER, JASPER
    (2002). *The Social Context of Rap in Tanzania.* MA Thesis, University of Antwerpen.
DU BOIS, ANDREW
    (n.d.). "N.D. Niggaz with Attitude or (NWA)."
    http://www.africana.com/research/encarta/tt_016.asp (24.01.2004)
ENGLERT, BIRGIT
    (2003). "Bongo Flava (Still) Hidden. 'Underground' Rap from Morogoro, Tanzania." *Stichproben. Wiener Zeitschrift für kritische Afrikastudien* 5, 72-93.
FABER, JÖRG
    (n.d.). "Cape Town's Hip Hop Scene." http://ntama.uni-mainz.de/hiphop/faber/index.html (18.2.2003)
FEMINA
    (2003). "HipHop. A Lifestyle." Femina 33 August/October, 46-51.
GEESTHUIZEN, THOMAS
    (2002). "HipHop in Tanzania."
    http://www.niza.nl/media/EA.hivhop/Ea2.Tanzania.html (27.5.2003)
KARIUKI, JOHN
    (2003). "World Music: Still Waiting for an East African Superstar." *The East African,* September 08-14, Part 2, I-II.
KLEIN, GABRIELE AND MALTE FRIEDRICH
    (2003). *Is this Real? Die Kultur des HipHop.* Frankfurt am Main: Suhrkamp Verlag.

KLOPPER, SANDRA
(2000). "Hip-hop Grafitti Art". In Sarah Nuttal and Cheryl-Ann Michael, eds. *Senses of Culture*. South African Culture Studies. Oxford: Oxford University Press, 178-196.

MAHABANE, ITUMELENG
(2003). "Being Broke is Childish. We Need to Start Looking Critically at the Reasons and Implications of Hip-Hop's Bling Bling Obsession." *YMAG* February/March 5: 43, 64-68.

MARASZTO, CAROLINE
(2002). "Sozialpolitische Wende? Zur Entwicklung des Rap im Senegal." *Stichproben. Wiener Zeitschrift für kritische Afrikastudien* 4, 81-104.

MESTHRIE, RAJEND
(2002). "South Africa: A Sociolinguistic Overview." In Rajend Mesthrie. *Language in South Africa*. Cambridge: Cambridge University Press.

MITCHELL, TONY (ed.)
(2001). *Global Noise: Rap and Hip-Hop Outside the USA*. Middletown: Wesleyan University Press.

NUTTAL, SARAH AND CHERYL-ANN MICHAEL (eds.)
(2000). *Senses of Culture*. South African Culture Studies. Oxford: Oxford University Press

REMES, PIETER
(1999). "Global Popular Music and Changing Awareness of Urban Tanzanian Youth." *Yearbook for Traditional Music* 31, 1-26.

REBENSDORF, ALICIA
(n.d.) "Representing the Real. Exploring Appropriations of HipHop Culture in the Internet and Nairobi." http://lclark.edu/~soan/alicia/rebensdorf.101.html (21.1.2004)

STANDLEY, JANE
(2000). "Hip Hop 'Comes Home'". *BBC News*, Monday, 20 November, 2000. http://news.bbc.co.uk/1/hi/world/africa/1032070.stm (18.2.2003).

STEPHENS, SIMON
(2000). "Kwaito." In Sarah Nuttal and Cheryl-Ann Michael, eds. *Senses of Culture*. South African Culture Studies. Oxford: Oxford University Press, 256-273.

TOROKA, ERIC
(2002). "Why Local Firms Ignore Tanzanian Artists." www.africanhiphop.com (9.10.2002).

UGASA, MOHAMED
(2003). "Ebbo Launches Privatisation Rap Single." *The Guardian* (Tanzania), January 16, 2003, 7.

WRIGHT, STEVE
(1999). "Kwaito: South Africa's Hip-Hop?" *CNN-WorldBeat Spotlight*. http://www.cnn.com/SHOWBIZ/Music/9906/09/kwaito.wb/ (18.2.2003)

YMAG
(2003). "Ladies First (Interview with Godessa)." *YMAG* February/March 5: 43, 54-56.

Specific Internet sites:
http://www.darhotwire.com/where_at/tma.html, 2.6.2003
http://www.madunia.nl/projects/struggling.htm, 2.6.2003
http://www.madunia.nl/projects/halisi.htm, 2.6.2003
http://www.daveyd.com/raphist1.html

Internet in General:
http://www.africanhiphop.com
http://www.mzibo.net/frame.html
http://www.darhotwire.com/v2/go/burudani/bongoexplosion.html
http://www.madunia.nl

CD:
Rough Guide to African Rap. Rappers, Rebels, Ragamuffins. 2004. World Music Network, Great Britain.

… 99

How Asterix Learnt Swahili: The Tanzanian Appropriation of a French Comic

JIGAL BEEZ
Bayreuth, Germany

Introduction

As a comic figure *Asterix* has crossed many borders. His adventures made him roam as far as America and India. Not bad for a globetrotter living in the year 45 BC! The commercial success of *Asterix* exceeds even his travels. This "French trivial epic" (Stoll 1974: passim) has been translated into more than one hundred languages and dialects worldwide (Selles 2002). Although he visited Egypt and Libya, *Asterix'* impact on the African continent is minimal. Because for African readers, *Asterix* is only accessible through the colonial languages Arabic, English, French, Portuguese and Afrikaans and not through any African language. However in the year 2000 the Gaul warrior entered Tanzania. He did it informally, without papers and without a permit, but with an awareness of the host culture, which he had never shown before. Asterix has been adopted by the Tanzanian comic artist Chris Katembo, who taught him Swahili and Tanzanian culture, making it easy for *Asterix* to disguise himself as an African cartoon. Katembo created the adventure comic *Komredi Kipepe na Kisa cha Bi Arafa* ('Comrade Kipepe and the episode of Ms. Arafa'). In this story, the well known Swahili comic figures *Kipepe* and *Madenge* rescue a kidnapped mganga, a traditional healer, called *Bi Arafa*. It has striking parallels to *Asterix* and *Obelix* saving *Getafix* out of the wraths of the Goths.

By comparing both narratives, particularly in their language and artistic realisation, this article aims to demonstrate how Katembo appropriates Goscinny's and Uderzo's classic comic volume *Asterix and the Goths* into an East African setting.

Comics have been studied in the field of popular culture for several years now, but most of these studies have been limited to Western society. The few publications that consider other parts of the world, tend to ignore Africa. Also scientists, who deal with African societies, do not seem to care much about comics. They may analyse, e.g. a new Swahili novel in detail, which is only read by a few literature scholars. However, for a scientific reputation it does not seem adequate to do research on comics, which are apparently read by millions of people of all walks of life. Nearly every Tanzanian knows the *SANI* comic magazine, but only a few East Africans could tell who the celebrated novelists are, about whose works several dissertations have been written. Nevertheless comics offer a vast source, not only for scholars of literature and art, but also for social scientists. Being a form of popular culture, they are part of the articulation, negotiation and consolidation of identities and can be used as an "analytic lens to understand socio-historical processes" (Mankekar 2002: 11733). Therefore the study of African comics can shed some light on discourses and developments in African societies. This paper focuses on the appropriation of aspects of Western popular culture by a Tanzanian artist.

Comics in East Africa

Following Scott McCloud's definition of comics as sequential art and his elaborations about signs and pictures which lead him to early rock paintings (McCloud 1994: 13, 149), one can conclude that not only the cradle of mankind, but also the cot of comic art, is to be found in East Africa. The rock paintings of Kolo in Central Tanzania are 3000 years old sequences displaying hunting scenes (Masao 1982: 46). Though there have been various works published about rock painting, little has been written about recent East African comics[1]. Knigge, who wrote a history of world comics, traces the beginnings of African comics back to the 1940s, where the strip *Mbumbulu* appeared in a colonial newspaper (Knigge 1996: 238). In East Africa there are also hints about Swahili comics which were published in *Askari*, *Heshima*, and *Jambo*, British journals for African soldiers in the second world war.[2] However, these comics were created by Europeans. The first known comics by East African artists were published in the 1970s. One of the earliest Swahili strips is E. Githau's *Juha Kalulu* ('Idiot Kalulu'), which was first published in the Kenyan newspaper *Taifa Leo* in July 1973 (Gikonyo 1986: 190). In Tanzania, David Kyungu is the pioneer of Swahili comics. Inspired by *Andy Capp*, he created the character of *Kalikenye* and started publishing his own works from 1976 onwards in papers like *Kiongozi*, *Lengo*, *Nchi Yetu* and *Daily News* (Kyungu 1993: no page numbers and personal comment in October 2002). The interest in these Swahili comic strips was so huge, that by 1980 a whole magazine dedicated to comics was founded. It is called *SANI*

---

[1] Only a few articles were published by Beck (1999), Beez (2003a, 2004), Beez and Kolbusa (2003), Gikonyo (1986) and Graebner (1995).
[2] I am grateful to Katrin Bromber for this information.

and still appears today. The fact that it survived all economic and political problems which hit Tanzania over the last 20 years, demonstrates how dedicated its readers are. *Mageuzi* (changes, reforms), the Tanzanian version of Gorbachev's perestroika, liberalized also the media sector and gave it a big push. More than thirty different Swahili comic magazines started appearing on the dusty streets of Dar es Salaam, the biggest Tanzanian city, where their colourful covers try to attract buyers for the price of currently 500 or 600 Tanzanian Shillings (around 0,50 to 0,60 €) which is equivalent to the price of a bottle of beer.

Although Beck states that "the influence of European, American, or Japanese comics other than daily newspaper strips seems to be rather small" (Beck 1999: 70) there are clear Western influences found in some publications. For instance, *Tintin*'s adventures and Hergé's style can be found in Anthony Mwangi's book *Safari ya Anga ya juu* ('journey to space') (Mwangi 1997). The *TITANIC* comic by Joshua Amandus Mtani is another example. He has drawn the story of the famous Hollywood movie into a comic, changing all the characters into Africans (Mtani 2000). Following this brief overview, the article will now turn to a story published in *SANI*, which was influenced by Goscinny's and Uderzo's *Asterix*.

The *SANI* magazine

The *SANI* magazine is said to be one of the oldest African comic magazines dating back to 1980. Over 70 issues have been published so far, which sold up to 60,000 copies per issue. *SANI*'s content comprises mainly of comic strips, often series, which are continued over several issues. But there are novels to be found as well as poems and riddles. Another regular feature found in the magazine are the pages dedicated to readers to greet each other and also to look for pen pals.

Each comic magazine has certain cartoon characters which are drawn over the years by different artists. The characters of *Madenge* and *Komredi Kipepe*, who are the heroes of the story that I am going to introduce, are drawn by Chris Katembo[3] since 1992. But he says these characters have been with *SANI* since the early issues in the 1980s. Chris Katembo was born in 1970. After finishing his primary education he visited several art schools and worked as an art teacher before joining *SANI*. His love for comics dates back

---

[3] I am very grateful to Chris Katembo for the valuable information he gave me during a talk and via email.

to his childhood days. Of course Katembo knows *Tintin* and *Asterix*, classic European comic heroes. But he says he only read four to five *Asterix* books, as they are rarely sold in Tanzanian bookshops and very expensive to Tanzanian standards. One of Katembo's favourites is *Asterix and the Goths*, which he used as a blueprint for the story *Komredi Kipepe na kisa cha Bi Arafa*. However, Katembo had no idea that the Gauls represent the French and the Goths the Germans.

Asterix' attraction to an East African audience

Asterix and the Goths started as a series in the French magazine PILOTE as *Astérix chez les Goths* on 18.5.1961 and was published as *Asterix* album No. 3 in 1963 (Uderzo 1986: 266). In *Asterix and the Goths*, the Gauls *Asterix* and *Obelix* accompany *Getafix* their village druid to his annual druid meeting at the holy forest of the Carnutes. There, *Getafix* is kidnapped by the Goths who want to use his secrets to rule the world. *Asterix* and *Obelix* follow the druid and free him by using his powers to cause civil war.

In the European cultural context the adventures of *Asterix* refer to real history, the Roman Empire and its rule over wide parts of the continent. Anybody who studied Roman history at school is easily amused by Goscinny's and Uderzo's stories. The story about the Goths gets its juice from the way the authors make fun of the warlike Goths whose descendents started two world wars in the last century.[4] But what makes this story interesting for an East African audience, forty years after its first publication in France? The answer lies in the fact that there are many similarities between *Asterix*' world and East African cultures, which makes it easy to appropriate.

First of all, *Asterix* is a warrior who frequently hunts with his friend *Obelix*. Warriors and hunters are honoured professions also in East Africa. Even *Asterix*' favourite prey, wild pigs, is commonly hunted and eaten by East Africans. Another protagonist, the druid *Getafix*, is a familiar character to Swahili speaking communities, who have *waganga* and *wachawi*, traditional healers and witches. *Getafix* wears a white gown, which resembles a *kanzu*, a traditional Muslim dress at the Swahili coast. Many famous *waganga* are known to wear this type of clothing, e.g. Kinjikitile, the prophet of the maji maji war (Beez 2003b: 108). Kinjikitile claimed to have a powerful war medicine, turning bullets into water. Thus *Getafix*' magic

---

[4] Some of the Gothic Characters resemble the German President Hindenburg and Adolf Hitler (Stoll 1974: 152).

portion, which makes *Asterix* invincible, fits well into the East African concept of war medicines, *dawa ya vita*. Another Gaul druid in the *Asterix* adventure possesses rainmaking powers just as many of their African counterparts. The fact that Gaul magicians meet in holy forests that must not be entered by strangers has similarities in East African concepts. The *kaya*-forests in Kenya or the *mshitu* and *mpungi*-forests of the Pare in Tanzania can be mentioned as examples (Sheridan 2000: 6).

Asterix' armoury contains spears, swords, shields and fists, the same weapons which are traditionally used all over Africa. That the Goths crush each other's head with a club is more exotic to the European audience than to an East African reader, who is used to see Maasai and also policemen with their *rungu* (club). The blowing of horns as a signal in *Asterix* might be fascinating for an European reader but *kupiga pembe* (blowing the horn) is common in East African rural areas, when announcements are made. Even the cooking styles in both cases are similar. *Getafix* prepares his magic portions on an open fire just like many East African women do their cooking today. Finally the open air banquets in the end of each *Asterix'* adventure have striking similarities to *nyama choma* (BBQ) events: meat is roasted and served with local brew. Like most East Africans, *Asterix* lives in a rural setting. His country Gaul is occupied by the Romans who have an urban culture. This situation reminds the reader of the colonial days in East Africa, whereby rural societies were colonized by industrialized societies. However the most humorous thing about *Asterix* is that the 'good boys' beat up the 'bad boys'. This is well appreciated worldwide.

The Swahili characters

According to the title, *Komredi Kipepe* and *Bi Arafa* are the main characters of Katembo's story. As mentioned earlier, *Komredi Kipepe* as a cartoon is a veteran in Swahili comic history, having appeared for the first time in the 1980s. His title *"Komredi"* is a humorous reference to the good old socialist days of Tanzanian Ujamaa. According to Katembo *"Kipepe"* is the name for loincloth in many southern Tanzanian languages. This cartoon is a cunning hunter running after the animals in amazing speed and swinging his characteristic club. Although *Kipepe* is brave and courageous he is often outwitted by the animals thus the readers of his stories have a laugh.

Bi Arafa is a new figure which was created by Chris Katembo specifically for this story. *Arafa* is a common female name along the East African coast. Katembo states that *Bi Arafa* is also a frequent name for female witches, *wachawi*. Its Arabic root means "the one who knows"[5] making it a perfect name for a wise healer. *Bi Arafa* is tall and thin, especially in the last picture of the episode, where she resembles the first Tanzanian President with her grey hair. Her statement against tribalism and fundamentalism reminds the reader of Nyerere's legacy.

Kipepe and *Bi Arafa* are accompanied by *Madenge*. Although *Madenge* is a school boy, wearing his characteristic black shirt and white shorts with suspenders, he is – historically speaking – as old as *Kipepe*, having been introduced to the Tanzanian readers in the 1980s. His name refers to his hairstyle. In his episodes, *Madenge* appears as a clever boy driving his parents and teachers nuts with his wit.

Kipepe, *Arafa* and *Madenge* belong to an ethnic group called Wabushi, which supposedly refers to the people from the bush. The Wabushi have appeared regularly in *SANI* for many years now. They are all rural characters appearing in the *SANI* magazine. But Katembo is using the Wabushi for the first time as an ethnic group. The Wabushi are the 'good guys' and the heroes of our story, representing the Gauls in Goscinny and Uderzo's story.

In the story of *Komredi Kipepe na kisa cha Bi Arafa*, *Kipepe* and *Madenge* escort *Bi Arafa* to a magicians competition in the forest of Gambush. Gambush is said to be the name of a real village in Mwanza region whose entire population consists of witches – *wachawi*. Thus Katembo takes a contemporary East African name as a translation for the antique name of the Gaul forest of Carnutes. *Bi Arafa* clearly takes over the part of the Gaul druid *Getafix*. Like him she is tall and slender. In the first pictures of the story she even wears the same dress: a white *kanzu* and a cape. Later she changes to a grey dress. Even her secret of a medicine that makes someone strong enough to uproot trees, is the same as *Getafix'* secret. As opposed to *Getafix*, *Bi Arafa* is a woman. Here Katembo shows gender consciousness, as most comics are dominated by male characters.

At first glance, *Kipepe* seems to play the role of *Obelix* and *Madenge* the role of *Asterix*. At least a comparison of Uderzo's and Katembo's drawings seems to suggest this as *Kipepe* often takes *Obelix'* position in a picture and *Madenge* poses like *Asterix*. Though they may take over poses in pictures, they still retain their own unique character which they developed over 20 years. For example *Kipepe* is more responsible. It is his idea to accompany *Bi Arafa* and protect her, while in the French comic this is *Asterix'* role.

---

[5] I thank Farouk Topan for this valuable information.

Madenge on the other hand seems to play *Asterix'* role. He is short and it is his smartness which rescues the heroes. Nevertheless his childishness resembles *Obelix'* naivety more than *Asterix'* sober reasoning.

An example of similarities between a drawing by Katembo and Uderzo can be demonstrated in pictures 1 (SANI 69: 29) and 2 (Uderzo/Goscinny 1971:25). The tree on the left can also be found in Uderzo's picture. For details Katembo adds flying birds which can be seen in many other pictures whereas these are not part of Uderzo's inventory for details. *Madenge*, just like *Asterix*, warns his comrade about approaching people. Even *Madenge's* arm position and the direction of his look resemble *Asterix*.

As *Getafix* is kidnapped by the Goths, *Bi Arafa* is also taken as a hostage by another ethnic group: the Wabarukuna. Katembo says the Wabarukuna is the nickname (*jina la utani*) for the Makonde, who live in Southern Tanzania. However, his Wabarukuna cartoons have their own character and are not meant to be a caricature of the Makonde. Like the Goths, the Wabarukuna are bold headed and dress in furs.

Material culture

Besides using Swahili characters for his story Katembo also appropriates features from the material culture of *Asterix*, translating them into a Swahili context. Goscinny and Uderzo used a Gothic helmet resembling German helmets from the first world war, as a symbol for a savage and war thirsty nation. This helmet was lost by a Goth during the capture of *Getafix* thus giving *Asterix* a hint of the kidnappers. But a helmet does not fit into an East African context. Thus Katembo created a special kind of spear, a very short one, as a symbol for the Wabarukuna. When this spear is found in the forest of Gambush, *Madenge* knows, that the Wabarukuna captured *Bi Arafa*. In Barukunaland a strange feature for East Africa appears in the form of thick stone walls. The Barukuna ruler lives in a stone palace. Although stonewalls are known in the coastal urban Swahili culture they surprise in the rural setting of the story. Also the V shaped doors, which resemble the Gothic palace in the French story, appear to be exotic to a Tanzanian context. As *Madenge* and *Kipepe* enter Barukunaland to follow *Bi Arafa* it is striking that the environment of Barukunaland resembles the way Uderzo portraits the Goths. Also the gag of an owl arguing with a woodpecker (*SANI* 66: 21; Goscinny; Uderzo 1971: 9), which is a running gag in many *Asterix* adventures, appears in Katembo's story. This is astonishing as an owl is a symbol for witchcraft and evil for many East Africans to the extent that they try to avoid it. In *SANI* No. 69 Katembo uses a light bulb as a symbol of a bright idea of *Madenge*. This is quite a modernisation of the *Asterix* theme. During *Asterix* times there were no light bulbs. If someone has an idea, Uderzo indicates it by an oil-lamp. But as Katembo's story is not playing in the past, he can use the symbol of a light bulb. Another form of appropriation of symbols is the trophy for the winner of the druid or *wachawi* contest. *Getafix* is awarded a small golden menhir for his craft. Menhirs are unknown in East Africa thus Katembo lets *Bi Arafa* be presented with a *tunguli*[6] *ya mpingo*, a gourd for local medicine made of ebony (Goscinny; Uderzo1971: 13, *SANI* 67). Ebony seems to be the appropriate symbol for honour in a Swahili context, whereas in French culture it is gold.

Serialization of the story

As mentioned earlier Katembo published his story as a series over seven issues. Thus he returns to the origins of *Asterix* as the adventure of *Asterix and the Goths* was first published as a series in the comic magazine PILOTE in 1961 and only later in 1963 as an album.

---

[6] Katembo uses the form tunguli. In the dictionaries the form tunguri is used (Johnson 1939: 480; TUKI 2001: 328). Katembo as many other Swahili speakers often interchanges /l/ and /r/. Another example will be discussed later.

But Katembo has not as much space as Goscinny and Uderzo had, because PILOTE was published more frequently than *SANI*. Therefore Katembo has to squeeze a comic of 48 pages into nine pages. As a result much of the story telling cannot be done in pictures but has to be written in special frames and boxes. There is also the need for text frames because of the serialisation of the story. Katembo has to keep the tension high at the end of each issue in order to keep the reader eagerly waiting for the next issue, whereby at the beginning of each new issue he explains what has been happening so far. Besides texts Katembo also uses pictures at the beginning of a new episode to get the reader back into the story. In *SANI* No. 70 the story ends with a Barukuna guard blowing a horn. The same horn blower is shown in the first panel of the story in *SANI* No. 71 together with an explanation of what happened last.

Additional to narrating the story in text frames, Katembo also shortens the episode by drawing various sequences in one panel. For example in *SANI* No. 70 the beating up of the Wabarukuna is combined in one picture with the stealing of their clothes as a disguise for *Madenge* and *Kipepe*. *Asterix* and *Obelix* need a full page for this (Goscinny; Uderzo 1971: 25f).

Action scenes

Although the Swahili comic has developed its own code for fighting scenes[7] Katembo is close to the original in the first violent scene of his episode as a comparison of picture 3 and 4 indicates: a spear is cracking on the right side of the panel. Both drawings are dominated by a cloud of dust out of which a foot and hands appear. *Obelix'* strong fist has been changed into a severely damaged Barukuna head. Whereas Uderzo only uses lines to indicate violent action Katembo adds splashing blood to illustrate that scene (*SANI* 70: 30; Goscinny and Uderzo 1974: 25). The signs of violence are more drastic in Swahili than in the original *Asterix*. Uderzo and Goscinny indicate the results of violence by stars, broken weapons, torn clothes, black eyes and a tongue hanging out of the mouth. Katembo uses the more drastic Swahili code for violence, especially in the last fighting scenes. His victims fart in despair, they run around with missing limbs and axes, arrows and knives sticking out of their bodies. Their heads get chopped off and fly through the picture while their blood is dripping all over the scene as can be seen in picture 5. Also the sound words of the fight have been changed. Only BIMM! was used as by

---

[7] Instead of a soundword a noun describing trouble and violence is often written in the middle of a dust cloud, like *kasheshe*. Metaphors of violence like Kosovo, which became a synonym for trouble, are also popular.

Goscinny. BOUM! have become BOU!. The sound PAFF! Has been translated into the Swahili sound of KARB! Finally a new sound has been added. The breaking of the spear is silent in the original but Katembo added a KHA!. Another sound word change can be noted in the blowing of the signal horn. The sound of the horn changed from a BOOOOO BOOOO and BAAAOOOO BOOOAAA into a POOOOOM. The Swahili horn sound seems to be more melodic to the listener as Katembo adds musical notes and a clef which are missing in the Gothic sound. The rest of the picture have close similarities. The horn blower stands on top of a stone wall holding the horn in his right hand and the body turned slightly to the left. (*SANI* 70: 31, 71: 28; Goscinny Uderzo 1974: 28).

Body-language

The sequence of an interpreter interrogating *Bi Arafa* in the service of the Barukuna king seems to be taken from the *Asterix* album one by one. Two comparisons of this sequence can be found in pictures 6 to 9. In the pictures the positions of the figures and the way they hold their arms and heads do rarely vary from the original. But a closer look reveals striking differences. It is interesting that the body language of the interpreter is different as he translates the lie that *Bi Arafa* will give out her medicine. Uderzo stressed that lie with a heavy nodding and folded hands. This seems to have no Swahili equivalent as Katembo's interpreter stresses this positive statement by moving his hands downwards. Moreover the Barukuna interpreter is shaking all over the sequence, indicated by fine trembling lines, whereas the Gothic interpreter is not. Shivering seems to be the correct translation of body language for fear by Katembo. The translation in the speech balloons is more or less the same. The chief wants to know whether the magician is willing to share his or her knowledge. In the case of refusal he threatens to kill the interpreter as well. A threat which makes the interpreter not to translate the words of the magicians but to tell the chief what he wants to hear. Interesting is the translation of *Getafix*' strict "never" into "si, rahisi". That shows that even in a very pressed situation a Tanzanian would be so polite to avoid a strict "hata" or "hapana" ("no") but prefers to give a vague "it is not easy".

Katembo adds thought balloons to the interpreter (*SANI* 70: 31) which are not used by Uderzo and Goscinny. These thought balloons are filled with Swahili exclamations "leo" ('today', meaning 'what a day'), "duh" (expression of surprise) and "lo" (expression of consternation). Uderzo was able to express the stress and fear of the interpreter by changing his face colour into green and yellow. Further more Uderzo's interpreter's physiognomy was more detailed which allowed him to express fear with the eyes and uncertainty with the nose. Maybe fear is not expressed in green and yellow in African faces. Besides that *SANI* is published in black and white and its printing quality is rougher which might have hindered Katembo to work more on his interpreter's face.

Of course *Bi Arafa* does not give her secret to the Wabarukuna. *Madenge* has the idea of brewing a medicine to cause civil war in Barukunaland and escape while the Wabarukuna are busy killing themselves. This is a slight variation on the original theme, where the Goths started a civil war as they received the original magic portion due to their natural greed and thirst for war.

Speech-balloons

Katembo's speech-balloons have different styles. Sometimes they have the classic balloon shape as in the last picture. There they are round, the lines of the text follow the oval of the balloon (*SANI* 71: 29). In other cases as in the first picture of the episode in *SANI* No. 70 the balloon follows the text and its paragraphs, having a straight line at the top and the bottom and slightly rounded lines on the sides. A third balloon variety appears on page 31 of *SANI* No. 70. There, the balloons have a rectangular shape. There is no difference in the content of these three types of balloons evident. But there is a fourth balloon type with a zigzag-frame (*SANI* 70: 30 and 71: 28). The zigzag-frame indicates that the speaker is talking in a loud harsh voice to his audience.

One device of indicating different languages through lettering is taken from the *Asterix* volume. There the Goth talk is represented by Germanic fracture font, whereas the Gaul language is written in Latin script. In No. *SANI* 70 it is obvious that the Wabushi and the Wabarukuna do not understand each other and they need a translator. Katembo indicates the different languages by the size of the letters. The Wabarukuna only talk in small letters whereas the Wabushi talk in capital letters. But as the difference is not clearly visible many readers do not understand this means of lettering.

By drawing pictures in the balloons Katembo indicates the thoughts of their protagonists. In issue No. 69 *Madenge* has an idea indicated by a light bulb. In the following picture in issue 70 *Madenge* thinks of a cloud of dust, definitely indicating a fight.

Spoken language

The characters in *Asterix* stories are famous for their play on words, which are, as it is said, up to 80% untranslatable out of the French language and cultural context. Goscinny is parodying various accents, playing around with words, mixing modern and ancient forms. Therefore in all *Asterix* translations much of the verbal humour gets lost. But it can be said, that he and his comrades talk the standardized form of any languages avoiding swearwords, curses and slang. Thus making it readable for children without the danger of interference of any forms of censorship.

But *Madenge* and *Kipepe* use slang (*kihuni*), and street language (*kiswahili cha mitaani*). For example in *SANI* 66 *Madenge* says to *Kipepe* after they have fallen behind *Arafa* and her friend: "*Anko tukazane bwana, ona vigagu vinatuacha*" (uncle lets exert man, look the oldtimers leave us behind). *Anko*, with the meaning of "uncle", is the colloquial form of *mjomba* derived from English. *Kigagu* is slang for an old person.

In *SANI* No. 70 *Madenge* says "*Tulianzishe la kigetogeto ... tuyapangilie madili yetu*" (Let's start the ghetto-thing ... let's plan our deals). This talk would definitely be criticized and banned if bodies like BAKITA (Baraza ya Kiswahili ya Tanzania, the Tanzanian Swahili Council) had a say in comic production.[8] The "ghetto thing" and "deals" as slang for a wild beating are a quite recent development of Swahili language in an urban underground culture context. If a Swahili comic uses latest slang it is well received by the

---

[8] There is also a comic guarding the purity of Kiswahili: *Mzee kifimbo cheza* (Graebner 1995: 264). This *Mzee* is guarding the Swahili language from the dirty influence of uncivilized talk.

readers. Another example of colloquial Swahili, which would not make it into a serious public announcement, is the untranslatable language of the fighting Wabarukuna in the last part of the episode: *Umenipata mume mwenza kuna lingine sema basi – kutembea na mke wangu isiwe nongwa yaani mimi mume mwenza wako?* (You got me the co-husband, but there is another, what do you say to that? – To walk with my wife do not be disagreeable... this means I am your co-husband?).

This rude language of sexual hints and admitted adultery would hardly fit into the clean world of the asexual figures of *Asterix* nor would it be heard on official Swahili occasions. But of course it would give someone credit in street quarrels. This indicates that Swahili comics do not represent the polished language of officials as it is read and heard in newspapers, radio or television. But they use the language of the ordinary man, which is spoken in the streets. This is a remarkable difference to Goscinny's and Uderzo's story.

The last example of sexual language is an unwilling slip of Katembo's pen in the process of lettering. In the last picture of the episode *Madenge* justifies the civil war in Barukunaland by saying *kiranga haliliwi* (sexual mania is not being eaten). To the reader it appears as if the greed and brutality of the Wabarukuna is classified by *Madenge* as *kiranga*, which means "sexual mania" (TUKI 2001: 148). But according to Katembo it is not that rude. *Madenge* wanted to say *kilanga haliliwi*, naughtiness is not being eaten, which indicates that he is not tolerating the mean behaviour of the Wabarukuna. It is obvious that *Madenge* interchanges /l/ and /r/ as many East African Bantu speakers do.

The Moral Ending

Finally the moral of Katembo's story, which is shown in picture 10, is a different one compared to *Asterix*. Uderzo and Goscinny were just making fun out of their war thirsty and power gambling neighbours, the Germans, whose desire to rule the world could be traced back to the times of *Asterix*. The Gauls just started a civil war in the country of the Goths so that the Goths may be busy slaughtering themselves instead of disturbing the peaceful Gauls. But for Katembo it is also a lesson to stop tribalism and religious fundamentalism in order to avoid civil war. This is what *Bi Arafa* explains to *Madenge* and *Kipepe*: *Unasikia Madenge mjukuu wangu. Ukabila na udini ni sumu kali sana! Penye ukabila na udini hali kama hii ni rahisi ya kutokea. Nyie ndiyo taifa la kesho hivyo msikubali vitu hivyo viwili vikawasambaratisha kama hawa Wabarukuna.* (You listen *Madenge*, my grandchild. Tribalism and religious fundamentalism is a very strong poison. Where there is tribalism and religious fundamentalism a state like this is very likely to happen. You are really the nation of tomorrow. Therefore do not agree to these two things, they will divide you as it has happened to these Barukuna.).

Obviously many countries surrounding Tanzania suffer or have suffered from civil war, which is often explained by tribalism. What religious fundamentalism can cause is reported in the news from Ireland, Israel, Sudan, to name a few. *Bi Arafa* has similarities with the Father of the Tanzanian Nation Mwalimu Nyerere. She is slim and tall and has grey short hair. She is very wise and full of knowledge and obviously very respected, as the first Tanzanian president was. Nyerere's legacy is the fight for a peaceful and free nation. He always warned against tribalism and religious fundamentalism which could destroy the peace Tanzania is enjoying.

Conclusion

Katembo was inspired by a French comic episode, appropriating it in parts so closely, that the line to copyright violation is not always clear. But at the same time he translates it into a different cultural context and adds a moral notion, which was never implied in the original. Uderzo and Goscinny have always stressed that their characters are created just for entertainment[9]. But

---

[9] „Wir haben einzig und allein ein Ziel: selbst Spaß zu haben und anderen Spaß zu machen. Das ist unser bescheidener Beitrag während unseres kurzen Aufenthaltes auf diesem Planeten." (Our

Tanzanian artists rarely do *l'art pour l'art* or make fun just for the sake of laughing. They feel obliged to educate the society. The artist Ka-Batembo "dedicates his efforts to making comics for social change" (worldcomics 2001a). Especially as people are more interested in the cartoon characters of *Karikenye*, *Polo-Chakubanga* or *Bogi Benda*, than in politics. As David Kyungu states (Kyungu 1991: 9), the Tanzanian artists feel obliged to use them not only for entertainment but also for education. The popular Tanzanian cartoonist Kipanya says "*Watu wanazijua na wanaziheshimu katuni kwenye magazeti kama Kipanya, Bi Mkora (Majira) au Zero (Mtanzania) na tunaweza kuzitumia kuwaelimisha watu*" (Kipanya 2001: 6) (The people know and respect the cartoons in the newspapers like *Kipanya*, *Bi Mkora* or *Zero* and we can use them to educate the people.) Katembo follows this attitude by reviving Nyerere's appeal for unity and peace. By taking something foreign or global and making use of it in his own local society he is appropriating *Asterix* for the Tanzanian audience. Local appropriation has been defined as a "translation into the vocabulary and syntax of the appropriating environment" (Beck 2001: 67). This is exactly what Katembo does with *Asterix*. He translates not only the words of the comic hero, but tailors the whole story to fit into an East African cultural context. Moreover he develops a moral ending for the story, which can be interpreted as "further invention as part of appropriation" (Beck 2001: 77). He uses the story of *Asterix* and puts it in a familiar surrounding. With the new moral ending he explains global problems of civil war in a local way. It is obvious that the civil war of the Wabarukuna is caused by *Bi Arafa*'s medicine. In the same way it can be explained that the ongoing civil wars are caused by medicine as well. An explanation which is within the world of thought of many East Africans as many leaders are said to possess strong spiritual powers or work together with ritual experts to sustain their rule. But this might be an over-interpretation as Katembo himself had only the conflict in Morogoro region in mind when he drew his story. There, pastoralists and farmers were in fierce battle over land issues and Katembo wanted to give a warning of what internal quarrels can lead to. Katembo's story has a *mafunzo* for the reader, a lesson to be learned. Such lessons are appreciated by the Swahili audience as can be seen from their traditional *hadithi* (narrations), whether they are oral or written or in this case drawn.

Rose Marie Beck wrote an article about "Swahili Comic or Comic in Swahili?". Here she queries if the Swahili culture has developed special forms

---

one and only aim is to have fun for ourselves and to entertain others. This is our humble contribution during our short stay on this planet) (Uderzo 1986: 128).

of comic or if comics in East Africa are just ordinary western comics. Concerning *Kipepe,* it can be asked in a similar way: *"Asterix* in Swahili or a Swahili *Asterix?"* The answer is that Katembo has not simply translated *Asterix* into Swahili but has made a real *mswahili* out of him, a true East African.

References

BECK, ROSE MARIE
    (1999). "Comic in Swahili or Swahili Comic?" *AAP* 60, 67-101.
BECK, KURT
    (2001). "Die Aneignung der Maschine." In Karl-Heinz Kohl and Nicolaus Schafhausen, eds. *New Heimat.* New York: Lukas and Starnberg, 66-77.
BEEZ, JIGAL
    (2003a). "They Are Crazy These Swahili: Komredi Kipepe in the Footsteps of Asterix. Globalization in East African Comics." *International Journal of Comic Art* 5:1, 95-114.
    (2003b). *Geschosse zu Wassertropfen: Sozio-religiöse Aspekte des Maji-Maji-Krieges in Deutsch Ostafrika.* Köln: Köppe.
    (2004). "Großstadtfieber und Hexenmeister: Horror- und Fantasycomics aus Tansania." In Tobias Wendl, ed. *Africa Screams: Die Wiederkehr des Bösen in Kino, Kunst und Kult.* Wuppertal: Peter Hammer Verlag, 153-164.
BEEZ, JIGAL AND STEFANIE KOLBUSA
    (2003). *Kibiriti Ngoma: Gender Relations in Swahili Comic and Taarab Music.* Paper presented at the 13th Annual Meeting of the Pan African Anthropological Association in Port Elizabeth, South Africa, 29.06.-04.07.2003.
GIKONYO, WAITHIRA
    (1986). "Comics and Comic Strips in the Mass Media in Kenya." In Alphons Silbermann and H.-D. Dyroff, eds. *Comics and Visual Culture: Research Studies from Ten Countries.* München: Saur, 185-195.
GOSCINNY, RENÉ AND ALBERT UDERZO
    (1963). *Astérix chez les Goths.* Paris: Dargaud.
    (1970). *Asterix und die Goten.* Stuttgart: Ehapa.
    (1974). *Asterix and the Goths.* Leicester: Hodder and Stoughton.
GRAEBNER, WERNER
    (1995). "Mambo: Moderne Textformen und rezente Sprachentwicklung in Dar es Salaam." In G. Miehe and W. Möhlig, eds. *Swahili Handbuch.* Köln: Köppe, 263-277.
JOHNSTON, FREDERICK
    (1939). *A Standard Swahili – English Dictionary.* Nairobi: Oxford University Press.
KATEMBO, CHRIS
    (2000/2001). "Komredi Kipepe na kisa cha Bi Arafa." *SANI* No., 65-71.
KIPANYA, MASOUD
    (2001). "Kipanya ni nani?"*Femina* Feb-Apr. 2001, 4-7.

KYUNGU, DAVID
(1991).'*Mensch guck mich nicht so an!... ': Alltagsgeschichten mit spitzer Feder gezeichnet von David Kyungu.* Breklum: Breklumer Verlag.
(1993): *'Mensch guck mich nicht so an!... ': Karikaturen von David Kyungu.* Husum: LAG Soziokultur.
KNIGGE, ANDREAS C.
(1996). *Comics: Vom Massenblatt ins multimediale Abenteuer.* Reinbek: rororo.
MANKEKAR, P.
(2002). "Popular Culture." In Neil Smelser, ed. *International Encyclopedia of the Social and Behavorial Sciences.* Amsterdam: Elsevier, 11733-11736.
MASAO, FIDELIS T.
(1982). *The Rock Art of Kondoa and Singida: A Comparative Description.* Dar es Salaam: National Museums of Tanzania.
MTANI, JOSHUA AMANDUS
(2000). *Titanic.* Dar es Salaam: Mtani Artwork Production.
MWANGI, ANTHONY
(1997). *Safari ya Anga za juu.* Nairobi: Sasa Sema Publ.
SELLES, HANS
(2002). "Asterix around the World. http://www.Asterix-Obelix.nl/. Accessed 12th Jan.2002.
SHERIDAN, MICHAEL J.
(2000). *The Sacred Forests of North Pare, Tanzania: Indigenous Conservation, Local Politics, and Land Use.* Working Paper in African Studies 224. Boston: African Studies Center.
STOLL, ANDRÉ
(1974). *Asterix: Das Trivialmythos Frankreichs.* Köln: Du Mont.
THEIS, GEORG
(2002). http://www.Asterix-fan.de/sw/swahili. Accessed 15th May 2002.
TUKI
(2001). *Kamusi ya Kiswahili – Kiingereza: Swahili - English Dictionary.* Dar es Salama: TUKI.
UDERZO, ALBERT
(1986). *Uderzo: der weite Weg zu Asterix.* Stuttgart: Ehapa.
WORLDCOMICS
(2001a): http://www.worldcomics.fi/Katti1.html. Accessed 14th May 2002.
(2001b): http://www.worldcomics.fi/Katti2.html. Accessed 14th May 2002.

Notions on Time in Burkina Faso

EVELYN WLADARSCH
Heidelberg, Germany

1. Introduction

"What, then, is time? When nobody asks me, I know. If someone asks me to explain, I can not tell him." This famous statement of Augustine (354-430 AD) is surely still true. While time is an omnipresent, taken for granted phenomenon of life, it is also a great enigma of life.

Time plays a central role in and upon socio-cultural life. Investigating in ideas and practices pertaining to time reveals a lot about humans and the diverse ways they develop to make sense out of the world. In this article some features of time in rural Burkina Faso are presented in order to present a socio-cultural time concept, which differs considerably from our Western one.

First, the question will be addressed, to what degree time is a universal category and to what degree it can be seen as a culturally constructed category. Then some facts about Burkina Faso will be presented as general background, before the notions on time in this country are exposed. Finally it will be discussed, how the understanding of "other's" socio-cultural time can help to develop sensitivity, respect, and tolerance for other cultures.

2. Universal time – cultural time

Each culture has its own, unique temporal finger print. Knowing a culture means knowing the time values, with which they live (Rifkin 1987: 9).

In fact, time is surely a universal feature of human life, but its representations and meanings differ considerably from culture to culture (Gell 1992). As all human beings experience time, namely temporal states, sequences, changes and natural rhythms and everyone somehow orders events temporally, time can be taken as a universal comparative category for cross-cultural research. However the socio-cultural conceptualisation of time within the specific cultural context is variable and therefore interesting for anthropological investigation. The temporal organisation and co-ordination of activities, norms about appropriate sequence and duration of events, the dealing with punctuality or waiting or the extension and significance of past, present and future are all the results of social negotiation processes. Such normative terms alone, like "appropriate", "dealing with" or "significance" already assign the social nature of the concepts in question, and they should express the culture-specific appropriateness or significance, that means how cultures experience and conceptualise time, according to their desires or necessities (Aveni 1990: 168). Consequently, these collective products have to be understood in their connection to social processes, institutions and values.

Thus it can be assumed that time and some basic temporal aspects (like sequence, duration, and pace) are universal categories, which all human beings experience, though handling, and interpreting them differently. The sociologist Mannheim states:

> ...that every social fact is a function of the time and place in which it occurs. Time and place in their turn, however, have meaning only when related to the totality of a given society. (Mannheim 1953: 211)

He continues by calling this in fact not a new insight but a "trite assertion", which however has only been taken as a tentative hypothesis within social sciences (ibid.).

3. Burkina Faso – the country

The results presented in the following are based on my research in Burkina Faso, where I have passed three field stays. Burkina Faso, the former Upper Volta, is a landlocked country of the Sahel in West Africa. It is surrounded by Mali and Niger in the north and Ivory Cost, Ghana, Togo and Benin in the south. With about 12,6 million inhabitants (2002) covering an area of 274.122 sq. km, it is one of the most densely populated sub-Saharan countries in West Africa.

The society is characterised by a great ethnic variety. More than 60 ethnic groups peacefully cohabit in Burkina Faso. Each group has its own language and cultural particularities. Usually, the different ethnic groups live geographically separated from each other within the villages, but not isolated. In everyday life, all people freely and peacefully interact with each other.

Concerning religion, the large part of today's population follow Islam (50%), then indigenous beliefs called Animism (40%) or Christianity (10%); traditional believe systems – usually subsumed under the term 'animism' – are formally diminishing, but are still present and powerful in everyday live.

As a consequence of the colonial history, the official language is French. Besides, there are three major local languages: Mooré in the centre, Dioula in the West and Fulfulde in the North of the country. Dioula is one of West Africa's major lingua francas and is commonly used for commerce and communication between groups with different mother tongues. Dioula is spoken not only in Burkina Faso, but also in Ivory Cost and parts of Senegal, Gambia, and Mauritania.

The social organisation is dominated by traditional structures, which co-exist with the formal political and administrative system. Every village has an official administrative representative as well as a *dugutigi* (Dioula),[1] a traditional village chief.

The field research was conducted in and around the town of Nouna, in the country's north-west. Nouna is the capital of the Kossi province, with about 22.000 inhabitants in Nouna, and 230 000 overall the province. In Nouna electricity and running water are available to a limited number of richer families. The town of Nouna has an important market that is frequented by the whole region. As there are also several services, administration, police and banks, it is a place where monetary income is gained and spent. Furthermore several schools reside in Nouna: primary schools, colleges and high schools, as well as a professional training school. Nouna is not only the region's educational, but also health centre, with the district's hospital. The surrounding villages on the other side, are totally rural, most of them having neither electricity nor running water, and the population lives from subsistence farming.

4. Time concepts in Burkina Faso

It is impossible to present *the* time concept, as time is always manifold and diverse. In this context, different temporal aspects are used and gain significance in different contexts of life (and of course there are also individual differences). Adams (1994: 509) illustrates this by showing that when we (Westerns) explicitly talk about time, we refer to time as an objective, natural, quantitative, linear fact, but in quotidian life we also speak of "good" and "auspicious" times, our lives are guided by various cycles (annual, week, tax year,...), and everybody experiences the relativity of the flow of time.

---

[1] In the following presentation some Dioula words and expressions will occur, which are written in "italics".

The cultural conception of time in Burkina Faso is also rich, colourful, diverse, and heterogeneous. I tried to give due consideration to this complexity by illuminating the topic from different angles. The following aspects played a key role in my investigation, regarding time concepts:

Firstly, time is located within the local ontology in order to provide a general comprehension with respect to the main features of the dominant world view and to identify the meaning of social time within this cultural context. Secondly, the structure of time is investigated. This refers to the configuration of socio-culturally meaningful phases, intervals and rhythms, which serve as frame of orientation, as they divide the continuous flow of time into pertinent parts or stages. Thirdly, temporal norms and practices in quotidian social life are exposed, like the ways of spending time and of organising interactions.

4.1. Levels of temporality in ontology

The three levels of temporality will now be presented, against the background of the prevailing notions on the cosmological order. The isolation of different spheres, being characterised by each specific aspects and properties of time is surely an analytical separation. This should help to understand how and where basic temporal features, like the flow of time, periodicity, and unchanging stability are located. On the basis of this theoretical differentiation the position of social time will be exposed.

The terrestrial world: passing time

The terrestrial domain is mainly the sphere of human life, where time is principally sensed in linear terms, as irreversibly *passing*, and *changing*.

Obviously, it is realised that people are born, grow up and die in the end. The other characteristic of this human world is the fact that life is subject to change, with the fact that changes or any other developments can not be undone. Questions about the past, people usually begin to answer with the expression that "the past and today can not be the same", with the explanation that there are not the same people living, and a lot of things changed. The same expression is applied toward the future, saying that it can not be the same as today. The old days will not come back, and children's lives already differ from their parents' one. For example, their behaviour is less influenced by traditions and traditional values (e.g. they do not have respect for the old people), and they have new possibilities, like school attendance. This development is seen as a proceeding, ongoing course. Human life and behaviour is changing permanently. Nowadays, the local population is well aware of the deep-going impact of Modernism on their culture. People refer to "the Whites", thus to Western influences, as the main cause for changes, which lead to a decline of the traditions and result in changed behaviour.

Another fact, implicitly expressing the linear view towards time and especially ideas of "progress" or "evolution", is the idea that a person's life always builds upon his parents' ones and is thus developing ahead. The word for progress or development is *nyɛtaali* and means literally "something that goes good/good going thing". It is wished that things go better, that children overtake their parent's achievements. An old man explained:

> In former times people cultivated with their hands,... we have ploughs and cows and we want that our children have tractors.

Therefore it is important to build up something, to leave this as a good starting point for the children. However, the underlying notion of progress is characterised as a stepwise proceeding, and not so much as an ongoing evolution from a lower to a higher level, towards a better world, how it was typical in the European Enlightenment and afterwards.

There is a proverb expressing that what is done can not be undone:

| *"Jii min bonna,* | Water that is spilled, |
| *an te se ka cɛ."* | you can not pick up. |

Once something has happened, it is impossible to turn back time. You have to accept the new situation as such, and continue on the basis of this new conditions, if you like it or not.

Thus, on the level of human life, time is conceptualised as linear, irreversible, proceeding and changing. This pertains to individual lives as well as to the development of the entire society.

The natural world: cyclical rhythms

In the domain of nature, time is characterised as *repetitive* and *stable*: The flow of time is structured by recurring phases or cycles, and these rhythms are fixed and invariable. While human life is seen as constantly changing, the broader sphere of the natural world recognised as providing a rigidly structured frame. People frequently stated: "The world (nature) did not change, but the humans changed."

The natural cosmos refers to the celestial bodies (sun, moon, stars) and to natural phenomena on earth (wind, clouds). It is said that their regular, repeating movements prove that the natural world stays the same. The most important cycle is the year, besides there are the moon phases and the day. Each natural cycle is composed of two complementary parts: the two seasons during the year, waning and waxing moon and day and night.

The time of nature is also *passing* (constant alternation of the paired halves of each cycle), however it is *not changing* like human time (the phases stay the same). It can be characterised as rhythmic or cyclical, and thus repetitive in contrast to people's linear, and irreversible time.

Natural time is not separated, but thoroughly interwoven with humans' lives, as people live embedded within nature. It serves as frame of reference and orientation, structuring and guiding social life.

The transcendent world: eternal time

The third level of temporality is located in the transcendent world, the sphere of God and supernatural beings, like spirits and ancestors. Transcendent time is *constant, immutable* and *eternal*, neither passing nor changing.

God as the ultimate ground of all things, the creator of the universe is beyond and independent of the categories of time space and cause (Gyekye 1987: 70). He is infinite and eternal and he created the spirits as well, but now they also exist in the transcendent sphere. God and the supernatural beings are eternal and their existence is rather a presence – they are omnipresent, have always been and will always be. While human existence can rather be characterised as life, with a beginning (birth), a changing period in between and an end (death). After death, a human may become an ancestral spirit according to animistic believes, or he may go to God, in Christian and Muslim believes. In both cases the person's form of existence changes, as he transcends into the eternal, immortal unchanging sphere.

However, the situation is even more complex. The existence of the "timeless", perpetual world, is perceived as the guarantee for the continuity of the natural and the terrestrial, human world. Time will continue to exists, it is said that there will be many days to come.

The transcendent world is the realm of pure being or existence and its time is "timeless" as it is outside passing time, and is eternal, permanent and enduring.

The distinction between these three domains of temporality is mainly an analytical one. They are in fact not separated, nor can they be understood in isolation. They are embedded, interwoven and interdependent, with each aspect gaining relevance in different spheres of life. It is unwarranted to regard human time (individual and social) detached from natural time, or leaving ontological issues out of consideration.

Here social time is constituted in combination of natural and terrestrial temporal features, and will be the topic of the following chapters.

4.2. Structuring time: human time and natural time combined

The two modes of temporality – natural and human time – are closely interwoven within the realm of social life, and are surely embedded within transcendental time. The continually recurring natural cycles provide a structure for temporal orientation in human life.

In order to make the continuous flow of time tangible, people intersect time by creating and defining caesura, and turning points, and by patterning time through regularly repeating events. Each moment, or period gets a meaningful sense within that frame, and persons, events, or actions can be localised within this structure.

Natural rhythms

Natural rhythms are inescapable. All biological beings are submitted to their particular biological clocks with, for instance, waking and sleeping phases. Within this context, I concentrate on rhythms in the natural environment. The most fundamental ones are the day and night cycle, the moon phase, and especially the seasons.

In Burkina Faso the most important structuring element within the flow of time is seasonality: the division of the year into a dry and a rainy season, forming the two complementary parts of one annual cycle. People state that "time is divided in two parts". The seasons and especially the reoccurrence of the rainy season offer the time frame for concrete considerations and everyday life. The rainfall and the following harvest are the outstanding events of the year; the rest of the year is either a 'leaving from' or an 'approaching to' the rainy period. People's tasks during the rainy season have a clear order and sequence, finishing with the harvest. In the dry season people are more liberate in the choice of how to fill their days, while "waiting" for the next rain falls. The rainy season – May to October – is the time for agricultural activities. As the large part of the rural population lives from subsistence farming, it is not surprising that the rainy period is considered to be the more important part of the year. During this time the food supply for the whole year has to be grown. The success of the farming activities that means a good and sumptuous harvest, is decisive for the group's survival for one year. This importance is well expressed in the Dioula term *balo* which means 'food' and also 'life'. The rainy season is called "the year's water" and people refer to this period of the year as "time of work", describing the way of living during this period, characterised by hard agricultural work. On the other side, the dry season – November to April – is called "time of the sun", simply referring to the dry, warm and sunny climate. It is perceived as the time of waiting and inactivity. In people's perception, the year begins with the end of the harvest (October/November), and ends with the end of the rainy period. This expression of saying "when the year is cut" (that means when it is finished), clearly shows, how the length of the year, and the importance, and 'real' presence of time is perceived and constituted through the concentration on the activities, that guarantee the society's survival and existence. Simultaneously with the millet, the old year is "cut", and with the new harvest a new year starts. Hence, time is evoked throughout these activities and their sequence.

Qualities of time

Another aspect, that structures time, is by asserting distinct qualities to different times. Time can not only be looked at in a quantitative way (counting days, numbering years or measuring duration), but also under qualitative aspects. Do different times have particular properties? In Burkina Faso the week's days are attributed different qualities. The days are classified into 'light', 'very light', 'heavy', and quite 'neutral' days. Wednesday and Saturday are considered as extremely light days, Monday and Thursday are also light, Friday is a very heavy day, and Tuesday and Sunday are neutral. Light days are advantageous for beginning an activity, and the action will go easily ahead. Monday and Thursday are very suitable for sowing, thus the beginning of cultivation. Wednesday and Saturday, that have even less weight, have the tendency to repeat or continue events. Therefore condolence visits should not be done on these two days, because they bear the risk that within a short period other deaths will follow. At the same time, Saturday is a very auspicious day for weddings, because its repetitive tendency promises a good marriage. Friday is a very heavy day, and is characterised as mighty, important, beneficial and dark. One should not start a work or activity on Friday, because it will probably not succeed, and it will take a long time. However, if something which was started on a Friday succeeds, it is said to be very stable, and will not break easily.

Hence, the different qualities attributed to the single days of the week, structure the continuous time flow and serve as frame of orientation for people's behaviour and activities.

Life stages

The time of a human life span is also structured into pertinent phases, which are – naturally – not repetitive but successive. One life course is finished with death, and the iterative rhythm relates to other persons, especially to one's children who will follow the same life stages from birth to death. There are various ways to define and mark different life phases and to equip these stages with distinct social meanings, rights, and obligations.

Each society offers a temporal frame for classification and interpretation of age and life phases. In fact, the socio-cultural construction of life stages and definitions of social age are a well-known theme in anthropology. While birthday and chronological age are very important in Western societies, most cultures are indifferent towards counted life years (Elwert and Kohli 1990: 3ff). There are rather life stages, and the transcendence into the next stage is socially marked by celebrations (e.g. initiation, marriage), and are expressed by visible signs (e.g. hair, clothing, body decoration) (Splitter 1990: 115).

There are identifiable life phases in Burkina Faso, but these are not linked to numerical counted life years, and abstract counting of years is totally irrelevant. I could distinguish three main, culturally relevant stages: child, adult and old person.

The first phase is subdivided into childhood and youth, and ends with marriage. I would still classify them under one category, as juveniles are often referred to as "children" (*denmisaw*), especially in delimitation to adults. Childhood is a sphere of freedom and learning. Children are free in so far, as they do not have responsibilities, no particular duties, and failures are forgiven easily, because they are not yet mature. They are not yet complete, grown-up persons, and therefore they are met with forbearance. However, childhood is also the time of socialisation, where children have to learn the cultural norms, values, and adequate behaviour. They have to learn and accept obedience and respect towards elders, and to start helping their parents in everyday activities. Through observation and imitation they gradually grow into their (gender) roles and tasks, and thus they adapt to, and integrate themselves into the social order.

Juveniles are still classified as children, because they are not yet mature. There are words for 'young man' (*kamelen*), and 'young girl' (*sunguru*), and people naturally differentiate between small children and youths. The terms *kamelen* and *sunguru* of course somehow refer to a particular age, roughly 14 to 20 years, but the decisive feature is the status of being unmarried. A 16 years old *married* girl, would never be said to be a *sunguru*. Correspondingly, a 25 years old man who is not yet married is still a *kamelen*.

Hence, adulthood is obtained through marriage, and not on the 18th or 21st birthday, as is usual in Western societies. But what is common in both cases is that adult status means a social transcendence to a new position with specific rights, obligations, and responsibilities. The term for adult is *mogo nyakalanni*, and literally means "person with open eyes" and is further explained as "ripe person", and "person who knows (everything)". Males become now responsible for their wife and their family, while the principle change for a woman is the local movement to her husband's household. Marriage is almost automatically linked to reproduction, and getting children is the next step that should – theoretically – directly follow marriage. Only with the birth of the first child, thus with parenthood a person can acquire the status of full personhood. This holds especially true for women, as only a mother is understood as a 'complete' woman. With the marriage the state of adolescence is left behind and one becomes a man (*cɛ*) or a woman (*muso*) and with the first child one becomes father (*facɛ*) or mother (*bamuso*). Children are then the supplement, who make a man and a woman complete. This idea is well expressed on the linguistic level, were the prefix "fa"- or "ba"- is added.

The last life stage of old age is perceived to start with chronological mark of about 45 to 50 years, and with the social mark of own grandchildren and the menopause for women. Old people (*mogokoroba*) have the highest status within society, they are seen as wise, and with a great amount of experience and knowledge, and are highly respected as complete and ripe persons. Old men decide over all affairs and problems of their extended family. As the head of the family they have the role of advisors, and the other members of the family are obliged to inform and consult them, and follow their decisions. The society is based on seniority, and authority increases with age.

Life phases are thus not chronologically determined periods, but rather indicate different degrees of "knowing the world" and of maturity.

4.3. Temporal norms and habits

Societies have established norms, routines, and practices, which provide guidelines for their members, about the expected and accepted ways of organising and conducting activities. To illustrate such temporal norms and habits, the culturally appropriate pace of living, and the division between working and leisure time are presented.

Pace of living

The experience of time is strongly influenced by a society's (relative) speed of living, accepted norms about the appropriate rate, duration, and the resulting behaviour. Following Levine, a culture's social time differs in many aspects, but the most significant distinguishing factor is the pace of life (Levine 1996 and 2000).

> The pace of life is virtually inseparable from the entire experience of social time, which in turn frames the totality of both our deepest relationships and our personal experience. (Levine 1996: 119)

Levine conducted a cross-cultural study in 31 countries, comparing the pace of living. As indicators he observed the accuracy of bank clocks, to explore the public interest in clock time; then he measured the average walking speed of pedestrians and the speed of post clerks, selling a stamp (Levine 2000: 37f, 179ff). The choice of the indicators is, however, open to critique, because they are very specific, not generally reflecting a society's speed of living, and they also adopt typical Western features as universal parameters (e.g. the general existence of public clocks). Levine's approach examines only the quantitative aspect of time and pace, neglecting the qualitative part of people's experience, if a society's members perceive their lives as fast and hurried or not.

In spite of these difficulties with Levine's approach, some impressions with regard to those indicators shall be given, although no similar measurements were conducted in this study. With respect to accuracy of clocks it is easy to state that there are no public clocks within the study area in Burkina Faso. There are two banks in the province capital Nouna, but none of them having a public clock on the outside of the building. In general, clocks are not widespread in this poor, rural region, and often rather fulfil the function of a status symbol or jewellery, than of measuring time.

For the speed of walking pedestrians and postal clerks, only a rough and subjective comparison to the Western, especially German setting, can be drawn. Apparently, walking and physical movements in general are much slower and less hurried in Africa, compared to Germany. Hectic behaviour is rather met with surprise or smiled at. Two Africans told me independently that they remarked that "the Whites" walk and move so fast, that they are always in a hurry, even if there is nothing important to do. An African would move so quickly only in case of real emergency or urgency.

In the post office you always have to wait even if you are the only customer. Furthermore it is impossible just to walk in and ask for a stamp. First the greetings have to be exchanged, as a foreigner you have to answer questions about your country and usually people chat a little bit before the request can be uttered (e.g. asking for a stamp). Without any hurry the clerk will then open a drawer, tear off one stamp, close the drawer, then he will give it to you, wait until you fixed it on your letter before he asks for the money; giving the change also takes some time for opening a drawer, counting the amount, closing the drawer, recounting the money and then passing it over. And it is not at all unusual that during this interaction the clerk starts doing another job or leaving the room and coming back only a few minutes later. I never saw someone being really upset or angry about this – compared to Western standards – slow procedure, as it is the "normal" pace of life there.

In fact, people in Burkina Faso usually do not feel time pressure, due to the widespread absence or low importance of clocks, schedules and time tables. As there are generally no imposed dead lines for the completion of tasks, no hurry emerges to finish activities as soon or fast as possible. Only natural demands or the nature of the task itself may require a special pace. For example the millet has to be sown when the rains start and the climatic conditions prescribe, if people have to hurry or not, to bring in the harvest; or a mat has to be woven before the grass becomes too dry. Otherwise it does not matter too much, if the mat is finished today or the next day. Instead of aiming at shortening the production time, it is important to do a good job. And this necessitates that one "takes the time" to – in this case – properly weave the mat; it will be done when it is finished. In the end, the weaver is paid for the mat and not according to the time he spend on this task. This attitude is also related to learning. One takes as much time as it takes, to learn for example a handicraft or a language. It just takes as long as it takes. If skills are required, which are not yet (completely) learned, people will improvise. People are not lazy, but they are not hurried, because a person without a clock, has always time (Aschoff 1992: 133).

Working time and leisure time

The term "leisure time" may be misleading here, as it is a culture specific, Western category. In industrialised, Western societies, the idea of leisure time gains its meaning in the light of the way working time is understood and organised (Habermas 1958: 219).

In the Burkinabè context, there is no word for leisure time, but it generally has the meaning of "having no work" or more precisely, "having no *real* work". It is thus contingent to the local notion of what is defined as real work. The seasonal division of the year is perceived as a separation into a time of work, the rainy season, and a period of no work and leisure, the dry season.

In daily life however, no clear separation is made. During the rainy season, people do not have a lot of spare time due to the farming activities, but this situation is the same for everyone. Thus, no choice between work and private life is posed. In the dry season it appears that even in the setting of offices, which exist in cities, private conversation is not limited to lunch time, but takes place also during the working hours. There is not such a clear line drawn between working and social or private time, as is usual for Western, industrialised societies. Indeed, it is really impolite to talk only about business, without any personal conversation preceding and following the 'official' part.

As even in the context of employment, working time and leisure time are not separated so clearly, working time is also not quantified and counted in time units but rather in work units. This becomes obvious in the modes of payment. People are paid for a job, a task, not in time intervals, like hour or day.

Helpful in this context is Hall's distinction between "monochronic" and "polychronic" time (Hall 1983: 43ff), which is basically an analytical differentiation, highlighting two extreme poles, while social reality is always somewhere in between. Following Hall, monochronic time is dominant in Western cultures and is defines as "one thing at a time". Events are scheduled as separate items and managed with timetables. On the individual's level this attitude is manifested by the desire to complete a tasks once it is initiated; uncompleted projects make people nervous, they are experienced as somehow immoral, wasteful or even threatening (Hall 1983: 31). Therefore they organise their time and work off one task after the other, as the completion of an activity is socially expected and honoured (Rifkin 1988: 68). Polychronic time, on the other side, means being involved in several things at once and switching between the different occupations according to the external demands (Hall 1983: 43). It is rather this position that applies to the context of Burkina Faso. People do not feel the psychological drive to bring a work to its end as fast as possible. As mentioned above, traditionally no "dead lines" exist, but things are done when it is the right time for them: The harvest is cut when it is ripe and one chats with the neighbour when he passes by. The construction of a house starts when one has some money to buy bricks, it is interrupted when there is no more money and will be continued when some money is available again. Meanwhile other projects may be taken up and for instance a bike is bought from financial surplus and the completion of the house may wait.

Hence, the cultural setting offers norms and values that direct people's perception and interpretation of urgency, priorities and of appropriate time allocation, duration and speed. The social codex of behaviour expresses and guides a framework within which social life happens and people interact with each other.

Thus, time pressure and social norms of punctuality are not experienced in the same way as in Western industrialised societies, where self-imposed time pressure and punctuality are established virtues. Temporal co-ordination and synchronisation of events or meetings are not fixed in the precise way of clock time and waiting is a general feature and accepted part of everyday life. Time is not handled as a rare resource. People do not experience the need to use and fill every hour or minute with purposeful actions. More correctly it is to state, that the social normative expectations of how to spend time ingeniously, differ compared to Western ideas. In Western contexts any activity should have an aim or inherent purpose (which is usually defined in economic, productive terms). This intention ranges from relaxation to productivity, but should always be justifiable, in the light of socially accepted norms of individual role and performance. Whereas, the rural society in Burkina Faso is directed by other values. Here people are expected to spend a lot of their (working-free) time with their social group of relatives and friends. Further there is no "action-imperative", that means people are not expected and driven to be in action the whole time. "Being together" is more important than "doing" something. "Good" performance is estimated rather by means of social norms and duties, than of efficiency or success in the job.

5. Conclusion

Time is an integral part of socio-cultural life. The examples from Burkina Faso have outlined, that the diverse temporal ideas and practices are embedded in a society's basic world view, its ideals about the aims of life, its economics forms, its plans and expectations. Regarding "others'" notions on time requires necessarily a reflection of one's own, often unconscious assumptions. One realises the cultural relativity of own, taken for granted categories, norms, values and patterns of behaviour. Being open and trying to understand why other societies expose other modes of handling time and seeing, on which (different) basic attitudes towards life these are founded, can help to develop respect and tolerance.

The occupation with time can be an excellent access to intercultural competence. One could become sensitive for the fact that the same behaviour might be interpreted totally different in other cultural context. Western persons from industrialised countries may evoke suspicion with their hurried, impatient behaviour. On the other side, they may realise that waiting or silence is not everywhere something negative, but may be a neutral or even positive sign, a part of communication, or indicating approval. Concentrating on time helps to learn the "silent rules" in interpersonal relations. For instance the norms of punctuality, that means what is perceived as "in time", how long, and in which contexts (e.g. private, in business), facilitate comprehension and interaction.

Understanding different cultural notions on time requires time, as these ideas are not easily observable. It surely takes time to watch, listen, and ask to grasp priorities, habits, interpretations, and norms in other societies. The effort, however, is worthwhile!

References

ADAM, BARBARA
    (1994). "Perceptions of Time." In Tim Ingold, ed. *Companion Encyclopedia of Anthropology*. London, New York: Routledge, 503-526.
ASCHOFF, JÜRGEN
    (1992). "Die innere Uhr des Menschen." In Jürgen Aschoff, ed. *Die Zeit: Dauer und Augenblick*. München: Piper, 133-144.
AVENI, ANTHONY F.
    (1990). *Empires of Time: Calendars, Clocks, and Cultures*. London: I.B. Tauris & Co Ltd Publishers.

ELWERT, GEORG AND MARTIN KOHLI
(1990). "Vorwort." In Georg Elwert, Martin Kohli, and Harald K. Müller, eds. *Im Lauf der Zeit: Ethnographische Studien zur gesellschaftlichen Konstruktion von Lebensaltern*. Saarbrücken: Breitenbach, 3-10.
GELL, ALFRED
(1992). *The Anthropology of Time*. Oxford/Providence: Ber Publishers.
GYEKE, KWAME
(1987). *An Essay on African Philosophical Thought: The Akan Conceptual Scheme*. Cambridge: Cambridge University Press.
HABERMAS, JÜRGEN
(1958)."Soziologische Notitzen zum Verhältnis von Arbeit und Freizeit." In Gerhard Funke, ed. *Konkrete Vernunft: Festschrift für Erich Rothacker*. Bonn: H. Bouvier u. Co., 219-232.
HALL, EDWARD T.
(1983). *The Dance of Life: The Other Dimension of Time*. Garden City, New York: Anchor Press/Doubleday.
LEVINE, ROBERT V.
(1996). "Cultural Differences in the Pace of Life." In Hede Helfrich, ed. *Time and Mind*. Seattle, Toronto, Göttingen, Bern: Hogrefe & Huber Publishers, 119-142.
(2000). *Eine Landkarte der Zeit: Wie Kulturen mit Zeit umgehen*. München, Zürich: Piper.
MANNHEIM, KARL
(1953). *Essays on Sociology and Social Psychology: Collected Works, Vol. 6*. London: Routledge.
RIFKIN, JEREMY
(1988). *Uhrwerk Universum: Die Zeit als Grundkonflikt des Menschen*. München: Kindler.
SPLITTER, GERD
(1990). "Lebensalter und Lebenslauf bei den Tuareg." In Georg Elwert, Martin Kohli, and Harald K. Müller, eds. *Im Lauf der Zeit: Ethnographische Studien zur gesellschaftlichen Konstruktion von Lebensaltern*. Saarbrücken: Breitenbach, 107-123.

Cultural Approaches to Second Language Varieties of English: A Call for New Methodologies and a Review of Some Findings on (West) African English

HANS-GEORG WOLF
Hong Kong, China

Introduction

Arguably one of the most fascinating fields in the study of the English language are the so-called 'New Englishes,' i.e., the second languages varieties of English that have emerged as a result of British colonial history.[1] The second language varieties of English spoken in West Africa, i.e., in The Gambia, Sierra Leone, Liberia, Ghana, Nigeria, and Cameroon,[2] are particularly intriguing because of the complex linguistic situation in this region and the interplay with English-oriented pidgin and creole varieties spoken in these countries.

Yet, though Schmied (1991: 204) already pointed out that "being a relatively new research area English in Africa can be used as a testing ground for concepts, methods and theories that have been developed in other areas and historical periods,"[3] little, in fact, has been done outside of the traditional scope of descriptive sociolinguistics. Numerous studies exist which deal with grammatical, lexical and phonetic phenomena of African English (see, e.g., Lucko, Peter, Wolf (eds.) 2003; Asante 1995; Simo Bobda 2001, 2000,1994), attitudinal questions (see, e.g., Igboanusi (ed.) 2001; Efurosibina 1994), and problems of language policy (see, e.g., Roy-Campbell, 2001; Bamgbose 2000, 1994; Igboanusi 1997), but sociolinguistic research not only on African English, by and large, seems to miss out on the "cultural turn" in linguistics, as noted by Auer (2000). This is quite surprising, as the speakers of the New

---

[1] A related term used in the field is 'World Englishes,' which includes, however, the first-language varieties as well.
[2] Although Liberia was not a British colony but rather a settlement of freed American slaves, it needs to be included here for historical, sociolinguistic, and structural similarities as well as geographical proximity. The anglophone part of Cameroon, technically, was not a colony but a League of Nations mandate and later a UN Trusteeship territory. In reality, it was administered as part of Nigeria (see Wolf 2001).
[3] One should note that the language, not the speakers of African English, are the testing ground, as is often sadly the case in the pharmaceutical field.

Englishes have a cultural background quite different from that of first language speakers of English in the "Western world." It is a rhetorical question to ask if an investigation of the varieties of English can afford to eclipse cultural questions in a globalized world where conflicting cultural values move to the center of attention, even more so as English is *the* medium of international communication.

There is no excuse that linguistic theories and methodologies are missing which could be drawn from and utilized in the endeavor to broaden the focus on the New Englishes in general and on African English in particular. I find two approaches particularly useful, namely Corpus Linguistics and Anthropological or 'Cultural' Linguistics, for that matter (see Palmer 1996, 2004, for the disciplinary scope). These two approaches cannot only provide insights in themselves, but can be combined in a meaningful way, as I hope to exemplify.

After a brief discussion of 'culture' in the study of L2 varieties of English, in a condensed form I will present findings from my own research – where I utilized the very methods just mentioned – which highlight some culture-specific aspects that surface in the English of speakers of West African English (WAE) and which may serve as a model for culture-oriented studies on other L2 varieties of English (see Wolf 2001, 2002, 2003; Wolf and Simo Bobda, 2001; Polzenhagen and Wolf 2002).

Some Notes on the Role of 'Culture' in the Study of the New Englishes

The indigenous culture of L2-speakers of English poses no theoretical problem for those who find the English language to be isomorphic with Western culture; if English is inextricably tied to Western beliefs and values, then those who adopt English in other parts of the world will adopt the beliefs and values of the West as well. The spread of English is seen, in one way or another, as a form of imperialism or neo-colonialism, resulting in the eradication of the autochthonous cultures and in a conceptual alienation from the home culture. Some of the prominent proponents of this position are, for example, Phillipson 1992, Skutnabb-Kangas 2000, Mühlhäusler 1996, und Ngugi wa Thiong'o 1995 (also see Lucko 2003, for a critical discussion). Yet these scholars not only neglect that more often than not, non-native speakers of English usually maintain their mother tongue, which would, given the implicitly assumed identity of language and culture, safeguard their native culture, but also that English can be used as a means to express different cultural concepts in different cultural settings and thereby already has undergone considerable transformation. As McConvell (1994) heeds, "the linking of language and culture can have negative effects if not sensitively handled by linguists. A number of Aboriginal people in Australia who speak English are offended by suggestions that they have "lost their culture" because they no longer speak their ancestral language."

A more differentiated, and what I find, more realistic look at the New Englishes – the term itself indicates that the varieties in question have a new quality – recognizes the tremendous change the English language has undergone in different settings across the globe, and terms like *indigenization, contextualization* and *acculturation* used in the description of these varieties attest to this change (see, e.g., Kachru 1994, 1982; Wolf 2001: 244-245). Inevitably, questions of culture come into play, as these changes are mainly induced by the cultural background of the speakers. The role of culture in the formation of the New Englishes, however, seems to be more addressed and discussed in literary studies, where post-colonial literature has emerged as a new branch of scholarship (see, e.g., Ashcroft et al. 1995), and the points of contact between the (literary) study of the New Englishes and cultural studies is being considered (see Dissanayake 2000).

Though sociolinguists increasingly recognize the importance of culture in their field of research (see, e.g., Schmied 1991, Pütz, ed. 1994), culture so far has been outside the scope of most sociolinguistic studies on the New Englishes. Culture is often only mentioned as a factor responsible for phonological, lexical, and grammatical variation, as can be illustrated by a quote from Quirk (1981: 152), who refers to Indian English: "The natural processes of language-culture interaction have produced a large number of phonological, grammatical, lexical and stylistic features ...". The category culture is similarly presupposed in works that focus on cross-cultural communication in English, where different cultural backgrounds of the speakers involved are seen as problematic, and where "intercultural competence" is demanded, yet where a systematic attempt at understanding the cultures in question is lacking (see, e.g., Smith, ed. 1981, Garcia and Otheguy, eds. 1989, House 1999, Gnutzmann 1999, Doyé 1999, and Wolf 2001: 2).

This is the point where Corpus Linguistics and Cultural Linguistics come in. From my point of view, these newly emerging paradigms in linguistics can greatly benefit the study of the New Englishes with respect to coming to an, albeit tentative, understanding of the culture of their speakers. The methods developed in these fields allow rigorous systematic empirical analyses and help to avoid the "mushiness" of cultural studies approaches some linguists may feel uneasy about.

Exemplary Findings from Corpus Studies

In the blossoming field of Corpus Linguistics, only very few studies have worked with computer corpora to investigate aspects of culture in the field of varieties of English (and vice versa), though Aston and Burnard (1998: 15-16) have mentioned their usefulness for comparing, as they call it, "geographical varieties and languages." In this respect, the study by Leech and Fallon (1992), entitled "Computer corpora – what do they tell us about culture?" is seminal.[4] For those not conversant with Corpus Linguistics, corpora are large compilations of texts, drawn from a specific genre or representing a variety of genres. Some computer software is then used to process these corpora, enabling the linguist, for example, to make wordlists, compute collocations (different words that frequently occur together), and to perform a number of other tasks.

My own intuitions and experience with Cameroon English led me to check the frequency of certain words, which are part of the common core of English, i.e., appear in all varieties of this language, but which I suspected to be more frequent in Cameroon English than in British English and American English, the most prominent native varieties of English. My basis of comparison was the Corpus of English in Cameroon (CCE)[5], with 898,572 tokens[6] (as calculated by WordSmith, the computer software used), and the combination of the FROWN corpus, which is based on American English, with the FLOB corpus, which is based on British English (2,064,764 tokens together). My rationale was that the combination of the two is a good representation of "western" varieties of English.

---

[4] From a comparison of the BROWN corpus, which is based on American English (compiled in 1961) and the LOB corpus, which is based on British English (compiled in the early 1970s), Leech and Fallon, judging from lexical frequencies, concluded, for example, that the US culture at that time was "masculine to the point of machismo."
[5] Shortly before its completion, the work on this corpus, as part of the International Corpus of English, stopped. Thus, only "unofficial" copies of it exist. I owe thanks to Josef Schmied, TU Chemnitz, from whom I received a copy of this corpus.
[6] Roughly, tokens are the individual words in a corpus.

The program I used for the computations is WordSmith. One advantage of it is that it allows you to compute key words (see, Scott 2001, for an overview of this program). Key words are words which occur significantly more frequently in one corpus (in my case, the CCE) than in the reference corpus (the FLOBFROWN corpus). The basic assumption is that the lexicon of a language or variety is closely related to the culture of a society, and that key words are especially socio-culturally significant (see Wierzbicka 1997: 1, 11-17). Of course, the text types or genres a corpus represents need to be taken into consideration, but the CCE and the FLOBFROWN are similarly designed (for more information, see Wolf 2003).

As indicated above, prior to my corpus analyses, I had suspected that terms relating to the domains of community/family and witchcraft (and there is a relation between the two, see below) would be more prominent in Cameroon English, because I found frequent references to these domains in newspapers, novels and in conversations with speakers of Cameroon English (and other varieties of WAE). And indeed, my investigations of the CCE confirmed my prior intuitions. The following findings are excerpted from an article of mine (Wolf 2003), and a paper held at the *Sociology of Language & Religion International Colloquium*. Roehampton, England (Wolf 2002). Due to the more general and non-specialist nature of this volume, I refer the reader to these works (and also to Wolf 2001) for the technical and statistical details of my studies. Words that appeared as "key," i.e., are significantly more frequent statistically in the CCE than in FLOBFROWN, include the terms *God* and *gods*,[7] *universe, nature, earth, community, communal, family, kin, kinsman, kinship, relatives, lineage*, and also *brotherhood*. The occurrence of *God/gods, universe, nature, earth* and *community* needs to be seen in the perspective of a holistic cosmology, which maintains the interrelatedness of all things (see Wolf 2001: 276-280, and below). As will be shown later, in the Cameroonian context (as well as in the general African one), 'family' and 'community' is not neatly distinguished. Furthermore, terms that relate to the continuation of the family are significantly more frequent in the CCE. Thus one finds *marriage* and *marital, husband* and *wife, procreation, maternity, parent* and *parenting, birth, child, neonate, newborn, offspring*, and *filial*. The key words, *childless, orphan*, and *orphanage* are an indirect attestation of the importance of the family and its continuation.

---

[7] That both God and gods appear as key words reflects the coexistence of monotheistic and polytheistic beliefs.

In the African family structure, the elders occupy an important position and *elder*[8], not surprisingly, is also a key word. The reason for the prominence of the elders is that, because of their age, they are believed to be closer to God and the ancestors (see Wolf 2001: 285-286). The ancestors are seen as a link to the realm beyond and both *ancestral*, *ancestor* and *living-dead* are key words as well. 'Link' should not be understood in a metaphorical sense, as ancestors are conceived as part of present reality (see Wolf 2001: 282-285). If ancestors assume their presence, they often appear as *ghost*(s) or *spirit*(s). Elders and people of special power are highly esteemed because they are held to be able to control spirits. The role of these *mediums* or *fetish priest*(s) is ambiguous, since they can put their power to good use and bad use. On the one hand, they have the power to *heal*, mostly with *herbs*, and are considered *healer*(s), on the other hand, they can invoke *demon*(s) and are considered *witch-doctor*(s).

It is not that these words appear as key only in the CCE. Smaller, more specialized corpora based on other varieties of WAE (Corpus Ghana, Corpus Nigeria), which were compiled at Humboldt-University, Berlin, support these findings and indicate their validity for WAE in general. These corpora, do not consist of more than one or two genres of text (on-line newspaper articles, contribution to email-lists); yet the fact that many of the terms are key even in general news reports strongly confirms the trend (see, e.g., Wolf 2003).

Here, I have presented not more than a sketchy and general explanation of the way traditional cultural beliefs are reflected in the lexicon of a variety. After all, the aim is to demonstrate how differences in lexical frequency can be read as cultural differences. Certainly the actual belief-system of Cameroonians or (West)Africans is much more complex and has become interwoven with occidental religious ideas but also with Islam, as I have argued elsewhere (Wolf 2002). Continued cultural contacts inevitably result in cultural adaptations and fusions, and my brief account should not be understood as "essentialist," to use a term popular in literary studies. Yet again, if key words are really seen culturally significant, and I firmly believe that they are, then the fact that they are key has to be explained in one way or another. This is where the other method I suggest for the investigation of cultural differences in the varieties of English comes in. Without some prior understanding of the cultures involved in the first place, the interpretation of key words elicited from computer corpora is not much more than educated

---

[8] As most other key words mentioned here, I lemmatized the relevant items in both the CCE and the FLOBFROWN, i.e., the different forms of a word (e.g., plural forms) are subsumed under one lemma.

guessing. If a stock of vocabulary reflects cultural concepts (Eastman 1979: 216), then we also have to look at what these concepts are and how they relate to one another.

The Metaphor/Cultural Model Approach in a Cultural View on West African English

Lakoff and Johnson (1980: 22), the founding fathers of the dominant paradigm in contemporary metaphor research, have argued that "the most fundamental values in a culture will be coherent with the metaphorical structure of the most fundamental concepts in the culture." This certainly holds true for the concepts expressed in Cameroon English, though it is not always clear to what extent they are metaphorical. One may revise Lakoff and Johnson's statement to "the most fundamental values in a culture are coherent with the conceptual structure in the culture." Lakoff and Johnson's theory of metaphor, and the theories of numerous other cognitive linguists, psychologists and anthropologist coming from the same school of thought, rest on the assumption that language is part of thought and that by analyzing language, one can arrive at the underlying conceptual structure of its speakers. This does not imply, however, that a language is isomorphic with the conceptual system of one culture, as proponents of the 'cultural-imperialism-view' would have it. Different languages can have a similar, and in turn, different varieties of one language may have an altogether different conceptual base, as is the case for various varieties of English.

According to Lakoff and Johnson's cognitivist view, a conceptual structure or 'conceptual domain' – and we can call it a metaphorical conceptual structure if more than one domain is involved – can generate countless linguistic expressions, which in turn can be systematically related to one another on the basis of this conceptual domain and attest to its existence. My examples below will concretize my explanations (some also appear in Wolf 2001: ch. 5). I follow the convention to present the concepts/metaphors in small caps, and the linguistic examples in italics.

Such a cognitive analysis requires the intensive study of texts (including spoken language) produced in a given variety, to make estimations about the systematicity and the status of the concepts in that variety. The interpretational process is bidirectional; the linguistic investigations allow us to arrive at the underlying concepts, the knowledge of which in turn enables us to understand the meaning of certain utterances.

Though numerous more culture-specific concepts and conceptual metaphors have been extracted from African English by now (see, e.g., Polzenhagen and Wolf 2002), I will concentrate only on those that directly relate to the key words I made note of earlier. Furthermore, the reader should be aware that these concepts and metaphors form systematic and intricate relationships, whose complete description would go well beyond the scope of this paper.

The concept that captures the holistic cosmology noted above is HUMANITY IS IN COMMUNITY WITH GOD/THE GODS AND SPIRITS AND THE WHOLE UNVIVERSE. Linguistic expression brought forth by this conceptualization are, for example:

> *In the universe, everything is ONE united. Man, animals, plants, fishes, water, air, etc. are one from the same source* (CCE 52828);
>
> *human kinship with the universe* (CCE 14559);
>
> *the union of heaven and earth ... the relationship, so to speax [sic] between supernatural forces and human beings with the cosmic continuum* (CCE 13174);
>
> *the sense of community is not restricted to relations with human beings alone. There is community with nature* (Opoku 1993: 77).

While in the "Western" world, 'family' and 'community' form two distinct conceptual domains, in traditional and localized African settings, 'family' and 'community' constitute only one domain. Thus, KINSHIP IS COMMUNITY and COMMUNITY IS KINSHIP are interchangeable metonymies. Kinship terms reserved in the West prototypically for relatives related by blood and adoption are freely used in reference to members of the same community, as, for example, evidenced in

> *I greet my fathers* (Oyono 1968; cit. in Mbangwana 1992: 95; cf. p. 177f.);
>
> *to kill our own brothers and sisters, the suffering people* (Butake 1993: 26);
>
> *the family head of the Bakweri community* (Andu 1998: 5);
>
> *children are introduced to adult kin as 'other' fathers and mothers and to their children as brothers and sisters* (CCE 17719);
>
> *Santa people whose son was a prime minister* (Ntoi 1998: 8);
>
> *three policemen molesting their grandson* (Kwendi 1998: 10).

This concept of community and kinship may be extended to broader communities, such as the state, and citizens referred to accordingly as *brothers and sisters*, and the president as the *father* of the nation (see Schatzberg 2001; Wolf 2001: 293-295, 2003; Polzenhagen and Wolf 2002).

Through children, the community is continued. Children are conceived as God's/the gods gift to the community and as a link to God/the gods. This can be condensed in the concept CHILDREN LINK THE COMMUNITY TO GOD/THE GODS AND PERPETUATE THE COMMUNITY. The following quotes express this concept.

> To live in the African traditional context is to participate in the protection of life, the survival of the family and the continuity of the community .... To share in the child is seen as the field that we share with God (in Masamba ma Mpolo 1994:18).
>
> The fact that a couple has no children is interpreted as sufficient proof that they are bad people and their 'badness' is being punished with childlessness (CCE 19359).
>
> The link between humans and God is via filiation (CCE 17307).
>
> procreation is ... a divine obligation and children are ... the seed of immortality (Musopole 1994: 11).

Consequently, the ultimate purpose of marriage is for the partners to become parents, i.e., to have children, and the concept THE PURPOSE OF MARRIAGE IS TO HAVE CHILDREN generates texts like

> For West Africans, the marriage contract foreshadows the child. The main purpose of marriage is child bearing (CCE 836,533).
>
> High fertility is regarded as a measure of divine or ancestral approval for a couple's marriage and life-style (CCE 836,617).
>
> The most basic socially acceptable family unit is established by a man and woman in marriage ... Bachelorhood, spinsterhood, or single parenthood is not a normal, expected social status and is best avoided. An unmarried, childless person is never accorded full adult status, and marriage alone confers only proto-adult status (CCE 820,023).
>
> Parenthood is a primary reason for marriage (CCE 820,358).

Age, coupled with parenthood, confers a status of respect on elders. If one were to use a sociological category, in traditional society, older people are hierarchically higher than younger ones. The elders have known the ancestors and usually precede the younger members in passing to the realm of the ancestors. ELDERS ARE PERSONS OF AUTHORITY underlies the following passages:

> Parental authority does not cease when children are adults but continues to be asserted when the offspring is trying to make his or her own way in life ... As long as one's parents are alive, "a child is always a child" and must come under "some" sphere of parental authority (CCE 845,025).
>
> The social system is characterised by deference to and locus of authority in elders, especially parents (CCE 820,823).

understanding the significance of respect for seniority and obedience to elders and superiors is one of the keys to decoding West African behavior (CCE 843,843).

A short excerpt from a Zambian novel shows that this concept exists across sub-Saharan Africa. The passage is about "a conflict ... between the dead [the ancestors] and the living" (Luangala 1991: 48). In this conflict,

> only the elders in the family ... would meet to plan the line of action taken. The eldest among the members of the family was the leading figure whose decisions at the most crucial moments were virtually unquestionable (Luangala 1991: 48).

This authoritative link does not stop with the elders; it extends to the ancestors. There is no impermeable boundary between the visible world and the world of the ancestors, and the ancestors continue to be present in the life of the people as ancestral spirits. I have termed this conceptualization (from a secular Western perspective, this would be a mix of conceptual metaphors, with 'ancestors,' 'spirits,' and 'present reality' as three distinct domains) ANCESTORS ARE SPIRITS and SPIRITS ARE PART OF PRESENT REALITY (Wolf 2001: 283-285). Expressions of this conceptualization abound in the literature:

> The departed ancestors are part of this constellation of living spirits (Masamba ma Mpolo 1994: 24).
>
> My return to the land of the living have [sic] been due to the disapproval of the Greater Caouncil [sic] of the spirits, which had decided that I was too young to do any useful work on the plantation (CCE 14677).
>
> Ancestors and gods keep a watchful eye on the living (CCE 17628).
>
> The ancestors live (Opoku 1993: 75).
>
> Calling on the deities or ancestors to pour blessings on the living (CCE 61757).

And again examples from Zambian English:

> We should go and consult our ancestral spirits to ask them to explain to us what it is particularly that has angered them (Luangala 1991: 61).
>
> ...When the ancestral spirits were thoroughly convinced that he had paid well enough for his offence (Luangala 1991: 50-51).

The elders can mediate between the ancestors and the living, but also other persons of respect, like traditional healers and traditional doctors (cf. Alobwede d'Epie 1982: 9):

> The children ask their guardian in this world [the eldest person] to lead them to the place where they can meet their ancestors. Did they not say that it was those who were about to enter another world who knew where the entrance was (Luangala 1991: 62; also see Kalu 1993: 115).

in the family, the Diokpala 'head of the lineage' as well as the paterfamilias 'head of the nuclear household' become quasi-priests, who ... pour libation to the 'living-dead' ancestors (Kalu 1993: 115).

kings incarnate their cultural heritage and are intermediaries between the living and the ancestral spirits and deities (CCE e.g., 17625).

the ancestors and gods keep a watchful eye on the living through the mediation of the king (CCE 17629).

The conceptual core of these expressions is PERSONS OF RESPECT ARE MEDIATORS BETWEEN THE SPIRITS AND THE LIVING. Since there are good spirits and bad spirits (cf. Alobwede d'Epie 1982: 8-9), the supernatural power of these persons has two sides. On the one hand, it is a power to *heal*, reflected in their being called *traditional healers/doctors* or *herbalists*. Their ability to control bad spirits, on the other hand, is usually associated with witchcraft, a force disruptive to the community or fatal to individuals (see, e.g., Wolf 2001: 288-289). In reference to this negative side, these persons are often called *witchdoctors, witches, wizards* or *sorcerers*. Concepts of illness and death, especially of children and healthy adults, are thus linked to concepts of witchcraft (DEATH OR ILLNESS OF A YOUNG PERSON OR HEALTHY ADULT IS CAUSED BY WITCHCRAFT), as the following quotes illustrate:

Aina is ... sickly and dull in school .... The mother begins to worry and therefore goes to a herbalist who prescribes some medicine, to no avail. In the end, ... the mother attributes his [sic] *son's predicament to the second wife's jealousy. She must be a witch. Another herbalist is consulted who confirms that Aina's problem is the handiwork of an evil force.* (Gbadegesin 1991: 111).

At this stage of his illness, family members and friends feared that the musician had been bewitched (CCE 53087).

A session of public and daytime 'witch-doctoring' was organised in the village in the presence of everyone in the course of which the herbalist told the villagers that Kambang was killed by 'kong', an expression used to mean that the person was killed through the practice of witchcraft. Right there on the spot, the witch doctor pointed out three people in the crowd whom he said had caused the death of the youngster (Corpus Calixthe).

Four persons have been arrested ... on suspicions that they used mystical powers to kill a village youngster ... the News Agency of Cameroon ... reported (Corpus Calixthe).

His second wife Zama had also died. But she had died while still very strong and healthy. She had been bewitched by her grandmother. Her grandmother had eaten human meat somewhere from the other witches and she had promised that she would also kill her own relative and that they would share the meat. The other witches had chosen Sicholo's second wife who was very fat then. They bewitched her and she died after a very brief illness (Luangala 1991: 45).

Witchcraft is evoked when community values are broken, e.g., certain taboos have not been observed, or when negative emotions, e.g., jealousy, lead a member of the family/community to seek the help of a witchdoctor to further his or her ends (see Wolf 2001: 288-299).

The conceptualizations introduced here are but a small part of a coherent network of concepts which are expressed in African varieties of English. Although the examples were mostly culled from Cameroon English, the fact that identical concepts are expressed in a Southern African variety of English strengthens the argument of a basic cultural unity of their speakers (see Wolf 2001: 275-276).

Conclusion

In this paper, I tried to exemplarily show how the application of methods from disciplines other than descriptive sociolinguistics can be used to broaden the understanding of the New Englishes and their speakers with respect to the variable 'culture.' Though the focus has been on African English, these methods could similarly be used in the investigation of, say, South Asian English or East Asian English. The lexical analysis of computer corpora based on second language varieties of English in comparison to native varieties of English, and the analysis of texts produced in the respective second language varieties from a cognitivist perspective do not only stand for themselves, but mutually enhance each other. Lexical frequency reflects the preoccupation of the speakers with certain themes and problems, and a corpus analysis allows us to make statements about them. A survey of the conceptual patterns that underlie certain expressions, in turn, provides insights into the meaning systems of the speakers of the varieties in question and thus can tell us why certain lexical items are more prominent than in other varieties.

Furthermore, with culture being the main concern, these approaches can establish points of contact with literary and cultural studies and in that sense are truly interdisciplinary.

References

ALOBWEDE D'EPIE, CHARLES
(1982). "The Language of Traditional Medicine: A Study in the Power of Language." Thèse d'Etat, University of Yaunde, Cameroon.
ANDU, EZIEH C.
(1998). "New Head for Bakweri Community in Muyuka." *The Herald*, March 18-19, 5.
ASANTE, M.Y.
(1995). "Ghanaian English: Motivation for Divergence from the Standard in Certain Grammatical Categories." PhD Thesis, University of Tübingen.
ASHCROFT, BILL, GARETH GRIFFITHS AND HELEN TIFFIN (eds.)
(1995). *The Postcolonial Studies Reader*. London: Routledge.
ASTON, GUY AND LOU BURNARD
(1998): *The BNC Handbook: Exploring the British National Corpus with SARA*. Edinburgh Textbooks in Empirical Linguistics. Edinburgh: Edinburgh University Press.
AUER, PETER
(2000). "Die Linguistik auf dem Weg zur Kulturwissenschaft?" Freiburger Universitätsblätter 147, 55-68.
BAMGBOSE, AYO
(1991). *Language and the Nation. The Language Question in Sub-Saharan Africa*. Edinburgh: Edinburgh University Press for the International African Institute:
(2000). *Language and Exclusion. The Consequences of Language Policies in Africa*. Münster: LIT Verlag.
BUTAKE, BOLE
(1993). "Shoes and Four Men in Arms." (manuscript). Now published in Bole Butake (1999). *Lake God and Other Plays*. Yaounde: Editions CLE, 115-142.
DISSANAYAKE, WIMAL
(2000). "Cultural Studies and World Englishes. Some Topics for Further Exploration." In Larry E. Smith and Michael L. Forman, eds. *World Englishes*. Honolulu: University of Hawai'i Press, 126-145.
DOYÉ, PETER
(1999). "English as a Global Language. Implications for the Cultural Content of Teaching and Learning". In Klaus Gnutzmann, ed. *Teaching and Learning English as a Global Language. Native and Non-native Perspectives*. ZAA Studies. Tübingen: Stauffenberg, 93-105.
EASTMAN, C. M.
(1979). "Language Resurrection: A Language Plan for Ethnic Interaction." In Howard Giles and Bernard Saint-Jacques, eds. *Language and Ethnic Relations*. Oxford: Pergamon, 215-221.
GARCIA, OFELIA AND RICARDO OTHEGUY (eds.)
(1989). *English across Cultures – Cultures across English. A Reader in Cross-cultural Communication*. Berlin: Mouton de Gruyter.

GBADEGESIN, SEGUN
 (1991). *African Philosophy. Traditional Yoruba Philosophy and Contemporary African Realities.* New York: P. Lang.
GNUTZMANN, KLAUS
 (1999). "English as a Global Language. Perspectives for English Language Teaching and for Teacher Education in Germany." In Klaus Gnutzmann, ed. *Teaching and Learning English as a Global Language. Native and Non-native Perspectives.* ZAA Studies. Tübingen: Stauffenberg, 157-169.
HOUSE, JULIANE
 (1999). "Misunderstanding in Intercultural Communication. Interactions in English as Lingua Franca and the Myth of Mutual Intelligibility." In Klaus Gnutzmann, ed. *Teaching and Learning English as a Global Language. Native and Non-native Perspectives.* ZAA Studies. Tübingen: Stauffenberg, 73-89.
IGBOANUSI, HERBERT
 (1997). "Language and Nationalism. The Future of English in Nigeria's Language Policies." *Context: Journal of Social and Cultural Studies* 1(1): 21-34.
 (2001). *Language Attitude and Language Conflict in West Africa.* Ibadan: Enicrownfit.
MCCONVELL, PATRICK
 (1994). "Endangered Languages." http://www.linguistlist.org/issues/5/5-832.html, 11-21-94, accessed January 15, 03.
KACHRU, BRAJ B.
 (1982). "Introduction: The Other Side of English." In Braj B. Kachru, ed. *The Other Tongue. English Across Cultures.* Oxford: Pergamon, 1-12.
 (1994). "The Speaking Tree. A Medium of Plural Canons." In James E. Alatis, ed. *Educational Linguistics, Crosscultural Communication, and Global Interdependence.* Georgetown University Round Table on Languages and Linguistics 45. Washington DC: Georgetown University Press, 6-22.
KALU, OGBU U.
 (1993). "Gods as Policemen. Religion and Social Control in Igboland." In Jacob K. Olupona and Sulayman S. Nyang, eds. *Religious Plurality in Africa: Essays in Honor of John S. Mbiti.* Religion and Society, 32. Berlin: Mouton de Gruyter, 111-131.
KWENDI, J. T.
 (1998). "Meta Drivers, Please Change." *The Herald*, March 4-5, 10.
LAKOFF, GEORGE AND MARK JOHNSON
 (1980). *Metaphors We Live By.* Chicago: University of Chicago Press.
LEECH, GEOFFREY AND R. FALLON
 (1992). "Computer Corpora – What Do They Tell Us about Culture?" *ICAME Journal* 16, 29-50.
LUANGALA, JOHN
 (1991). *The Chosen Bud.* Lusaka: Kenneth Kaunda Foundation.
LUCKO, PETER
 (2003). "Is English a 'Killer Language'?" In Peter Lucko, Lothar Peter and Hans-Georg Wolf, eds. *Studies in African Varieties of English.* Frankfurt/M.: P. Lang, 152-165.

LUCKO, PETER, LOTHAR PETER AND HANS-GEORG WOLF (eds.)
(2003). *Studies in African Varieties of English*. Frankfurt/M.: P. Lang.
MASAMBA MA MPOLO, JEAN
(1994). "Spirituality and Counseling for Healing and Liberation." In Emmanuel Lartey, Daisy Nwachuku and Kasonga Wa Kasonga, eds. *The Church and Healing. Echoes from Africa*. New York: P. Lang, 10-33.
MUSOPOLE, AUGUSTINE C.
(1994). *Being Human in Africa. Toward an African Christian Anthropology*. New York: P. Lang.
MÜHLHÄUSLER, PETER.
(1996). *Linguistic Ecology. Language Change and Linguistic Imperialism in the Pacific Region*. London: Routledge.
NGUGI WA THIONG'O
(1995). "The Language of African Literature." In Bill Ashcroft, Gareth Griffiths and Helen Tiffin, eds. *The Postcolonial Studies Reader*. London: Routledge, 285-290.
NTOI, KAY JOSEPH
(1998). "NorthWesterners Caused Achidi Achu to Lose his Post." *The Herald*, March 4-5, 8.
PALMER, GARY B.
(1996). *Toward a Theory of Cultural Linguistics*. Austin: University of Texas Press.
(2004). "Anthropological Linguistics." Manuscript submitted to Dirk Geeraerts and Hubert Cuyckens, eds. *Handbook of Cognitive Linguistics*. Oxford: Oxford University Press.
PHILLIPSON, ROBERT
(1992). *Linguistic Imperialism*. Oxford: Oxford University Press.
OPOKU, KOFI ASARE
(1993). "African Traditional Religion. An Enduring Heritage." In Jacob K. Olupona and Sulayman S. Nyang, eds. *Religious Plurality in Africa. Essays in Honor of John S. Mbiti*. Religion and Society, 32. Berlin: Mouton de Gruyter, 67-82.
OYONO, M.
(1968). *Until Further Notice*. London: Methuen. Cit. in Paul Mbangwana (1992). "Some Grammatical Sign-posts in Cameroon Standard English." In Josef J. Schmied, ed. *English in East and Central Africa II*. Bayreuth African Studies Series, 24. Bayreuth: Bayreuth University, 93-102.
POLZENHAGEN, FRANK AND HANS-GEOR WOLF
(2002): "A Cognitive Linguistic Account of Socio-cultural Concepts. Expressions of Witchcraft, Magical Leadership, and Corruption in African Varieties of English." Paper presented at the 35th SLE Meeting, Rethinking Language and Mind. Potsdam. 22.-25. Juli, 2002.
PÜTZ, MARTIN (ed.)
(1994). *Language Contact and Language Conflict*. Amsterdam: John Benjamins.

QUIRK, RANDOLPH
(1981). "International Communication and the Concept of Nuclear English." In Larry E. Smith, ed. *English for Cross-cultural Communication*. London: Macmillan, 151-165.
ROY-CAMPELL, ZALINE M.
(2001). *Empowerment through Language. The African Experience – Tanzania and Beyond*. Trenton, NJ : Africa World Press.
SCHATZBERG, MICHAEL G.
(2001). *Political Legitimacy in Middle Africa. Father, Family, Food*. Bloomington: Indiana University Press.
SCHMIED, JOSEF J.
(1991). *English in Africa. An Introduction*. Burnt Mill, Harlow, Essex: Longman.
SCOTT, MIKE
(2001)."Comparing Corpora and Identifying Key Words, Collocations, Frequency Distributions through the WordSmith Tools Suite of Computer Programs." In Mohsen Ghadessy, Alex Henry, and Robert Roseberry, eds. *Small Corpus Studies and ELT: Theory and Practice*. Studies in Corpus Linguistics. Amsterdam: John Benjamins, 47-67.
SIMO BOBDA, AUGUSTIN
(1994). *Aspects of Cameroon English Phonology*. Bern: P. Lang
(2000). "Comparing Some Phonological Features across African Accents of English." *English Studies* 81:3, 249-266.
(2001). "East and Southern African English Accents." *World Englishes* 20:3, 269-284.
SKUTNABB-KANGAS, T.
(2000). *Linguistic Genocide in Education or Worldwide Diversity and Human Rights?* Mahwah (NJ): Lawrence Erlbaum Associates.
SMITH, LARRY E. (ed.)
(1981). *English for Cross-cultural Communication*. London: Macmillan.
WIERZBICKA, ANNA
(1997). *Understanding Cultures through their Key Words. English, Russian, Polish, German, and Japanese*. Oxford Studies in Anthropological Linguistics, 8. Oxford: University Press.
WOLF, HANS-GEORG
(2001). *English in Cameroon*. Contributions to the Sociology of Language 85. Berlin: Mouton de Gruyter.
(2002). "Religion and Traditional Belief in (West) African English." Lead-paper presented at the Sociology of Language & Religion International Colloquium. Roehampton, England, June 20-22.
(2003). "The Contextualization of Common Core Terms in West African English: Evidence from Computer Corpora." In Peter Lucko, Lothar Peter, and Hans-Georg Wolf, eds. *Studies in African Varieties of English*. Frankfurt/M.: P. Lang, 3-20.
WOLF, HANS-GEORG AND AUGUSTIN SIMO BOBDA
(2001). "The African Cultural Model of Community in English Language Instruction in Cameroon. The Need for More Systematicity." In Martin Pütz, Susanne Niemeier, and René Dirven, eds. *Applied Cognitive Linguistics. Theory, Acquisition and Language Pedagogy*. Berlin: Mouton de Gruyter, 225 –259.

CORPORA AND SOFTWARE

CORPUS OF ENGLISH IN CAMEROON (CCE)
Designed as part of the International Corpus of English. Compiled by Tiomajou, David et al. Diskette.

CORPUS CALIXTHE
(1998) Compiled by Bettina Peters and Susan Navissi. Humboldt University Berlin.

CORPUS GHANA
(1999/2002) Compiled by Jana Trommer and Susanne Gehl. Diskette. Humboldt University Berlin.

CORPUS NIGERIA
(1999/2001) Compiled by Jana Trommer and Thomas Gonsior. Diskette. Humboldt University Berlin.

THE FREIBURG – BROWN CORPUS OF AMERICAN ENGLISH (FROWN).
(1999) Compiled by Christian Mair et al. (1999). University of Freiburg, Germany. On ICAME collection of English language corpora, 2nd ed. CD-ROM. The HIT Centre. University of Bergen, Norway.

THE FREIBURG – LOB CORPUS OF BRITISH ENGLISH (FLOB)
(1999) Compiled by Christian Mair et al. (1998). University of Freiburg, Germany. On ICAME collection of English language corpora, 2nd ed. CD-ROM. The HIT Centre. University of Bergen, Norway.

SCOTT MIKE AND OXFORD UNIVERSITY PRESS
(1998). WordSmith. CD-ROM. Oxford: Oxford University Press.

151

Deeper Insights through Triangulation: Experiences from a Sociolinguistic Study on Pidgin English in Cameroon*

ANNE SCHRÖDER
Halle, Germany

1 Introduction

The following paper highlights methodological insights gained during a sociolinguistic study on "The Status, Functions, and Prospects of Pidgin English in Cameroon", which was conducted between April 1999 and September 2001.[1] The study is based on the concept of *Grounded Theory* (Glaser and Strauss 1967) and thus qualitative in nature. Qualitative research very often combines various sources of data as well as different research methods, and since the combination of qualitative and quantitative methods is particularly effective, the study presented in the following consists of qualitative and quantitative data. The process of combining different methods is also referred to as *triangulation*, as it allows the researcher to approach the research question from different angles. As this paper will show, on the basis of two illustrative examples, the combination of qualitative and quantitative methods proves extremely useful because it allows for a more adequate analysis and evaluation of the situation than either part of the data could provide if analysed separately.

2 Background information on Cameroon and the linguistic situation

The data for the study was collected in the Republic of Cameroon, which is located on the Bight of Biafra between Equatorial Guinea and Nigeria and has common frontiers with Gabon, the Democratic Republic of Congo, the Central African Republic and Chad. It is one of the more densely populated

---

* I would like to thank Naomi Hallan for comments on an earlier draft of this paper. I remain solely responsible for all remaining shortcomings.
[1] For a report on the entire study, cf. Schröder (2003a). The data presented in the following was collected during two research trips of eight months altogether in 1999 and 2000. I would like to thank the German Academic Exchange Service (DAAD) for granting me a scholarship of eight months for field research.

African countries and its literacy rate is one of the highest among the countries of the African continent. Cameroon is also one of the most linguistically diverse African countries: in addition to the approximately 280 indigenous languages (ILs), the country has two official European languages – English and French.[2] In contrast to other African countries, e.g. Nigeria, where identities are primarily based on ethnic affiliation and IL-language background, in Cameroon identities are established on the basis of official language background. Thus, – at least at a national level – Cameroonians define themselves as 'anglophones' or 'francophones' rather than as, for instance as 'Meta' or 'Bamvele'. In this context, Cameroon Pidgin English (CamP) and some other ILs function as Languages of Wider Communication (LWCs), and the linguistic situation can best be described by a modified version of Bamgbose's *three language model* (Bamgbose 1991: 54), with one or more languages spoken at the local, regional, national and international level:

Figure 1: *The linguistic situation in Cameroon*[3]

local level	• indigenous languages (ILs)
	• CamP (in urban areas)
regional level	• CamP
	• other LWCs, e.g.: Duala, Bulu, Ewondo, Ewondo Populaire, Mungaka, Fulfulde
	• (English and French)
national level	• French
	• English
	• CamP
international level	• English
	• French

Figure 1 illustrates that CamP seemingly holds a prominent position in the linguistic make-up of the country. However, the important function CamP apparently fulfils at all levels of the above model is not reflected in the official status of this language, since it is almost completely ignored at the official level and only unofficially tolerated elsewhere, for instance in the educational sector (cf. Schröder 2003a: section 4.2.1. and 5.3).

---

[2] Cf. Wolf (2001: 149/150) for an account of the various estimates made for the number of languages spoken in Cameroon and ibid. (47-143) for an excellent summary of the historical events leading to Cameroon's present linguistic situation.
[3] Diagram adapted from Schröder (2003a: 121).

3 Background information on the study

This general "indifference of the Cameroonian authorities" to CamP (Mbangwana 1983: 90), also presents a sharp contrast to the treatment this language receives in the linguistic literature. In the relevant publications on CamP, this language is often described as the most widely spoken language in Cameroon (e.g. Todd 1982, Povey 1983, Tiomajou 1991, Chumbow and Simo Bobda 1996, Ayafor 2000, to name but a few). In addition, it is frequently referred to as a neutral means of communication, spoken by all Cameroonians irrespective of their educational and official language background[4] and neutral to ethnicity and religion (cf. e.g. Féral 1980, Mbangwana 1983, Todd 1984, Chumbow and Simo Bobda 1995).

3.1 Research questions and research design

In the academic community in general, Pidgin and Creole languages have long been acknowledged as fully functional means of communication. The questions which thus arose and which the study tried to answer was: Why is there "so much resistance to recognising such a widespread *lingua franca*" (Chumbow and Simo Bobda 1996: 419), and why is there such a striking discrepancy between official acknowledgement by the Cameroonian government and private use or academic interest in this language?

In order to discover explanations for these contradictions, we intended to give an exhaustive description of CamP's present status and functions, which would subsequently allow for an evaluation of its prospects. Since there was practically no empirical data available on language use in Cameroon in general – the latest reliable survey was carried out in the 1970s (Koenig, Chia, and Povey 1983)[5] – the aim of the present study was to collect new and adequate empirical data for a realistic assessment of the present sociolinguistic situation.

The present study was carried out in 8 out of the 10 Cameroonian provinces. Thus, in contrast to most previous studies on CamP, which concentrated on the anglophone part and on the francophone part adjacent to the anglophone provinces of the country, the present study includes francophone provinces, which have so far been neglected or excluded. It was hoped that the inclusion of these provinces, i.e. the Eastern Province, the

---

[4] Cf. Schröder (2003b) for a critical discussion of these claims.
[5] Thus, almost all publications on CamP rely either on this survey published in 1983 or on subjective, impressionistic personal observations.

Southern Province, the Central Province and one of the three Northern provinces,[6] would provide a national picture of CamP's role and functions and correct possible distortions caused by the bias in previous studies towards the anglophone part of the population and the country.[7]

Since it was believed that CamP's status and functions in the linguistic make-up of the country – and thus its prospects – are primarily determined by language-external rather than by language-internal factors, the research question was considered to be more social than purely linguistic in nature. Therefore the most adequate analytic tools seemed to be empirical research methods developed in and for the social sciences. Qualitative methods and the concept of *Grounded Theory* were felt to be particularly appealing as the researcher, rather than testing a hypothesis or assumption, tries to gain new insights by evolving a theory from the data (Glaser and Strauss 1967: 1). The collection of data, their analysis and processing as well as the final interpretation and emergent theory are closely related. (Strauss and Corbin 1998: 12) In addition, the analytic tools chosen were mostly interactive and thus the scope of the investigation could be extended from research *on* and *for* social subjects to research *with* the informants (cf. Cameron et al. 1993). The aim was – wherever possible – to hand over authority and control to the informants.

3.2 Research methods

Although empirical research has often been divided into qualitative and quantitative approaches, with the tendency to view these as "mutually exclusive epistemological camps" (Silverman 1997: 25), many researchers have concluded that these two different approaches and consequently their research methods, do not necessarily oppose or exclude each other, but should rather be seen as complementing each other in many areas (e.g. Glaser and Strauss 1967, Kardoff 1995, Lamnek 1995a, Mayring 1996, Oswald 1997, Engler 1997).

> [...] there is no fundamental clash between the purposes and capacities of qualitative and quantitative methods or data. What clash there is concerns the primacy of emphasis on verification or generation of theory – to which heated discussions on qualitative versus quantitative data have been linked historically. We believe that each form of data is useful for both verification and generation of

---

[6] The three Northern provinces (Adamawa, North and Far North) are linguistically relatively homogenous.
[7] For the distribution of the research locations, cf. Map 9 in the appendix of Schröder 2003a.

theory, whatever primacy of emphasis. Primacy depends only on the circumstances of research, on the interests and training of the researcher (...). In many instances both forms of data are necessary – not quantitative used to test qualitative, but both used as supplements, as mutual verification [...]. (Glaser and Strauss 1967: 17/18)

3.2.1 Qualitative research methods

As the basis of *Grounded Theory* is qualitative research methods, 'primacy of emphasis' in the present study was laid on qualitative data. "Interviews are one of the most commonly recognised forms of qualitative research method" (Mason 1996: 39), and "[i]n particular, open-ended interviews [...] [are] most useful for suggesting new or altered dimensions to be explored" (Bouchard Ryan 1979: 154). For the purpose of the present study, a thematic, topic-centred, semi-structured approach was chosen.[8] Although qualitative interviews should be comparatively informal in style and resemble "a conversation or discussion" (Mason 1996: 38), an interview guide with a range of topics and a structured list of questions was nevertheless used. However, the order of the topics discussed was not fixed but evolved with the conversation. The informants were free to add topics they considered relevant and they determined both the development of the conversation and the amount of time spent on any particular topic.[9]

The present study consists of 52 interviews, which were conducted by the author in a relatively unconstrained atmosphere, since confidentiality and anonymity were assured. According to the official language background of the interviewee, the language of the interviews was either English or French. Given the multilingual character of the country, this approached Kirk and Miller's call for conducting qualitative research with people "in their own language" (Kirk and Miller 1986: 12) as much as was possible under the circumstances. The interviews lasted between 30 minutes and an hour and were tape-recorded. After transcription they were read into and evaluated with WinMAX, a program designed for computer-assisted analysis of qualitative data.[10]

---

[8] For different types of qualitative interviews, cf. e.g. Mayring (1996:49-57).
[9] However, I agree with Dingwall (1997:59/60) that one should keep in mind that "an interview is not a conversation" and that interviews therefore may be "fraught with problems because of the activity of the interviewer in producing them".
[10] Cf. Kuckartz (1999a) for a description of the program and Kuckartz (1997) or Kuckartz (1999b) for an introduction to methods and techniques of the computer-assisted evaluation of qualitative data.

3.2.2 Quantitative research methods

Parallel to the qualitative data collection a self-administered questionnaire survey was carried out. To keep the length of the questionnaires practicable, the survey consisted of two standardised written questionnaires.[11] There was considerable and intentional overlap between many questions on the two questionnaires and the topics dealt with in the qualitative interviews. So-called 'hybrid questions' (Schnell, Hill, and Esser 1993: 342)[12] were used wherever possible to alleviate most of the disadvantages of closed questions.[13] In addition, the informants had space for comments at the end of each questionnaire and could thus – if they wished – express themselves in their own words.

The quantitative part of the present study consists of 1103 respondents for Questionnaire A and 865 respondents for Questionnaire B. Both questionnaires were made available in English and French and, in general, informants filled in only one of the two questionnaires. The questionnaires took approximately 60 minutes each to complete. The answers to the questionnaires were coded (cf. Fink 1995a: 90) and the codes were entered into an SPSS (Statistical Package for the Social Sciences) data entry sheet. All subsequent statistical calculations were carried out using this program.

3.3 Triangulation

As mentioned in the introduction, qualitative research very often draws on different data sources and combines various methods (Marshall and Rossman 1995: 99 ff.). This allows the researcher to approach the research question from different angles, although total agreement of the results is not necessarily to be expected.

> Aber die Ergebnisse der verschiedenen Perspektiven können verglichen werden, können Stärken und Schwächen der jeweiligen Analysewege aufzeigen und schließlich zu einem kaleidoskopartigen Bild zusammengesetzt werden. (Mayring 1996: 121) [The results of approaches from different perspectives can be compared, which can make the strong and the weak points of the different

---

[11] Questionnaire A and Questionnaire B. In the following when referring to questions on these questionnaires, they will be abbreviated as QA and QB with the number of the respective question following, e.g. QA1 refers to question n° 1 on Questionnaire A.

[12] I.e. an 'other' category (Fink 1995b: 73) was added, which respondents could specify.

[13] Some of these well-known disadvantages are: frustration of the informants because their preferred answer is not given as a choice (Neuman 2000: 261) and therefore loss of information (Fink 1995b: 73) or invalidity of the results (Atteslander and Kopp 1995).

approaches visible and can eventually provide a holistic, albeit kaleidoscopic, picture. My translation.]

This combination of different methods and sources of data is called *triangulation*, cf. e.g. Jick (1983: 135), Lamnek (1995b: 402), Mayring (1996: 121/122). "The triangulation metaphor is from navigation and military strategy that use multiple reference points to locate an object's exact position." (Jick 1983: 136)[14] Triangulation can refer to the combination of several qualitative methods, but also to the combination of qualitative and quantitative approaches. (Flick 1998: 259) Thus Neuman (2000: 124/125) distinguishes several types of triangulation. He refers to the combination of qualitative and qualitative research styles and data as *triangulation of methods*, which he distinguishes from *triangulation of measures*, *triangulation of theory*, and *triangulation of observers*.[15] The combination of qualitative and quantitative data and methods[16] is particularly recommended (Mayring 1996: 121/122), because "the different methodological perspectives complement each other in the study of an issue and this is conceived as the complementary compensation of the weaknesses and blind spots of each single method" (Flick 1998: 259). In my opinion, however, the purpose of triangulation should *not* be primarily to "judge the efficacy or validity of the different methods and sources by comparing the products" (Mason 1996: 148). To refer to 'triangulation as validity check', as for instance does Layder,[17] restricts its usefulness:[18]

---

[14] Cf. also Tashakkori and Teddlie (1998: 41) and Lamnek (1995a: 248).
[15] Tashakkori and Teddlie (1998: 41), referring to Denzin (1978), distinguish four basic types of triangulation:
1. data triangulation, i.e. the use of a variety of data sources in a study
2. investigator triangulation, i.e. the use of several different researchers in a study
3. theory triangulation, i.e. the use of multiple perspectives in interpreting the results of a study
4. methodological triangulation, i.e. the use of multiple methods to study a problem
Cf. also Schründer-Lenzen (1997: 107/108).
[16] Also referred to as across methods triangulation, as opposed to within methods triangulation, where either multiple qualitative analytic tools or multiple quantitative analytic tools are combined (cf. Jick 1983, Tashakkori and Teddlie 1998: 42).
[17] Cf. also Tashakkori and Teddlie (1998: 82): "[...] if a measurement is accurate, it should be repeatable over time or obtainable with an identical method of measurement. [...] This is simply a type of triangulation of measurement simultaneously with two or more identical methods in the same group or situation, or with the same method on more than one occasion." This is not the type or use of triangulation we have in mind here.
[18] Cf. also Bloor (1997: 38ff) for a critical comment on 'triangulation as validation exercise'.

A number of writers have used combinations of methods and data as a means of confirming or disconfirming a finding or hypothesis initially produced by the use of one particular method. For example, in-depth interviews may be used to check patterns or findings generated through participant observation, or simple forms of counting may check the generality of a qualitative insight [...]. Thus, if the use of other methods turns up the same finding or result, then it is confirmed. If it does not, then the initial finding may be discarded as an artifact or aberration caused by the method used. (Layder 1993: 121).

Triangulation can be much more than this as it can enhance the validity of the study as a whole "in the sense that [...] social phenomena are a little more than one-dimensional" and that the investigator needs "to grasp more than one of those dimensions" (Mason 1996: 149).

4 Triangulation in action

This 'multi-dimensionality' of social phenomena and thus of some of the research questions can be illustrated by two examples from the sociolinguistic study of CamP. As we will see in the following, the triangulation of quantitative and qualitative data allows for a more holistic and adequate analysis and evaluation of the issues than either set of data on its own would have been able to provide.

4.1 Example 1: Attitudes towards multilingualism

It is a well known fact that language attitudes are crucial for any sociolinguistic concern and at the same time extremely difficult to assess.[19] [20] This is particularly true in a multilingual country such as Cameroon, where speakers' attitudes to multilingualism are important for any language policy or language planning activity.

Consequently informants in the present study were asked to express their opinion on the multilingual state of their country. On Questionnaire A, they could answer the following question:

---

[19] Cf. e.g. Baker (1992), Holmes (1976), Nader (1968), Pütz (1995), St Clair (1982), Schmied (1985), Sure (1991).
[20] 'Attitude' in itself is a problematic term, as it is often used interchangeably with terms such as 'opinion', 'belief', 'preference', 'feeling', 'value' (cf. Fink 1995b: 66).

QA15: Many languages are spoken in Cameroon. Do you think this is a good thing?   Yes   No

QA15: Beaucoup de langues sont parlées au Cameroun. Pensez-vous que ce soit une bonne chose?   Oui   Non

As we can see in Table 1, 74.7% of all informants and 81.3% of all valid cases answered this question in the affirmative:

Table 1: QA15/frequencies

	Count	%	% of valid cases
yes/oui	824	74.7%	81.3%
no/non	190	17.2%	18.7%
not answered	89	8.1%	-
total	1103	100%	1014

There are no significant differences between anglophones and francophones with regard to this question, as 72.8% (353) of all anglophones and 76.4 % (424) of all francophones ticked 'Yes' or 'Oui' as an answer to this question. The same holds for the educational background of the informants. If we consider those with further or higher education, the differences between diploma college graduates, who gave the lowest percentage of affirmative answers (67.7%), and master's degree holders, who gave the highest percentages (82.8%), would be significant, if bachelor's degree holders were not ranged in-between these two groups (73.4%), which makes clear, that the attitude towards multilingualism cannot be correlated to the level of education.[21] The geographical distribution of the respondents also seems unimportant with regard to QA15:

---

[21] This can also be seen in the rest of the sample: 76% (373) of the high school students (first cycle or less), 70.3% (109) of the high school graduates (A-level), 73.1% (136) of the university students without bachelor and 74.1% (20) of the doctorate holders answered the question in the affirmative.

Table 2: Crosstabulation QA15 and place

	yes/oui			no/non			not answered		total	valid cases
	count	%	% of valid cases	count	%	% of valid cases	count	%		
Bamenda	135	71.8%	*77.1%*	40	21.3%	22.8%	13	6.9%	188	175
Buea	77	74.0%	83.7%	15	14.4%	16.3%	12	11.5%	104	92
Douala	112	71.8%	80.0%	28	17.9%	20.0%	16	10.3%	156	140
Dschang	156	73.2%	78.0%	44	20.7%	22.0%	13	6.1%	213	200
Yaoundé	156	73.2%	84.3%	29	13.6%	15.7%	29	13.6%	214	185
Ebolowa	55	*88.7%*	*91.6%*	5	8.1%	8.3%	2	3.2%	62	60
Bertoua	60	*81.1%*	82.2%	13	17.6%	17.8%	1	1.4%	74	73
Maroua	68	*79.1%*	81.9%	15	17.4%	18.1%	3	3.5%	86	83
n..i.	5	83.3%	83.3%	1	16.7%	16.7%	0	-	6	6
total	824	74.7%	81.3%	190	17.2%	18.7%	89	8.1%	1103	1014

Table 2 suggests that respondents from Ebolowa, Bertoua and Maroua are slightly more positive towards the multilingual state of the country than respondents from other places, but these results are caused in part by the fact that the total number of informants almost equals the number of valid cases. The geographical differences with regard to attitudes towards multilingualism are less acute (at least between Bertoua, Maroua and the other places), when only the valid cases are taken into consideration. Significant differences can only be observed between Bamenda and Ebolowa.

On the basis of this quantitative analysis alone we could thus reasonably conclude that Cameroonians, irrespective of their official language and educational background or the area in which they live, see multilingualism and the multilingual state of their country as 'a good thing'.

However, the analysis of the qualitative part of the study allows for a more differentiated picture. In the interviews, informants were asked the same question, to which they usually gave a 'yes *and* no'-answer. Thus, they chose an option that was not available to the respondents in the quantitative sample and as a result of this, made obvious that an answer to this question is not easily given:

TEXT: lecturer, anglophone 1 (Bamenda) (492/498)
It is like a coin, it has two sides. If, you know, sometimes *it is difficult to communicate* with people, to make them understand you. That is where the difficulty lies and that makes it a bad thing. Bad in quotes. But for this, they have, it makes people have their *identity and for the cultural diversity* all that, I think it is good.

TEXT: lecturer, francophone (Dschang) (423/442)
Ah, vous savez, c'est difficile. Je vais vous répondre sur *deux aspects*.
[...]
Moi, je ne sais pas s'il faut dire *une bonne ou une mauvaise chose*.

TEXT: lecturer, anglophone (Yaoundé) (680/681)
Ehm. I think *one cannot say that it is a good or a bad thing*. [...]

TEXT: teacher, francophone (Buea) (199/200)
Une *bonne chose*, je peux dire oui. Et aussi une *mauvaise chose*.

TEXT: teacher, francophone (Bertoua) (305/332)
C'est une bonne chose, <pause> si chacun ne cherche pas à se replier sur soi-même. Vous comprenez? *Mais, ça devient très dangereux*, si au delà, de la vogue, de la considération, de la prise de la langue comme un instrument permettant la communion entre deux êtres vivants, vous cherchez autre chose, d'impérialisme, ou bien triomphe de telle langue, de ceci, de tel tribu, là ça devient dangereux. Mais quand on prend la langue comme un instrument de paix, parce que là où il y a la communication, il n'y a pas de tension. Mais là où il n'y a pas de communication, les gens sont énervés, et qu'est-ce qu'ils disent? C'est quoi? Qu'est-ce qu'il dit? On est plus tendu, il y a risque d'explosion. Donc, moi, chacun a un rôle qui permet aux hommes de diminuer les tensions, de se comprendre, de communier de communier. Là vraiment, il faut prendre ça très au sérieux. Pour moi donc, une langue qui me permet de communiquer avec l'autre est un

instrument à ne pas négliger. Et comme toutes les langues ont cette vocation la, *la multitude de ces langues-là, si on sait en faire un bon usage pourrait nous empêcher des désagréments. Mais si chacun considère cela comme une arme, en ce moment là ça devient dangereux*. Un réservoir, le Cameroun ne serait qu'un réservoir d'armes dangereux. Vous comprenez?

TEXT: teacher, anglophone (Ebolowa) (605/616)
I think *it would have been good, to an extent. But unfortunately I think that practically it is not good* because the language difference tries to maybe bring in many other differences. It brings in the differences in reasoning and so on. It even brings about tribalistic feelings and so on. So because you don't speak my dialect, we are not friends, or we cannot be friends, I must treat you as an, as an enemy. *So that is the bad side of it*. Otherwise I would say that so many languages could only be, could only portray the richness of Cameroon. Yes, unfortunately, it brings in those bad effects and so on.

TEXT: principal, francophone (Yaounde) (438/444)
Oui, c'est une très bonne chose. *C'est une grande richesse du point de vue culturel*. C'est une *très bonne chose que nous ayons beaucoup de langues. Mais euh... c'est aussi quelque part une mauvaise chose* dans la mesure où ces ..., ces langues peuvent apparaître comme des *espèces de barrières entre les gens* de cette zone et les gens de l'autre zone.

TEXT: lecturer, anglophone (Dschang) (369/372)
Well, you see, *multilingualism in itself* is a reflection of the *cultural richness* of a people, but it can act as a *disincentive* for choosing a national language [...]

As we can see from these quotations, multilingualism can be and is indeed judged negatively. As informants elaborate, multilingualism is depicted as a reason for national disintegration and tribalism or for the creation of communication barriers:

TEXT: professor, francophone (Dschang) (471/473)
Au point de vue de *l'unité, de l'homogénéité de la nation*, ce n'est pas une, ce n'est pas une bonne chose.

TEXT: lecturer, anglophone (Yaoundé) (686/704)
[...] What is negative about that is that with every language comes a peculiar culture and people tend to identify more with that culture and that language when it comes to dealing with somebody from outside of that language. If you come from Nso where I come from and then I am supposed to employ two people and I see one is from Nso, so I, the tendency for me is to see whether this guy from Nso can be taken rather than looking at who is the better out of the two. That is a negative part of it.
[...] But
then, when those languages are translated into ***tribes*** and ***tribalism*** then that becomes, you know, it becomes negative.

TEXT: teacher, anglophone 1 (Yaoundé) (919/928)
[...] But if you from the onset
say to me, if there were fewer languages in Cameroon, then I don't think the problems we are having in Cameroon now would have come up. Because the problems we are having now mostly with this democracy that we have multi-partism, we tend to see that everything moves with ***tribal links***. You want to support a person because he or she comes from your place. But if we had few languages, I don't think this one would have been the case.

TEXT: professor, anglophone (Bamenda) (303/322)
[...] It's quite a difficult for an
educator as I am. Because ***the fewer the languages, the easier one can communicate*** and instructions can pass. But when you have a wide variety, you cannot even harmonise the culture based on linguistic background and it makes it very difficult.

Text: teacher, anglophone 1 (Bamenda) (541/543)
It's not. It keeps the people so divided.
Because that Home Language is already ***a barrier***. So ***it keeps us divided***.

TEXT: teacher, anglophone (Bertoua) (466/470)
[...] But the fact that we have
different, different people, and small small groups talking different, ***different languages, makes people to at least create some little, little unnecessary barriers amongst themselves***.

TEXT: high school student, anglophone 1 (Bamenda) (333/339)
[...] because you can leave from here and go somewhere, like there're some, in some villages most of the people they speak only their own dialect, know how to speak their own dialect, they don't even know Pidgin. When you go there, even try to speak just the Pidgin, they wouldn't understand, *except you learn their own then that's the only chance that you can communicate*.

The last informants' opinions, i.e. that the multitude of ILs in Cameroon makes communication difficult and creates communication barriers, is shared by many informants. Thus, the call for a single, unifying and integrative language for all Cameroonians can be heard.

TEXT: lecturer, francophone (Dschang) (424/429)
[...] Cela serait une bonne chose
si les Camerounais, si c'était une particularité des Camerounais. C'est-à-dire, de parler *une langue partout* où tu passes, on sait: ça, c'est un Camerounais. *Communication générale*. Partout, tous les camerounais pouvaient s'exprimer dans cette langue-là, c'est bien.

TEXT: teacher, anglophone (Buea) (288/297)
[...] Yes, but with
reference to the multilingual nature of Cameroon, it isn't really very good for the country as such. If we had *a common language in the whole country*, I think if would be better, it would be more of a *unifying factor*. You know, language is one of the most, is the most important cultural identity, or to identify somebody, one of the greatest aspects you can use to identity him is his language, with language. So *if people have one language, they have that sense of belonging*, well.

However, in agreement with official language policy towards the ILs,[22] informants also believe that the multiplicity of languages protects national unity by impeding concertation between dissidents from separate ethnic groups:

TEXT: teacher, francophone (Buea) (200/204)
Une bonne chose pourquoi? Si on regarde
politiquement parlant, ça nous divise et *cette division*

---

[22] I.e. government's 'phobia of national disintegration' and its subsequent refusal to support and adopt ILs (cf. Chumbow and Simo Bobda 1995: 10).

nous aide. Parce que c'est difficile de réunir des gens pour faire des troubles. Il y a ce côté là- ça. C'est pour moi, je trouve ça positif.

Despite all the negative factors of multilingualism mentioned in the interviews, the overall attitude towards the multitude of ILs seems to be rather positive. The ILs are seen as a source of cultural richness and identity as they represent a link of the individual to her or his cultural heritage:

> **TEXT: professor, francophone (Buea) (294/297)**
> Ah, non, non, non, non, non! Moi, je pense
> plutôt qu'en fait *la diversité* il n'y a que ça qui soit
> *riche*.

> **TEXT: lecturer, anglophone (Yaoundé) (695/699)**
> But the positive part of it is
> that, like I said, each language comes with a culture
> and therefore that is that cultural variation which
> when you put together gives you this *very rich melting pot of cultures*.

> **TEXT: professor, anglophone (Buea) (596/598)**
> Oh, of course, I think it's a good thing! I
> think it's a good thing, because it makes for a lot of
> *culture variety*, which I enjoy [...]

> **TEXT: professor, francophone (Buea) (356/358)**
> [...] telles qu'elles existent les langues
> nationales, elles permettent à *des cultures*, à des
> populations, à des individus *de s'identifier*.

> **TEXT: professor, anglophone (Dschang) (280/283)**
> [...] I think each person should have his
> *identity* and his secret, be able to communicate to his
> *kin and kith* in the language, that is his. In a secret
> language whenever he wants to.

> **TEXT: teacher, anglophone 2 (Bamenda) (464/474)**
> [...] The native languages are a sort of
> culture, because for us, somebody who does not have a
> culture is regarded as, is not regarded, is not
> regarded with any importance in the society. You must
> be able to say *the village from which you come*, or from
> where your parents came and if you always go back
> there, you should be able to speak that native
> language. Only then I know you're really respected in

our society. So in our society, *a person without his native language, means he has no culture* and such a person is not respected.

Informants also acknowledge that in many instances the ILs represent the only possible means of communication for and with people in the rural areas:

> **TEXT: high school student, francophone (Bertoua) (265/270)**
> <pause> Dans un certain contexte je trouve que c'est bon. Dans la mesure où *ça permet aux gens de communiquer*, oui. Et ce n'est pas tout le monde qui maîtrise par exemple l'éwondo qui est une langue de communication pour certains personnes. Donc la multitude des langues a un avantage quelque part.

However, the fact that an individual can be identified as a member of a particular ethnic group via the language she or he is speaking, is also seen as a handicap:

> **TEXT: high school student, francophone 1 (Dschang) (316/323)**
> [...] parce que les langues *maternelles créent souvent des problèmes entre les tribus. A chaque minute que tu vas causer ton patois, il y peut-être quelqu'un qui va te reprocher quoi.* Il va dire que ce n'est pas bon, de petites injures comme ça. Par contre, si on utilisait peut-être les deux langues nationales, on pouvait bien s'entendre avec tout le monde, pas de problème.

In sum, if we take all the various arguments given in the qualitative part of the study, we can see that most of them could be classified along two dimensions:

1. positive vs. negative effects of multilingualism

2. effects of multilingualism on the individual vs. effects at societal or national level

The multitude of the statements in the qualitative part of the study can thus be simplified in the following figure:

Figure 2: *Positive and negative effects of multilingualism*[23]

	positive effects	negative effects
national level	• cultural diversity/richness • national integration	• national disintegration • tribalism • inter-ethnic rivalries • educational problems
individual level	• ethnic and cultural identity • tradition • secrets • rural means of communication	• language barriers • problems arising out of ethnic identification

The analysis of the qualitative part of the study thus illustrates that Cameroonians seem to see the effects of multilingualism or the multilingual state of their country more negatively at the national level and more positively at the individual level. If we consider the results of the analysis of QA15 in Table 1 and thus the 81.3% of all valid cases who consider multilingualism 'to be a good thing' against this background, we can conclude that in responding to this question priority is generally given to the individual dimension of multilingualism.

The advantages of triangulation are clearly illustrated by this first example. The analysis of the quantitative data alone would have given a distorted picture of the situation as it would have left us with the impression that the multilingual state of the country is almost unanimously seen as positive. The analysis of qualitative data has made clear that many respondents have ambivalent feelings towards the multilingual state of their country. It has also shown where and how multilingualism affects people, at both individual and societal level. The combination of the two types of data and their analysis allows us to conclude that despite the negative effects multilingualism, at both individual and societal level, most Cameroonians consider the multilingual state of their country to be positive and that apparently priority is given to the individual dimension of the problem.

4.2   Example 2: The national language question

The advantages of triangulation can be further illustrated by a second and related example from the study. The quotations in the previous sections have

---

[23] Diagram taken from Schröder (2003a: 63).

shown that many Cameroonians feel that multilingualism, and consequently tribalism, represent a danger to the national unity of the country. However, very few Cameroonians would suggest that the official languages, English and French, were a solution to this problem.

Although in Cameroon, as in many other African countries, the promotion of these former colonial languages is encouraged on the basis of their allegedly neutral character, most Cameroonians have come to realise that "the presence of a 'neutral' foreign language as the official language of the state has done little to minimise the so-called 'tribal' and other cleavages" (Mansour 1993: 127). Tension between ethnic groups have increased since independence (Tchoungui 1983: 114), the official languages have come to serve as markers of an anglophone vs. a francophone identity (cf. e.g. Wolf 1997, Wolf 2001), and it seems as if national integration has been as much impeded as enhanced by the two official languages. Informants very often put forward what is elsewhere defined as the 'linguistic imperialism' and 'cultural alienation' argument against the continuing use of the official languages (Schmied 1991: 104) and they stress their need for an additional Cameroonian indigenous language as national language.

TEXT: university student, francophone (Dschang) (625/637)
Mais pour ce qui est des perspectives, pour
le Cameroun, je souhaite l'insertion d'une langue
nationale. Ce qui me satisferait, c'est l'insertion
d'une langue nationale. Pour, déjà, pour que le
Cameroun puisse s'affirmer comme un pays à part
entière, puisque *le français et l'anglais nous font,
nous mettent sous dépendance.* Déjà qu'on utilise *la
langue de quelqu'un*, bon on est obligé de la comprendre.
D'entendre ce qu'il dit, de suivre ce qu'il dit. Bon,
chacun doit pouvoir, chacun doit chercher à maîtriser
ces deux langues, français et anglais, pour le moment,
oui. Mais à la longue, *je souhaite l'insertion d'une
langue nationale.*

TEXT: lecturer, anglophone (Dschang) (385/396)
Well, you see, national does not exclude
international. The fact that there is a national
language, *the national language could be used for its
own purposes*. For instance, you see, there are secrets
of a country. *Each country has its secrets and those
are the secrets*, <incomprehensible> *the cultures of the
people*, the *traditions* and the, the *rites*; all those
things. You know, they *could be communicated in the
national language* because that's what you want the

people to know and the international languages could
still be used, you know, as not language of instruction
this time but as a school subject.

The informants thus affirm that the official languages are incapable of transmitting Cameroonian experiences and cultural values and that they would therefore welcome the introduction of an additional indigenous national language. Although many linguists believe that CamP would be a suitable and useful candidate for the position of such a national language (cf. e.g. Mbangwana 1983, Ayafor 2000), statements in the interviews suggest that for many Cameroonians CamP was not an eligible solution; negative judgements of this language abound:

TEXT: high school student, anglophone 1 (Bamenda) (262/267)
Informant: The first language I would like my children to
know is English; then second French before any other
language, but not Pidgin. I would not like them to even
know Pidgin.
AS: Why not?
I: I think, *it's very dirty*!

TEXT: high school student, francophone (Bertoua) (75/80)
I: Non, *ce n'est pas une bonne langue.*
AS: Ce n'est pas une bonne langue pourquoi?
I: Bon. Parce que le, le pidgin, on a remarqué que
le pidgin relève de ceux qui ne maîtrisent pas vraiment
l'anglais. Donc *le pidgin est en quelque sorte la
déformation de l'anglais.* Oui.

TEXT: university student, anglophone (Buea) (458/459)
I think I can define Pidgin as *a deviation from
English, good English.*

TEXT: lecturer, francophone (Dschang) (331/333)
C'est, je pense que c'est, c'est, c'est la,
c'est *une déviation de la langue anglaise.* Comment je
peux dire? Oui déviation.

TEXT: teacher, francophone (Ebolowa) (649/653)
[...] Bon ! il n'est ni
fran... *ni français, ni anglais.* Hmm hun ! c'est une
langue intermédiaire. Je vous ai dit que, *les bandits,
les petits badauds* ont instauré, puis ça s'est
développé. Oui !

TEXT: teacher, francophone 1 (Yaoundé) (315/317)
[...] Je ne vais pas maîtriser le Pidgin. Parce
que, parfois, on vous assimile à des bandits, on vous
dit que, *c'est la langue des bandits*.

TEXT: professor, francophone (Buea) (1019/1023)
[...] il aimait tellement le
pidgin qu'il a fini par épouser une femme nigérienne.
Malheureusement, *comme le pidgin est une langue de
pute*, sa femme aussi, elle l'a trompé et bon
finalement, ils ont quand même eu des enfants.

TEXT: lecturer, anglophone (Dschang) (306/314)
Like? No. I not talk of liking because, you
know, I have never really admired Pidgin English,
actually. So I would not like a variety. In fact, I
always, you know, think that *Pidgin English is the
broken part of good English*. As an educationist, I look
at it that way. Pidgin English, *it's not a language on
its own, it's a language that borrows a lot from many
languages* and perhaps acts as a lingua franca, but its
not a language that I admire personally.

TEXT: lecturer, anglophone (Buea) (533/541)
If I were asked to suggest a national language
in Cameroon, I would suggest a language like Fulfulde,
which I know is the most widely spoken African language
in Cameroon. I would also suggest, *I may not want to
suggest Pidgin because Pidgin, as I said, has got not
an African origin*. But if they care, they could still
implement it. But the one African language in Cameroon
which is spoken by a cross-section of African ethnic
groups is Fulfulde.

CamP is classified as a language of the uneducated, of those who have not mastered 'good English' and therefore have to rely on this 'deviation of English'. It is also referred to as the language of criminals and prostitutes and one can easily believe that this language is very unlikely to be an eligible candidate for a national language. The informants of the last two quotations also state more precisely that they reject CamP because of its lack of ethnic affiliation. The case of the last informant is all the more interesting as this informant is relatively open towards CamP as a medium of instruction, as he stated earlier in the interview, but would not readily accept CamP as a national language.

The analysis of the quantitative data of the study, however, suggests that matters are slightly different. The informants were asked:

> QA18: French and English are the official languages in Cameroon. In your opinion, which language has the status of a national language?
>
> QA18: Le Français et l'Anglais sont de langues officielles au Cameroun. Quelle langue, selon vous, a le statut d'une langue nationale?

This question had a hybrid format, i.e. the informants had the choice of ticking either of the LWCs, of adding any language they wanted in the 'other-category, please specify' or of ticking 'none'. Given the statements in the interviews quoted above, the results of the quantitative study come somewhat as a surprise:

Table 3: QA18/frequencies

language	count	%	% of valid cases
none	307	27.8%	34.2%
CamP	261	23.7%	29.1%
Duala	93	8.4%	10.4%
Ewondo	54	4.9%	6%
Ewondo Populaire	43	3.9%	4.8%
Fulfulde	38	3.4%	4.2%
Mungaka	26	2.4%	2.9%
Bulu	20	1.8%	2.2%
other	56	5.1%	6.2%
not answered	205	18.6%	
total	1103	100%	898 (100%)

As we can see in Table 3, despite its lack of ethnic affiliation CamP is by far the most frequently mentioned language among all those which are said to have acquired the status of a national language. On the basis of the quantitative data alone, we might therefore come to believe that CamP was indeed a suitable choice as a national language in Cameroon. However, Table 3 also shows that the number of informants who ticked 'none' as an answer to QA18 is even higher than those who believe CamP to have the status of a national language. Given the general tenor of the interviews, this cannot be interpreted as a general lack of interest towards the issue or a sign that the national language question is felt to be irrelevant. But, as the qualitative data of the study suggest, the informants are well aware that the choice of a single national language is very difficult to make:

> **TEXT: lecturer, francophone (Dschang) (473/478)**
> [...] Le
> Cameroun serait, on dit que c'est une Afrique en
> miniature. Alors cette diversité-là de culture, la
> diversité de langues, ça fait que, pour qu'on, pour que
> je parle d'*une langue qui a un rayonnement national au
> Cameroun, c'est très difficile.*

> **TEXT: professor, anglophone (Dschang) (298/312)**
> No, no, there is none, and *it would also be
> tragic accepting any one language out of the 250, 236
> or 286, I wouldn't, it would not be fair acquiring one
> as a national language.*

> **TEXT: professor, anglophone (Bamenda) (351/355)**
> I don't think it is easy
> because the problem definitely is that people start
> asking *why not my own language* and this is where they
> are finding it *difficult to break down the language
> barriers*.

> **TEXT: teacher, francophone 2 (Dschang) (348/353)**
> [...] parce que *le
> problème que nous avons actuellement, c'est choisir une
> langue nationale* que l'on peut enseigner à l'école. On
> ne sait laquelle. Il y en a tellement. On ne sait donc
> quelle langue nationale on peut enseigner. Or si on
> avait 2 ou 3 ça faciliterait la tâche.

These statements explain that the choice of a national language is rendered difficult by the linguistic diversity of the country and the threat of tribalism. However, some informants in the interviews also give a solution to the problem:

> **TEXT: university student, francophone (Buea) (338/353)**
> Mais il est vrai que c'est difficile, le Cameroun étant
> divisé par province, c'est vraiment, vraiment difficile
> de déterminer. Parce que *dans chaque province où tu
> vas, tu trouves qu'elle a une langue qui domine sa
> province*.
> [...]

Ou alors
qu'on divise le Cameroun par contrée. Ca veut dire
qu'on fasse par exemple, le grand Nord, le grand Sud,
l'Est et l'Ouest. *Et que chaque partie a une langue qui
la domine.*

TEXT: teacher, anglophone (Maroua) (116/121)
AS: And, you've travelled around in, as you said, 9 of
the 10 provinces, you know, and what languages did you
use while you were travelling around? What is the most
widely spoken language in Cameroon?
I: *In each of these regions it was a local
vernacular that prevailed.*

TEXT: teacher, francophone 2 (Yaoundé) (378/417)
S'il m'arrive de choisir quatre langues
nationales, surtout que ça entre facilement dans notre
contexte.
[...]
A des régions. Les langues, a chaque région
s'adapte une langue ou alors *une langue s'adapte à une
région.*

TEXT: principal, francophone (Yaoundé) (166/193)
Mais une langue qui aurait un statut national, c'est-
à- dire qu'on parlerait dans l'ensemble du pays, c'est
difficile. Mais on pourrait *– par zone géographique –
avoir une langue* qu'on pourrait appeler euh ... euh...
une espèce de lingua frenc...
AS: Franca.
I: Franca, voilà. Qu'on parlerait comme ça, qui
servirait de ... langue de communication à tout le
monde.
[...]
Mais *chaque région a ses particularités*. Mais je
veux vous dire qu'au Sud, la langue la plus parlée,
enfin au Centre et au Sud, c'est la langue éwondo ou le
bulu. Euh ... au Littoral, c'est le bassa et le duala.
Au Nord, c'est le fulfuldé et le haoussa.
AS: Et le pidgin se trouve où?
I: Bien, le pidgin donc se trouve ... dans ce que
je pourrais appeler, que j'ajouterais ici, n'est-ce-pas
euh ... ça, c'est le Cameroun, la zone anglophone, ça
se trouve principalement ici. Mais, dans ces zones
aussi là, ici, on parle aussi le pidgin.
AS: C'est le Littoral.

I: C'est le Littoral, voilà. Ici, aussi on en parle [...]

Thus, the informants seem to favour a solution to the problem which resembles the one found for Nigeria,[24] i.e. they see the choice of several regional LWCs as 'national languages at a regional level'[25] as an acceptable solution to the national language question. If we look at the quantitative data against this background, we can see that the acceptance of e.g. CamP as a national language varies from one region to another.

Whereas for instance 45.2% (85) of all respondents from Bamenda and 26.9% (28) of all informants from Buea believe CamP to have acquired the status of a national language, this is true for only 9.5% (7) of all informants from Bertoua and 10.5% (9) of the informants from Maroua. However, Ewondo Populaire and Fulfulde, two languages which (with a score of 4.8% and 4.2% respectively) score comparatively low in the national count for QA18 (cf. Table 3), receive high scores in Bertoua and Maroua respectively.

Table 4: Crosstabulation QA18 and place

	Bamenda	Buea	Douala	Dschang	Yaoundé	Ebolowa	Bertoua	Maroua	n.i.
CamP	*85* *45.2%*	*28* *26.9%*	37 23.7%	40 18.8%	43 20.1%	12 19.4%	*7* *9.5%*	*9* *10.5%*	0
Ewondo	5 2.7%	4 3.8%	10 6.4%	7 3.3%	20 9.3%	5 8.1%	3 4.1%	0	0
Duala	14 7.4%	14 13.5%	19 12.2%	13 6.1%	23 10.7%	0	7 9.5%	3 3.5%	0
Mungaka	12 6.4%	2 1.9%	1 0.6%	1 0.5%	9 4.2%	0	1 1.4%	0	0
Ewondo P.	3 1.6%	4 3.8%	0	6 2.8%	11 5.1%	1 1.6%	*17* *23.0%*	0	1 16.7%
Bulu	1 0.5%	0	0	3 1.4%	1 0.5%	10 16.1%	2 2.7%	0	3 50%
Fulfulde	1 0.5%	0	2 1.3%	3 1.4%	1 0.5%	0	2 2.7%	*29* *33.7%*	0
other	6 3.2%	10 9.6%	3 1.9%	20 9.4%	4 1.9%	2 3.2%	8 10.8%	3 3.5%	0
none	36 19.1%	22 21.2%	47 30.1%	90 42.3%	50 23.4%	20 32.3%	14 18.9%	27 31.4%	1 16.7%
n.a.	25 13.3%	20 19.2%	37 23.7%	30 14.1%	52 24.3%	12 19.4%	13 17.6%	15 17.4%	1 16.7%
total	188	104	156	213	214	62	74	86	6

---

[24] Similar proposals have been made by Bot Ba Njock (1966) and Gratien Atindogbe (at the 3L Conference 1999 in Yaoundé) for the choice of several media of instruction at a regional level.

[25] I am aware of the fact that, strictly speaking, this is a contradiction in terms. We can thus see that the structure proposed by Bambgbose (1991: 54) and adapted in Figure 1 with its division between the national level and regional level, at least in the Cameroonian context, is somewhat artificial. Because in Figure 1, the languages proposed in the following as 'national languages' (i.e. Ewondo Populaire and Fulfulde) are listed as languages at regional level.

If only the valid cases are taken into account, these numbers even amount to 52% of the respondents from Bamenda and 33% of the respondents from Buea, who consider CamP to have acquired the status of a national language (cf. Schröder 2003b: 322, diagram XII).

The same holds for the acceptance of Ewondo Populaire in Bertoua, which 28% of all respondents believe to have acquired the status of a national language (cf. Schröder 2003b: 323, diagram XIII) and for Fulfuldé, whose acceptance amounts to 41% of all respondents from Maroua (cf. Schröder 2003b: 323, diagram XIV), if only the valid cases are taken into account.

As we can see in Table 4, apart from Maroua and Bertoua, the general acceptance of CamP is comparatively high. However, Table 4 also clearly indicates that CamP is very unlikely to be accepted as a national language in all Cameroonian provinces. The quantitative data confirms what we concluded from the interviews to be a possible solution for the national language question, i.e. the introduction of several national languages at a regional level.

The triangulation of the qualitative and quantitative data has given us a more accurate picture of the attitudes that informants have towards the national language question. Because of the number of negative statements about this language, the qualitative data analysed on its own would have left us with the impression that CamP is probably not eligible as a national language. A superficial analysis of the quantitative data would have led us to suggest CamP as a national language without any restrictions. The combination of the two types of data has allowed for a more differentiated approach to both sets of data and has shown us that the national language question has to be answered at different levels.

Thus, triangulation of the two sets of data can also help us to explain the apparent glaring contradiction between the negative statements about CamP quoted above, some of which were even made by informants from Bamenda and Buea, and the surprisingly high figures for this language in Table 3. As elaborated elsewhere (cf. Schröder 2003a: sections 4.4. and 5.2.1.6), attitudes towards CamP are highly ambivalent or even contradictory and have to be approached at two levels. One of the informants already quoted above, demonstrates this ambivalence very clearly. This is a person who is, generally speaking, very open towards CamP, is actually in favour of its use a medium of instruction and, at one stage in the interview, defines CamP as an African language:

> **TEXT: lecturer, anglophone (Buea) (394/397)**
> Pidgin has got a European history. Pidgin has got a European background, but I believe *it is an African language. It has got a European origin, but it is an African language*,[...].

However, when he is asked to state his opinion on the national language question, he hesitates to include CamP in his considerations because of its 'European origin' and prefers a language such as Fulfulde as a national language (cf. p.170). We can thus see that CamP's 'Africanness' and acceptability is evaluated at two levels:

> **TEXT: professor, francophone (Buea) (447/460)**
> AS: Est-ce que, vous avez dit que *les langues comme le foufouldé portent...*
> I: *La marque de notre culture!*
> AS: Et que le pidgin ne porte pas cette marque, comme le français et l'anglais ne la portent pas?
> I: *Le français et l'anglais ne la portent pas du tout. Pas du tout. Le pidgin s'adapte peut-être mieux! C'est une langue qui est plus souple plus élastique, pour intégrer.* Mais, elle, elle intègre des intégrants. Je veux dire que, bon, c'est *une langue hybride*, c'est une pute, si vous me permettez l'expression. C'est une prostituée. Elle sert à toutes les sources. Finalement, elle ne sert à aucune source. *Personne ne peut dire que le pidgin est de chez moi*!

When compared to any of the ILs, CamP is primarily associated with its European origin and evaluated on the basis of its lack of ethnic affiliation. However, in comparison with the two official languages, primacy of attention is shifted to the fact, that this language has been appropriated by the Cameroonians and made suitable for the Cameroonian context and experience. Thus, Cameroonians also seem to express identity at two levels: firstly at the local level and secondly at a regional or national level.[26] The results of the quantitative analysis of QA18 in Table 3 therefore suggest that most respondents had the second level in mind when answering this question.

---

[26] Cf. Schröder (2003a) for details.

5 Conclusion

This paper has illustrated that qualitative and quantitative data are compatible and that triangulation of these two types of data can help to shed light on multi-dimensional phenomena. As we have seen, it is very often divergent results – as in the case of Example 2 above – which uncover previously unseen factors, such as the two level approach to the national language question and the inseparability of regional and national levels (cf. also fn. 25) The combination of different types of data "is useful whether there is convergence or not. Where there is convergence, confidence in the results grows considerably. [...] However, where divergent results emerge, alternative, and likely more complex, explanations are generated" (Jick 1983: 144). Thus, as this paper has demonstrated, triangulation in our sense is certainly not a validity test, but it can be "*relevant* to the issue of validity, in so far as [it] may yield new data that throw fresh light on the investigation and provide a spur for deeper and richer analyses. [...] it is not just that additional data are available for study, but also that these additional data may alter the researcher's perception of the initial data" (Bloor 1997: 49). We have seen that qualitative and quantitative data can be used not simply to supplement or complement each other but in a circular and evolving process (cf. Strauss and Corbin 1998: 34). We thus hope to have shown through this sociolinguistic study of CamP that qualitative approaches and in particular the triangulation of qualitative and quantitative data are valuable tools in sociolinguistic investigations and can provide new and more profound insights into sociolinguistic research questions in African countries and elsewhere.

References

ATTESLANDER, PETER AND MANFRED KOPP
    (1995). "Befragung." In E. Roth and K. Heidenreich, eds. *Sozialwissenschaftliche Methoden*. München: Oldenbourg, 146-174.
AYAFOR, MIRIAM
    (2000). "Kamtok: The Ultimate Unifying Common National Language for Cameroon." *The Carrier Pidgin* 28, 4-6.
BAKER, COLIN
    (1992). *Attitudes and Language*. Clevedon: Multilingual Matters.
BAMGBOSE, AYO
    (1991). *Language and the Nation. The Language Question in Sub-Saharan Africa*. Edinburgh: Edinburgh University Press.

BLOOR, MICHAEL
(1997). "Techniques of Validation in Qualitative Research: a Critical Commentary." In G. Miller and R. Dingwall, eds. *Context and Method in Qualitative Research*. London/Thousand Oaks/New Delhi: Sage, 37-50.
BOT BA NJOCK, HENRI MARCEL
(1966). "Le problème linguistique au Cameroun." *L'Afrique et l'Asie* 73, 3-13.
BOUCHARD RYAN, ELLEN
(1979). "Why Do Low-Prestige Varieties Persist?" In H. Giles and R. N. St Clair, eds. *Language and Social Psychology*. Oxford: Basil Blackwell, 145-157.
CAMERON, DEBORAH, ELIZABETH FRAZER, PENELOPE HARVEY, BEN RAMPTON, AND KAY RICHARDSON
(1993). "Ethics, Advocacy and Empowerment: Issues of Method in Researching Language." *Language & Communication* 13: 2, 81-94.
CHUMBOW, BEBAN SAMMY AND AUGUSTIN SIMO BOBDA
(1995). "The Functions and Status of English in Cameroon." Paper Presented at the English in Africa Conference. Grahamstown, South Africa, 11-14 September 1995.
(1996). "The Life-Cycle of Post-Imperial English in Cameroon." In J. A. Fishman, ed. *Post-Imperial English. Status Change in Former British and American Colonies 1940-1990*. Berlin, New York: Mouton de Gruyter, 401-429.
DINGWALL, ROBERT
(1997). "Accounts, Interviews and Observations." In G. Miller and R. Dingwall, eds. *Context and Method in Qualitative Research*. London/Thousand Oaks/New Delhi: Sage, 51-65.
ENGLER, STEFFANI
(1997). "Zur Kombination von qualitativen und quantitativen Methoden." In B. Friebertshäuser and A. Prengel, eds. *Handbuch Qualitative Forschungsmethoden in der Erziehungswissenschaft*. Weinheim and München: Juventa, 118-130.
FÉRAL, CAROLE DE
(1980). "Quelques Fonctions et Caractéristiques Structurelles du Pidgin-English Camerounais." *Ba Shiru: A Journal of West African Languages and Literature* 11: 2, 21-35.
FINK, ARLENE
(1995a). *The Survey Handbook*. Thousand Oaks/London/New Delhi: Sage.
(1995b). *How to Ask Survey Questions*. Thousands Oaks/ London/ New Delhi: Sage.
FLICK, UWE
(1998). *An Introduction to Qualitative Research*. London/Thousand Oaks/New Delhi: Sage.
GLASER, BARNEY AND ANSELM L. STRAUSS
(1967). *The Discovery of Grounded Theory. Strategies for Qualitative Research*. Chicago: Aldine.
HOLMES, JANET
(1976). "A Review of Some Methods of Investigating Attitudes to Languages, Dialects and Accents." In W. Viereck, ed. *Sprachliches Handeln - Soziales Verhalten*. München: Wilhelm Fink, 301-330.

JICK; TODD D.
(1983). "Mixing Qualitative and Quantitative Methods: Triangulation in Action." In J. Van Maanen, ed. *Qualitative Methodology*. Newbury Park/London/New Delhi: Sage, 135-148.
KARDOFF, ERNST VON
(1995). "Qualitative Sozialforschung – Versuch einer Standortbestimmung." In Uwe Flick et al., eds. *Handbuch qualitative Sozialforschung*. Weinheim: Beltz, 3-8.
KIRK, JEROME AND MARK L. MILLER
(1986). *Reliability and Validity in Qualitative Research*. Beverly Hills, CA: Sage.
KOENIG, EDNA L., EMMANUEL CHIA AND JOHN POVEY (eds.)
(1983). *A Sociolinguistic Profile of Urban Centers in Cameroon*. Los Angeles: Crossroads Press.
KUCKARTZ, UDO
(1997). "Qualitative Daten computergestützt auswerten: Methoden, Techniken, Software." In B. Friebertshäuser and A. Prengel, eds. *Handbuch Qualitative Forschungsmethoden in der Erziehungswissenschaft*. Weinheim/München: Juventa, 584-595.
(1999a). *Handbuch zum Textanalysesystem winMAX für Windows*. Opladen: Westdeutscher Verlag.
(1999b). *Computergestützte Analyse qualitativer Daten. Eine Einführung in Methoden und Arbeitstechniken*. Opladen: Westdeutscher Verlag.
LAMNEK, SIEGFRIED
(1995a). *Qualitative Sozialforschung. Bd. 1: Methodologie*. Weinheim: Beltz.
(1995b). *Qualitative Sozialforschung. Bd. 2: Methoden und Techniken*. Weinheim: Beltz.
LAYDER, DEREK
(1993). *New Strategies in Social Research. An Introduction and Guide*. Cambridge: Polity Press.
MANSOUR, GERDA
(1993). *Multilingualism and Nation Building*. Clevedon, Philadelphia, Adelaide: Multilingual Matters.
MARSHALL, CATHERINE AND GRETCHEN ROSSMAN
(1995). *Designing Qualitative Research*. Thousand Oaks/London/New Delhi: Sage.
MASON, JENNIFER
(1996). *Qualitative Researching*. London/Thousand Oaks/New Delhi: Sage.
MAYRING, PHILIPP
(1996). *Einführung in die qualitative Sozialforschung*. Weinheim: Beltz.
MBANGWANA, PAUL
(1983). "The Scope and Role of Pidgin English in Cameroon." In E. L. Koenig, E. Chia and J. Povey, eds. *A Sociolinguistic Profile of Urban Centers in Cameroon*. Los Angeles: Crossroads Press, 79-92.
NADER, LAURA
(1968). "A Note on Attitudes and the Use of Language." In J. A. Fishman, ed. *Readings in the Sociology of Language*. The Hague: Mouton, 276-281.

NEUMAN, LAWRENCE W.
(2000). *Social Research Methods – Qualitative and Quantitative Approaches.* Boston: Allyn & Bacon.
OSWALD, HANS
(1997). "Was heißt qualitative forschen?" In B. Friebertshäuser and A. Prengel, eds. *Handbuch Qualitative Forschungsmethoden in der Erziehungswissenschaft.* Weinheim and München: Juventa, 71-87.
POVEY, JOHN
(1983). "The Language Profile of Cameroon: An Introduction." In E. L. Koenig, E. Chia and J. Povey, eds. *A Sociolinguistic Profile of Urban Centers in Cameroon.* Los Angeles: Crossroads Press, 7-18.
PÜTZ, MARTIN
(1995). "Attitudes and Language: An Empirical Investigation into the Status and Use of English in Namibia." In M. Pütz, ed. *Discrimination through Language in Africa? Perspectives on the Namibian Experience.* Berlin: Mouton de Gruyter, 245-284.
SCHMIED, JOSEF J.
(1985). "Attitudes towards English in Tanzania." *English World-Wide* 6. 2, 37-269.
(1991). *English in Africa.* London: Longman.
SCHNELL, RAINER, PAUL B. HILL, AND ELKE ESSER
(1993). *Methoden der empirischen Sozialforschung.* München: Oldenbourg.
SCHRÖDER, ANNE
(2003a). *Status, Functions, and Prospects of Pidgin English. An Empirical Approach to Language Dynamics in Cameroon.* Tübingen: Gunter Narr.
(2003b). "Cameroon Pidgin English: A Means of Bridging the Anglophone-Francophone Division in Cameroon?" *AAA: Arbeiten aus Anglistik und Amerikanistik* 28:2, 305-327.
SCHRÜNDER-LENZEN, AGI
(1997). "Triangulation und idealtypisches Verstehen in der (Re-) Konstruktion subjektiver Theorien." In B. Friebertshäuser and A. Prengel, eds. *Handbuch Qualitative Forschungsmethoden in der Erziehungswissenschaft.* Weinheim and München: Juventa, 107-117.
SILVERMAN, DAVID
(1997). "The Logics of Qualitative Research." In G. Miller and R. Dingwall, eds. *Context and Method in Qualitative Research.* London/Thousand Oaks/New Delhi: Sage, 12-25.
ST CLAIR, ROBERT N.
(1982). "From Social History to Language Attitudes." In E. Bouchard Ryan and H. Giles, eds. *Attitudes towards Language Variation. Social and Applied Contexts.* London: Edward Arnold, 164-174.
STRAUSS, ANSELM AND JULIET CORBIN
(1998). *Basics of Qualitative Research.* Thousand Oaks/London/New Delhi: Sage.
SURE, KEMBO
(1991). "Language Functions and Language Attitudes in Kenya." *English World-Wide* 12: 2, 245-260.

TASHAKKORI, ABBAS AND CHARLES TEDDLIE
(1998). *Mixed Methodology. Combining Qualitative and Quantitative Approaches.* Thousand Oaks/London/New Delhi: Sage.
TCHOUNGUI, GISELE
(1983). "Focus on Official Bilingualism in Cameroon: Its Relationship to Education." In E. L. Koenig, E. Chia and J. Povey, eds. *A Sociolinguistic Profile of Urban Centers in Cameroon.* Los Angeles: Crossroads Press, 93-116.
TIOMAJOU, DAVID
(1991). *Bilingualism in the Mass Media in Cameroon: A Sociolinguistic Analysis of Cameroon Radio Television (CRTV).* Unpublished PhD dissertation, Yaoundé, Cameroon: University of Yaoundé I.
TODD, LORETO
(1982). "English in Cameroon: Education in a Multilingual Society." In J. Pride, ed. *New Englishes.* Rowley, Ma: Newbury House, 119-137.
(1984). *Modern Englishes: Pidgins and Creoles.* Oxford: Basil Blackwell.
WOLF, HANS-GEORG
(1997). "Transcendence of Ethnic Boundaries: The Case of the Anglophones in Cameroon." *Journal of Sociolinguistics* 1: 3, 419-426.
(2001). *English in Cameroon.* Berlin/New York: Mouton de Gruyter.

183

Black Scousers:
The Long Presence of British Africans in Liverpool

SEBASTIAN BERG
Chemnitz, Germany

City of Paradox

The story of Africa and Europe, of America and Europe, of the relationship of black and white people, of European wealth and the exploitation of Africa and Africans is the story of colonialism and the traces it has left to the present day. Liverpool is almost a symbol of this story, because of its central role in the slave trade.[1] From a present-day perspective, Liverpool's story is above all a story of many paradoxes: as 'capital of the triangular trade' it became, in the 18th century, one of Europe's richest cities. As the 'Bermuda triangle of British capitalism' it became, in the 20th century, one of (Western) Europe's poorest cities. For most of the 20th century, the population declined dramatically – from about 700,000 inhabitants in the 1900s to 450,000 in the 1990s. But still the city has notorious housing problems, high levels of unemployment, and has become almost synonymous with all kinds of social difficulties. With regard to Liverpool's black people, whose ancestors had come from West Africa, more paradoxes are to be found: In 2002, Liverpool City Council passed a Race Equality Scheme. In the introduction, it states:

> Liverpool is a premier European City and we have a strong legacy and history as a port. With this window to the world we have a strong, diverse set of different communities living and working in the city. We hope that through this scheme we will begin to truly address the needs of all these communities and to build on our commitment to promote Racial Equality. (Liverpool City Council 2002: 6)

This is paradoxical not only because Liverpool "will begin to truly address the needs" some 250 years after the first black people had arrived, but also because there were numerous similar declarations before. Black people in Liverpool form one of the oldest non-European minority populations in

---

[1] "Triangular trade" is the term for the business of exporting cheap goods to Africa, exchanging them for local people who were shipped to America where those who survived the passage were sold as slaves. The profit was used to buy commodities like sugar, tobacco and, especially, cotton. These goods were sold in Europe. The traders earned huge sums of money at the American and European end of the triangular journey. For the history of slavery and the slave trade see Blackburn 1998.

Britain.[2] Nevertheless, they are also one of the poorest. In a way, the black population is absolutely "integrated" – at least as long as one agrees with the statement in a report on their desperate situation in the city: "Those who believe that Britain's racial problems will disappear with integration, are proved wrong by the Liverpool experience. You cannot have greater integration than intermarriage [between black and white people, S.B.]" (Gifford et al. 1989: 42). For some time during the 1980s, Liverpool City Council was controlled by a Trotskyist group within the Labour Party, called the 'Militants' (cf. Steffen 1994: 197-221). After Margaret Thatcher's government had won the battle against and had ousted them, two of their leading figures wrote a book of self-defence. They described Liverpool 8, the place where most of the 'integrated' black people live, as "the most ghettoised area of Britain" (Taaffe/Mulhearn 1988: 244). Nevertheless, during their time of office they had been opposed to any special programmes for changing this. There are further paradoxes: Liverpool's black population is among the 'most-researched' ones in Britain. But there is not even consensus about its size – estimates range from 20,000 to 40,000 people.[3] The black population is extremely politicised but still politically heavily isolated. Sometimes white people regard them as part of the myth of Liverpool's exceptionalism, sometimes they are excluded from the city's self-image. Finally (and as indicated in this article's title), black people sometimes regard themselves as 'Black Scousers', referring for example to their impenetrable local accent. But sometimes they rather see themselves as people in exile, 'British Africans', who belong to a world-wide black diaspora and who are safe and at home only in 'their' part of the city: Liverpool 8.[4]

In this article, I try to explain some of these contradictions. Therefore, I will describe the emergence and history of the 'African presence' in Liverpool as well as the history and content of white reactions to this presence. Then, I will discuss developments during the last two decades, especially black people's political mobilisations and demands as well as white reactions to these. This historical approach will be used then to analyse the shape and the consequences of racism. It will also be used to question the usefulness of voguish concepts like 'multiculturalism' or 'integration'. What becomes obvious, I think, is that a strong political will is needed to confront

---

[2] There are communities of a similar age in London, Bristol, Tyneside, and Cardiff. For a comprehensive history of black people in Britain see Fryer 1984.
[3] The high number of 40,000 is given by the Liverpool Black Caucus (1986: 17), while the most recent estimate of Liverpool City Council is 5 per cent, which is a bit more than 20,000 (2002: 3).
[4] For the identities of black Liverpudlians see Ackah/Christian 1997.

the traces and scars left by past and present racism. Secondly, it becomes obvious that racism is closely linked with the processes of capitalism (boom and bust, production of social hierarchies, competition of individuals). Finally, it can be shown that stereotypes based on old-fashioned biological racism still have their effects and are still in use: in Liverpool's case they are constructed around supposed sexual and social pathologies.

Coming to the Capital

To call Liverpool the 'capital of the triangular trade' is by no means exaggerated. In the late 18th century, it organised 90 per cent of the British or 40 per cent of the whole European slave trade (Julienne 1994: 19). The city's rapid growth in the 18th century was a consequence of the trade. Streets in today's city centre, like Bold Street, Hardman Street, Blackburne Place, bear the names of dynasties of slave merchants (ibid.). Their businesses began to thrive after 1677, when slaves legally became 'goods' and 'commodities'. For trading with particular goods, companies could claim monopolies. Liverpool and Bristol did so for the slave trade. Liverpool soon outflanked its rival due to its sheltered port. In 1760, an observer gave the following account:

> Though few of the merchants have more education than befits a counting house, they are genteel in their address (...). Their tables are plentously furnished and their meats well served up, their rum is excellent, of which they consume large quantities in punch made when the West India fleet comes in mostly with rumes which are very cooling and afford a delicious flavour. I need not inform your Lordship that the principal exports of Liverpool are all kinds of woollen and worsted goods, with other manufacturers of Manchester and Sheffield and Birmingham wares etc. These they barter on the coast of Guinea for slaves and elephant teeth and golddust. The slaves they dispose of at Jamaica, Barbados and other West Indian islands for rum and sugar for which they are sure of a quick sale at home. This port is admirably well suited for trade being almost central in the channel so that in war time, by coming north about the ships have a good chance of escaping the many privateers belong to the enemy which cruise southward (...). Since I have been here I have seen enter the port, in one morning, seven West India ships. (quoted in Law 1981: 6-7)

The merchants not only traded slaves, but, as symbols of prestige, they owned black domestic servants themselves. Thus slaves formed the oldest section of Liverpool's black population. In the local newspaper, advertisements like the following appeared: "For sale a fine Negroe boy of about 4 feet 5 inches high. Of a sober, tractable, humane disposition. Eleven or twelve years talks English very well, and can dress hair in a tolerable way" (quoted in Law

1981: 99). It seems that the merchants liked such boys and in many cases regarded them as something like lap dogs. Once grown up, however, most were treated far worse. It was, for example, common to brand their foreheads. Some managed to escape and lived, half-hidden, in Toxteth Park, which was the poorest area of the city and not far from where their descendants are at home today (Ibid.: 13)

The second nucleus of the black population developed with African sailors who came in the 19th century. The slave trade had been abolished in 1807 (but was continued illegally), nevertheless the Elder Dempster Company still held a monopoly on the West African trade. White sailors regarded West Africa as a "white man's grave" because they often caught fatal diseases on the passages. In such cases, African sailors replaced them (Frost 1994: 91). The ships' captains liked these "Black Jacks" (as they called them) since they thought them less likely to drink and to misbehave. Supposedly, they were also better able to cope with the heat of both, the climate and the engine rooms of the steamships in use from the mid-19th century on. In Liverpool, they initially lived as transients in boarding houses, but often they later decided to stay. Except a few women employed in the boarding houses, the Africans were male. Many married white women. Having children, these couples contributed to the growth of Liverpool's black population through the 19th century (hence in a strict sense, the population became 'less black'). Until World War I, they worked almost exclusively as sailors. Opportunities to find employment elsewhere were extremely scarce (Ibid.: 92).

In 1911, there lived about 3,000 black people in Liverpool. By 1919, this number had grown to 5,000 (Gifford et al. 1989: 28). The reason for this increase was the war: black people replaced those factory workers who had become soldiers. Colonials took the occasion to settle and work in Britain. The numbers stagnated in the inter-war years because of lacking work opportunities and anti-immigrant laws, directed in particular against sailors. If black people became unemployed (as in the recession of the 1930s), they could be deported to the colonies as soon as they claimed social benefits. There were new jobs available during World War II, but soon afterwards Liverpool's long decline began. As a result, only very few of the 'typical' 1940s/50s New Commonwealth immigrants came to the city. The jobs on ships and in the docks disappeared in just a few years and it was difficult to find employment elsewhere – especially for black people. Abercrombie, the quarter of the city where they lived together with poor white people, was knocked down in the 1960s and they moved around the corner to Granby, part of Liverpool 8. In 1981, 20 per cent of Liverpool's population were unemployed, but in Liverpool 8 the number was 34.6 per cent (Gifford et al. 1989: 40) – and about 60 to 70 per cent of the young people in this area (Liverpool Black Caucus 1986: 17).

How did white people respond to the black presence? Not only slave merchants but the city as a whole profited from slavery. Also middle-class people bought small shares and thus participated in the trade – Liverpool developed into an early local shareholding society. Consequently, the city became a stronghold in the fight against the abolition of slavery. Many of the streets not named after slave merchants are named after local Members of Parliament who opposed the emancipation of slaves and the abolition of the trade (cf. Julienne 1994: 19). While the presence of a small number of slaves in upper-class houses was acceptable to white people, the presence of African sailors was less so, especially once they had begun to marry local white women. The following words stem from an Irish-Liverpudlian writer in the early 20th century. They demonstrate the uneasy feelings people had about these marriages:

> The fact, that most of the black fellows followed the sea had much to do with the local girls marrying them – much better, reasoned the girls to put up with a negro three months of the year (while drawing his steady salary) than to marry a young dock walloper and be continually starved and beaten. (quoted in Law 1981: 25)

While one could read this as admiration for the shrewdness of Liverpool women, it clearly reveals a total lack of comprehension of the idea that a white woman could really like or love a black man. Right from the start, racist myths disfigured these relationships. There was, especially in Victorian times, a certain fascination about black males' supposed sexual capacities. This, however, was suspected to cause moral and social problems, especially since many people believed that the white women having relationships with black men were prostitutes. The following quote is from a 1935 police report about a night club in the dock area with allegedly a "particularly revolting state of affairs":

> [It was] frequented by white and coloured and half-caste men and women. Nightly scene of obsessive drinking, foul language and filthy conduct, and dancing during which the grossest indecencies took place. Between and during the dancing indecent conduct between men and women was openly indulged in. The sanitary arrangements of this den were of the most primitive character. (quoted in Sherwood 1994: 15)

In port cities, clubs like this one were widespread. The reason for the police to single it out was that black people were involved, not the "indecent conduct" as such.

Most Liverpudlians were not happy with black and white people raising children in orderly families either. From the 1920s onwards, especially higher educated middle-class people engaged in a discourse on 'half-caste children'. They claimed these children to be degenerate and less healthy than others. On a 'meta-level' they argued that these children would never have chances of leading normal lives because of other people's prejudices. In the late 1920s some middle-class whites formed what they called the "Association for the Welfare of Half-Caste Children". They issued an "Investigation into the Colour Problem in Liverpool and other Ports" published by Liverpool University Press (Fletcher 1930). Their solution to the 'problem' of half-caste children's welfare was the suggestion to replace all black sailors working on Liverpool ships by white sailors.

This was not far from the ideas of many white sailors and dock workers. They opposed equal treatment of blacks and whites. In 1911, the National Union of Seamen achieved through strike action that black sailors were paid lower wages than whites. Later, however, they complained that blacks were employed as cheap labour. In 1919, at the height of the post-war recession, about 10,000 white people rioted in the area of black settlement. One man, Charles Wootton, was driven into the River Mersey and pelted with stones until he died.[5] After World War II, black people again were accused of stealing white people's jobs. The trade unions tried to keep them away from the few jobs created in the new lighter industries and the expanding public services. Further rioting occurred in 1948 (Liverpool Black Caucus 1986: 18).

Black people remained isolated. They shared with the poorest section of the white population what better-off whites regarded as a ghetto. The ideas of unstable families, undesirable sexual relationships, crime, and violence continued, though the term 'half castes' became slowly replaced by 'Liverpool-born blacks'. However, as late as 1978 a journalist described the situation in Liverpool in an article about Merseyside Police with the following words:

> Policemen in general, and detectives in particular, are not racialist [...]. Like any individual who deals with a vast cross-section of society, they tend to recognise that good and evil exist, irrespective of colour or creed. Yet they are the first to define the problem of half-castes in Liverpool. Many are the products of liaisons

---

[5] Today, the black population's independent community college bears his name.

between black seamen and white prostitutes in Liverpool 8, the red light district. Naturally, they do not grow up with any kind of recognisable home life. Worse still, after they have done the round of homes and institutions, they gradually realise that they are nothing. The negroes will not accept them as blacks, and the whites just assume they are coloureds. As a result, the half-caste community of Merseyside – or, more particularly, Liverpool – is well outside recognised society. (quoted in Gifford et al. 1989: 30)

Surviving on the Bermudas

In the 1980s, Liverpool's economic problems became even more severe. During this time the term 'Bermuda triangle of British capitalism' came into use. The city developed into a centre of opposition to the Conservative government in London and into a symbol of everything Margaret Thatcher and her political peers did not like. In journals there appeared headlines like "Thatcher to Liverpool: Drop Dead" (Jones 1985), or "Liverpool versus the 1980s" (Lane 1986). In the early 1980s, the Race and Social Policy Unit of Liverpool University showed in a substantial number of studies that the black population was disproportionately hit by economic decline and resulting social problems (e.g. Ben-Tovim 1983; Torkington 1983; Brown 1986).[6] Furthermore, they suffered from discrimination and disadvantages in all fields of public life – employment, education, housing, and health. In 1981, the 'Toxteth riots' (as they were called in the British press) had occurred[7] Therefore, the results of these studies managed to attract the attention of local politicians. The disturbances in Toxteth were on the one hand expressions of despair over the bleak socio-economic situation but on the other reactions to police behaviour. Police cars used to drive through Liverpool 8 and officers frequently stopped and searched young black men for ridiculous reasons. Britain's notorious Sus Law was always at hand to justify their provocative behaviour.[8] Margaret Simey, a Labour county councillor then and particularly concerned with police questions, told the following story:

> A typical tale of the time had it that a Black lad, returning from the laundrette with his mother's washing, was stopped by a policeman who enquired what was in the bag and to whom it belonged. The boy answered, adding that he lived just across

---

[6] The fieldwork in Liverpool contributed to one of the important Marxist analyses of racism and race relations in the 1980s: Gideon Ben-Tovim's and his collaborators' study *The Local Politics of Race* (1986).
[7] Toxteth is the name of a vague southern area of the city. Granby/Liverpool 8 is a part of Toxteth.
[8] Sus means "subject under suspicion" – the law could be used to control anybody disliked by the police.

the street and the officer was welcome to call and verify his story. Instead he was taken to the police station where, because of the rigour of his protest when stopped, he was charged with obstruction. His mother's arrival established the ownership of the washing all right but she expressed her indignation even more forcibly and was charged with disorderly behaviour. Both appeared in Court, were duly fined and placed on the records as 'criminals'. Neither charge related to the original reason for stopping the lad.

It was hard, on first hearing, to take this seriously [...]. Yet variations on this theme recurred so often [...] that it earned the label of the bagwash syndrome. (Simey 1988: 32)

A similar arrest in the summer of 1981 led to the Toxteth disturbances. The atmosphere was bitter because several youth clubs had been closed down by the police. Violence erupted, local people (black and white) attacked the police. A man was killed by a police van and houses were burnt down. British police used CS gas for the first time somewhere beyond Northern Ireland.

After the revolts it became obvious to Liverpool's local politicians that they had to do something in order to improve the situation of black people in the city.[9] As in other cities, the council tried to establish formal dialogue structures with the black population. In contrast to other cities, these attempts ended in confrontation rather than dialogue. The reasons for this can be found in the particular political strategies of the respective ruling parties. Until 1983, the Liberal Party held a majority of council seats. Their major interest was to maintain low rates.[10] From 1983 the council was under Labour control (the local party being dominated by the Trotskyist Militants). They were convinced that the main differences in society were class differences. Local politicians met with representatives of the black population in a 'Race Relations Liaison Committee'. The black activists' politics were strongly influenced by the US (and British) civil rights and black power movements. They demanded compensatory policies to redress the injustices of the past. The following years witnessed a continuous struggle between these two points of view. The Black Caucus (as the black representatives called themselves) wanted targets and timetables for increasing the number of black employees in the City Council. The Labour Party was opposed to this. The Black Caucus wanted 'ethnic monitoring' for the provision of social services in order to see whether providers considered, and dealt with, black people's

---

[9] For a detailed account of the controversies between the Militant Labour city council and the representatives of the black population see Berg 2000, especially pp. 251-280.

[10] Rates could be raised by local councils until 1989 when they were replaced by the Community Charge ("Poll Tax") and later the Council Tax. The amount is now regulated by central government.

needs. The Labour Party was opposed to this. The Black Caucus suggested a sheltered home for elderly black people, the Labour Party preferred to spend the whole housing budget on their 'Urban Regeneration Strategy'. The controversy reached its peak over the selection for the job of a Principal Race Relations Adviser (a race relations 'watchdog' in the city council). The Black Caucus wanted a person, who supported compensatory measures and who was local. The Labour Party wanted Sam Bond who was black, but from London, against compensatory policies and a follower of the Militant Labour line. After many allegations and counter allegations the communication between city councillors and black population broke down. While the early to mid-1980s were a time when several cities (for example London, Manchester, or Sheffield) introduced important programmes for their black people, Liverpool's Labour Party reinforced the view that the black population was not really part of the local working class, the people they claimed to fight for. After 1987, local councils had become too weak, in political as well as financial terms, in order to make a real difference. Thus although the new generation of Labour councillors elected in 1987 re-established dialogue structures, there was far less they could practically do.[11] Furthermore, many among these local politicians regarded Liverpool 8 as a ghetto whose problems were irrelevant for the city as a whole. Whereas in other cities black people made inroads into public sector employment, benefited from improved educational and social services, became in growing numbers elected as local councillors, and were promoted as an asset to local society in an increasingly cosmopolitan world, nothing like this took place in Liverpool. Even several interventions by the Commission for Racial Equality (Britain's central race relations 'watchdog') hardly changed the behaviour of the local administration (cf. Moore 1994).

In Liverpool, black people still have to fight their own struggles. To a certain degree, this might even be an advantage, because it gave Liverpool 8 a closely-knit social infrastructure with initiatives like Charles Wootton College, Liverpool 8 Law Centre, South Liverpool Personnel, Toxteth Health and Community Care Centre, and many others. Arguably, there is more congruence and solidarity here than among black people in other cities, where integration into council jobs and council politics caused splits along lines of class and influence. But on the other hand, the black population's social, economic, and political isolation remained through the 1990s. In the late

---

[11] The Militant councillors were barred from office in early 1987 because they had transcended legal limits in order to circumvent central government's financial restrictions (cf. Parkinson 1985, 1988).

1990s, there was one black councillor. Estimates about numbers of people in council employment vary heavily, but all indicate they are too low. In the mid-1990s, unemployment of black people was as high as 40 per cent. Black people still rely on white liberals in positions of power and on the Commission for Racial Equality for achieving political and social change (Christian 1997: 63). In 1861, a sympathetic policeman told Charles Dickens about the black people in Liverpool: "They generally kept together, the poor fellows, because they were at a disadvantage singly, and liable to slights in neighbouring streets." In 1998, Maria O'Reilly, the co-ordinator of Liverpool 8 Law Centre, told the newspaper *Independent*: "There are parts of North Liverpool where black people would not go alone after dark (...). Black families who have moved there also face a lot of harassment. What has improved in the last nine years? Next to nothing." (both quoted in Sengupta 1998: 4)

Community of Resistance

The Liverpool story is about the legacy of the slave and colonial trades and the related forced displacements and voluntary migrations of African people. Therefore it is the story of one of the oldest communities of British Africans in Britain. It is the story of people who were isolated through mechanisms of institutional racism (by politicians, trade unionists, the council bureaucracy), and criminalised (by the police). They reacted to all this with a lot of vigour. They formed – more intensively than many other 'black communities' – what veteran anti-racist activist A. Sivanandan called a "community of resistance" (1990: passim). Their successes, however, were only modest against politicians who prioritised low rates or, later, demanded unconditional support in the struggle with the Thatcher government or, still later, argued that Liverpool 8 should solve its problems on its own.

This means that integration (which, in order to make any sense at all, can only be defined as the possibility to participate in public life on an equal level) cannot be achieved as long as there is no political will to make it possible. Unfortunately, in the case of Liverpool, left-wing politics were primarily concerned with defending a white (male) working class in downward spirals of job insecurity, job loss, and poverty. The economic background to the neglect of black people's demands become clear enough once one looks at the dates of violent confrontations: 1919, 1948, and 1981 were points in time when economic problems became particularly severe. But as soon as one looks at the behaviour of the police, one notices that there is more to racism: it also includes discrimination based on negative stereotypes of pathological behaviour as result of undesirable sexual relationships, destroyed families, etc. Aggressive police behaviour towards black people provokes aggressive reactions, which seemingly prove the stereotypes and lead to even more aggressive policing. The point here is not about police bashing – but it seems sensible to assume that the police hold opinions that are widespread in society as a whole. This makes vicious circles of violence and counter-violence even harder to destroy.

Against this background, several of Britain's "race relations myths" need to be deconstructed:

1. The "immigration paradigm": Liverpool's example shows that minority people's problems do not automatically disappear after one or two generations, once immigrant children have adapted to 'British ways' – whether these are defined in terms of multiculturalism or not.

2. The idea that racism is either individual prejudice or deliberate 'blaming the victim' in order to explain away material inequalities which are inextricably linked with a capitalist economy: Liverpool demonstrates that both dimensions interact and reinforce each other.

3. The idea that social mobility is achievable without compensating for structural disadvantages: as long as there is economic marginalisation, it will be used as an argument for justifying racist exclusion.

Liverpool is also part of Northern England. The North's collective feeling of losing out, of being left behind, and the competition for scarce and poorly-paid jobs often takes the form of supposed competition between black and white people. Fascist groups use these feelings (as the confrontations in several Northern cities in the early summer of 2001 have shown), and they get support (as recent local elections have shown). Needed are both, policies to revitalise the social, economic, and cultural life of the run-down inner cities of the North, and to improve the situation of black people in the North. Unfortunately, today's understanding of 'integration' is a perverted one. From a new European far right (Le Pen, Fortuyn, Haider, Schill, etc.) to members of Britain's Labour government, the demand is on 'immigrants' to 'integrate' rather than on political actors to create conditions that allow equal participation in public life.[12] The response to such provocations is likely to be a "violence of the violated" (as Arun Kundnani [2001] pointedly called the

---

[12] For a detailed analysis on recent trends in British 'race relations' politics see Berg 2003.

disturbances of that year). The reasons for such violence are well summarised in a short poem by Leroi Cooper, written after the other disturbances – those of Liverpool 8 in 1981:

> *You wonder why we uprise*
> *Politically unstabilised*
> *Economically destabilised*
> *People dehumanised*
> *Youth criminalised*
> *Mentally vandalised*
> *Housing ghettoised*
> *Politically unrecognised*
> *And you wonder why we uprise.*
> (quoted in IRR 1986: 45)

References

ACKAH, WILLIAM AND MARK CHRISTIAN (eds.)
(1997). *Black Organisation and Identity in Liverpool. A Local, National and Global Perspective*. Liverpool: Charles Wootton College Press.
BEN-TOVIM, GIDEON (ed.)
(1983). *Equal Opportunities and the Employment of Black People and Ethnic Minorities on Merseyside*. Liverpool: Merseyside Association for Racial Equality in Employment, Merseyside Area Profile Group.
BEN-TOVIM, GIDEON ET AL.
(1986). *The Local Politics of Race*. Basingstoke: Macmillan.
BERG, SEBASTIAN
(2000). *Antirassismus in der britischen Labour Party. Konzepte und Kontroversen in den achtziger Jahren*. Frankfurt: Peter Lang.
(2003). "Multiculturalism and Racism in Blair's Britain." In Merle Tönnies, ed. *Britain under Blair*. Anglistik und Englischunterricht No. 65, 33-48.
BLACKBURN, ROBIN
(1998). *The Making of New World Slavery: from the Baroque to the Modern, 1492-1800*. London: Verso.
BROWN, WALLY
(1986). *Race, Class and Educational Inequality. A Case Study of Liverpool-born Blacks who have Experience in Higher Education*. Liverpool: Liverpool University, unpublished.
CHRISTIAN, MARK
(1997). "Black Identity in Liverpool. An Appraisal." In William Ackah, and Mark Christian, eds. *Black Organisation and Identiy in Liverpool: A Local, National and Global Perspective*. Liverpool: Charles Wootton College Press, 62-79.
FLETCHER, MURIEL
(1930). *Report on an Investigation into the Colour Problem in Liverpool and other Ports*. Liverpool: Liverpool University Press.

FROST, DIANE
(1994). "Ethnic Identity, Transience and Settlement: The Kru in Liverpool since the Late Nineteenth Century." In David Killingray, ed. *Africans in Britain*. Ilford: Frank Cass, 88-106.
FRYER, PETER
(1984). *Staying Power. The History of Black People in Britain*. London: Pluto Press.
GIFFORD, TONY ET AL.
(1989). *Loosen the Shackles. First Report of the Liverpool 8 Inquiry Team into Race Relations in Liverpool*. London: Karia Press.
INSTITUTE OF RACE RELATIONS
(1986). *The Fight against Racism. A Pictorial History of Asians and Afro-Caribbeans in Britain*. London: Institute of Race Relations.
JONES, MERVYN
(1985). "Thatcher to Liverpool: Drop Dead." *New Socialist* 33, 26-29.
JULIENNE, LOUIS
(1994). "Liverpool's Slave Trade Echoes in the Present." *Black Housing*, July-September, 19.
KUNDNANI, ARUN
(2001). "From Oldham to Bradford. The Violence of the Violated." *Race and Class* 43, No. 2, 105-110.
LANE, TONY
(1986). "We are the Champions. Liverpool versus the 1980s." *Marxism Today*, January, 8-11.
LAW, IAN
(1981). *Race and Racism in Liverpool, 1660-1950*. Liverpool: Merseyside Community Relations Council.
LIVERPOOL BLACK CAUCUS
(1986). *The Racial Politics of Militant in Liverpool. The Black Community's Struggle for Participation in Local Politics 1980-86*. London: Runnymede Trust.
LIVERPOOL CITY COUNCIL
(2002). *Race Equality Scheme 2002 and Race Equality Action Plan 2002-2005*. Liverpool: Liverpool City Council.
MOORE, ROBERT
(1994). "Crisis and Compliance. The Liverpool Non-Discrimination Notice 1989-1994." *New Community* 20: 4, 581-602.
PARKINSON, MICHAEL
(1985). *Liverpool on the Brink. One City's Struggle against Government Cuts*. Hermitage: Policy Journals.
(1988). "Liverpool's Fiscal Crisis. An Anatomy of Failure." In Michael Parkinson et al., eds. *Regenerating the Cities. The UK Crisis and the US Experience*. Manchester: Manchester University Press, 110-127.
SENGUPTA, KIM
(1998). "Liverpool's Blacks Still Facing Hard Times." *Independent* 25.03., 4.
SHERWOOD, MARIKA
(1994). *Pastor Daniels Ekarte and the African Churches Mission, Liverpool 1931-1964*. London: Savannah Press.

SIMEY, MARGARET
> (1988). *Democracy Rediscovered. A Study in Police Accountability.* London: Pluto Press.

SIVANANDAN, AMBALAVANER
> (1990). *Communities of Resistance. Writings on Black Struggles for Socialism.* London: Verso.

STEFFEN, JENS-PETER
> (1994). *Militant Tendency. Trotzkismus in der Labour Party.* Frankfurt: Peter Lang.

TAAFFE, PETER AND TONY MULHEARN
> (1988). *Liverpool. A City that Dared to Fight.* London: Fortress Books.

TORKINGTON, N. PROTASIA K.
> (1983). *The Racial Politics of Health. A Liverpool Profile.* Liverpool: Merseyside Area Profile Group, Department of Sociology, Liverpool University.

Not just Making the Faces Black: The Representation of African Americans in Contemporary Crime and Detective Fiction

KATRIN FISCHER
Chemnitz, Germany

ABSTRACT

This contribution to *Crossing Borders* approaches Africa from an entirely different perspective, and it does so in basically two respects: First, it shifts the prime focus of attention from the African to the North American continent and concentrates on the African *American* experience. With this, the article echoes a central premise of postcolonial literary theory: There are creative strategies common to writers belonging to marginalized and/or subordinated groups within all societies harmed by the remains and experiences of colonialism and/or racism. The most important of these strategies is appropriation – the transformation of a genre or a literary form through a new style, a different content, and/or a more political intention. This can be found not only in African literature but also in African Caribbean and – most notably – in African American writing. Secondly, this article puts a genre of popular culture at the center of interest, namely that of contemporary crime and detective fiction, which gives visibility and voice to authors and protagonists who are not of Anglo-American descent. Bringing these two angles of vision together results in a thorough exploration of the substantial critical potential of recent detective fiction, especially as regards the treatment of ethnic minorities and women in American society and literature.

Black characters appeared early on in the genre, and African Americans have been prolific writers of detective fiction almost from its beginnings in the 19th century. This paper traces milestones in the development of African American detective fiction (as a unique form of postcolonial literature), and it discusses the critical and subversive potential inherent in modern detective fiction written by African Americans. In studying the changing portrayal of Blacks and in examining more closely Valerie Wilson Wesley's on-going series about Black private investigator Tamara Hayle, the paper explores how the genre can be an effective device for discussing distinct African American concerns and cross-cultural themes. It argues that detective fiction – traditionally supposed to be apolitical and restricted to its basic formula – can be considered a barometer of changes of racial attitudes and indeed assume the function of a social document.

> The white woman, the African American, the gay man, the lesbian, abject characters who once inhabited the periphery of the detective's world, now take the center and appear as discursive subjects.
>
> Jeffrey Langham[1]

Chester Himes (1909-1984), considered to be one of the first African American mystery novelists and famous for his violence-laden, hard-boiled novels about Black detective duo Grave Digger Jones and Coffin Ed Johnson,[2] once remarked, with notable understatement: "I haven't created anything whatsoever, I just made the faces black, that's all."[3] The significance of Himes's Harlem detectives to the sub-genre of hard-boiled crime fiction proves the author's modest self-assessment wrong. He and other African American writers, both before and after him, have made important and unique contributions to the detective genre. Their first experiments with elements of the mystery and crime story reach back to Pauline Elizabeth Hopkins' (1859-1930) short stories "Talma Gordon" and "The Mystery Within Us", both published in 1900.[4] In "Talma Gordon", Hopkins addresses issues of miscegenation and explores the theme of the 'tragic mulatto'[5], who is torn between two different cultures. She also makes use of the locked-room device, successfully established earlier by Edgar Allan Poe (1809-1849) in his famous short story "The Murders in the Rue Morgue" (1841).[6] As Poe rose to fame as the 'father' of the detective story, so Hopkins can rightfully be

---

Thanks are due to Sebastian Berg for his helpful comments and critical response. I am grateful to Naomi Hallan for checking my manuscript from a native speaker's point of view.

[1] Jeffrey Langham, "Subject to Interrogation," *Multicultural Detective Fiction: Murder from the 'Other' Side*, ed. Adrienne Johnson Gosselin (New York: Garland, 1999) 107.

[2] For Himes see Peter Freese, *The Ethnic Detective: Chester Himes – Harry Kemelman – Tony Hillerman* (Essen: Blaue Eule, 1992) 15-90.

[3] John A. Williams, "My Man Himes: An Interview with Chester Himes," *Amistad 1*, eds. Johan A. Williams and Charles F. Harris (New York: Random House, 1970) 49.

[4] For Hopkins see John Cullen Gruesser, ed., *The Unruly Voice: Rediscovering Pauline Elizabeth Hopkins* (Urbana: U of Illinois P, 1996).

[5] For a discussion of the theme of the "tragic mulatto" see Frankie Y. Bailey, *Out of the Woodpile* (New York: Greenwod, 1991); Sterling Brown, "Negro Character as Seen by White Authors," *The Journal of Negro Education* 2 (1933): 179-203.

[6] In "The Murders in the Rue Morgue" Poe's detective, C. Auguste Dupin, investigates the razor-slashing deaths of two women in a seemingly inaccessible apartment. A body found in a sealed room adds the question of 'how' to the reader's curiosity about 'who done it.'

claimed as "the foremother of African American mystery fiction."[7] Among her distinguished literary heirs are Rudolph Fisher,[8] the above-mentioned Chester Himes, George Schuyler, Walter Mosley,[9] Eleanor Taylor Bland, Nikki Baker, Barbara Neely,[10] Valerie Wilson Wesley – on whose series about Black private investigator Tamara Hayle this essay will especially focus – and many others.

In approaching contemporary African American detective fiction as written by Valerie Wilson Wesley, it is important first to reconsider some aspects of the representation of Blacks in literature in general and in traditional detective fiction in particular. African American authors have been writing mystery fiction almost from its beginnings in the 19th century. Black characters also appeared early on in the genre – consider, for instance, Poe's Negro slave Jupiter in "The Gold Bug", one of the author's five tales of ratiocination.[11] Characters like Jupiter were created by white and African American authors alike, and they tended to fit popular stereotypes. For a long time, the depiction of Blacks in fiction was shaped by Euro-centric images of 'the Other' and – as Frankie Y. Bailey notes – restricted to variations of either the rural plantation slave or the urban slum dweller.[12] In his classic essay "Negro Character as Seen by White Authors" Sterling Brown explores common stereotypical images of African Americans in literature and differentiates the contented slave, the wretched freeman, the tragic mulatto, the exotic primitive, the brutish Negro and the local color Negro.[13] Writers freely took advantage of these and other ingrained racial clichés in order to

---

[7] Paula L. Woods, introduction, *Spooks, Spies & Private Eyes: An Anthology of Black Mystery, Crime, and Suspense Fiction of the 20th Century*, ed. Paula L. Woods (Edinburgh: Payback, 1996) xiii.
[8] For Fisher see Charles Heglar, "Rudolph Fisher and the African American Detective," *The Armchair Detective* 30:3 (1997): 301-305.
[9] For Mosley see Thomas Michael Stein, "The Ethnic Vision in Walter Mosley's Crime Fiction," *Amerikastudien – American Studies* 39.2 (1994): 197-212.
[10] Bland's novels depict detective Marti MacAlister, a middle-class African American policewoman. She first investigates in *Dead Time* (New York: St. Martin's, 1992). Baker's detective series starts with *In the Game* (Tallahassee: Naiad, 1991) and focuses on issues facing African American lesbians. Neely's detective character is Blanche White, a middle-aged African American domestic worker, who solves her first case in *Blanche on the Lam* (New York: Penguin, 1992).
[11] With his 'tales of ratiocination,' Poe created the detective story as a separate genre. The canon consists of three short stories starring Auguste Dupin: "The Murders in the Rue Morgue", "The Purloined Letter", "The Mystery of Marie Rogêt". Some critics – among them Dorothy Sayers – also include "Thou Art the Man" and "The Gold Bug".
[12] See Bailey, *Out of the Woodpile* xii.
[13] Brown, "Negro Character as Seen by White Authors" 179-203.

meet the primarily Anglo-American mystery readers' expectations, or, as Sally Munt has phrased it: "Writers have capitalized on a clichéd racism, using exotic characters to reinforce the White reader's comfortable conformity."[14]

The prototypical detective – anticipated by Poe's Parisian aristocrat Auguste Dupin and incarnated by Doyle's Sherlock Holmes, or, on the hard-boiled side, Chandler's Philip Marlowe and Hammett's Sam Spade – is invariably of white Anglo-Saxon ethnic origin and of male gender. He is a man whose superior mental capabilities make him a paragon of intelligence and rationality. He is a close reasoner, a born logician, an almost superhuman mastermind. At the opposite end of the scale are non-whites and females, who are often cast as incapacitated by their race and gender. As Sally Munt puts it: "Black man, because of his construction as non-thinking, non-rational, and non-literate, cannot deliver the denotation 'detective' easily."[15] Munt's statement holds true not only for African Americans but also for members of other ethnic minority groups and for women. In her essay "Desires and Devices: On Women Detectives in Fiction" Brigitta Berglund observes that "the overwhelming majority of detectives in fiction have until quite recently been men." Women, Berglund continues, "have been victims, or they have been perpetrators, but they have not, on the whole, been detectives – that is, they have not been given the most important part to play."[16] One of the traditional roles of women in crime fiction is as the investigator's ever-available secretary, and the hard-boiled detective's sexist attitude towards women is widely known: Hammett's Sam Spade and his equally tough and macho colleagues are made to regard members of the 'weaker sex' as "either children, sisters, angels or babes."[17] In these circumstances creating a non-white *and* female detective – who is not weak at all, but rather independent of male guidance and protection, and who herself is most successful in a male profession – appears to be a double violation of the genre's conventions.

Modern crime fiction from the 1970s onwards challenges traditional role scripts and power conceptions. It undermines binary oppositions between male and female, white and non-white, good and evil. Increasingly, it gives

---

[14] Sally R. Munt, "'A change is gonna come'? Race politics in crime fiction by women," *Murder by the Book? Feminism and the Crime Novel* (London: Routledge, 1994) 85.

[15] Sally R. Munt, "'A change is gonna come'? Race politics in crime fiction by women," *Murder by the Book? Feminism and the Crime Novel* (London: Routledge, 1994) 85.

[16] Brigitta Berglund, "Desires and Devices: On Women Detectives in Fiction," *The Art of Detective Fiction*, ed. Warren Chernaik, Martin Swales, and Robert Vilain (New York: St. Martin's, 2000) 138.

[17] Samuel Coale, *The Mystery of Mysteries* (Bowling Green: Bowling Green UP, 2000) 11.

visibility and voice to authors and protagonists who are not necessarily male and/or of Anglo-American descent. Thus, the popular genre participates in a broad trend towards diversity in literature and society. Alfred Hornung observes that: "In the course of the 1980s, the center of mainstream literature, formerly occupied by mostly male authors, loses its dominant, hegemonic position and leaves room for formerly marginalized female and ethnic authors."[18] A steadily growing appreciation of diversity in American society – whether it is cultural, religious, political, or sexual – is reflected in crime fiction. In 1977, Marcia Muller (1944-) broke new ground with the introduction of Sharon McCone in *Edwin of the Iron Shoes*. Sharon is considered the first female hard-boiled private eye of detective fiction. She can also be regarded a predecessor or early example of later female *ethnic* detectives,[19] because her heritage is Scots-Irish and Shoshone Indian.[20] The modern-day criminal investigator is no longer required to be white Anglo-Saxon and male. He or she may be an African American (as, for instance, Wesley's detective Tamara Hayle), a Native-American (as, for instance, Aimée and David Thurlo's Navajo Ella Clah),[21] an Australian Aborigine (as, for instance, Arthur W. Upfield's half-Aborigine 'Bony'), a Chicano (as, for instance, Lucha Corpi's Gloria Damasco), a homosexual (as, for instance, Barbara Wilson's lesbian Pam Nilson),[22] or even – as Robin Winks suggests –

---

[18] Alfred Hornung, "Postmodern – post mortem: Death and the Death of the Novel," *Neo-Realism in Contemporary American Fiction*. Ed. Kristiaan Versluys (Amsterdam: Rodopi, 1992) 97.
[19] The ethnic detective is defined by Peter Freese as "the criminal investigator who not only solves a murder mystery, be it by means of superior ratiocinative powers or daringly active interference, but who also introduces the reader to an unknown ethnic culture and thus assumes the function of a cultural mediator." (Freese, *The Ethnic Detective* 9)
[20] A talk between Sharon McCone and Gloria, daughter of Mexican immigrants, in *Wolf in the Shadows* reveals Sharon's ethnic origin: "How do you [Gloria] know I've [Sharon] had it so easy? You don't know anything about me – haven't even bothered to ask. I haven't experienced as much hardship as you, but my life hasn't been so wonderful, either. Especially not when it comes to prejudice. You may have noticed, although you never remarked on it, that I have Indian blood – I'm one-eighths Shoshone. Bigots don't like half-breeds – or eighth-breeds." (Marcia Muller, *Wolf in the Shadows* [New York: Mysterious, 1994] 81.)
[21] For an exploration of the representation of Native Americans in contemporary crime and detective fiction see Katrin Fischer, *'Time to Tear Down Barriers': Raum, Kultur und 'indianische' Identität im Kriminalroman* (Essen: Die Blaue Eule, 2003).
[22] In *Sisters in Crime* Maureen T. Reddy explores the potential of feminist crime fiction. With regard to crime fiction featuring lesbian detectives she writes: "Whereas hard-boiled detective fiction in particular, and conventional crime fiction generally, tends to objectify women as lawless, immoral predators who use their sexuality to destroy men, lesbian feminist crime fiction redefines the threat lesbians, and potentially all women, pose to men, which is actually threefold: (1) the threat of indifference; (2) the threat of changing the relations of the sexes by placing women at the center of concern; and (3) the threat of radically altering social power

"a dwarf, a child" or "a machine."²³ The fundamentally Western detective genre is no longer restricted to pre-coded representations of 'the Other.' In fact, it can serve as a valuable means to illuminate minority cultures that have long been neglected in North American literature and society. There are endless variations on the detective fiction formula, but – as Stephen Soitos and other critics note – in the finest examples of detective fiction answering the central question 'Who done it?' is closely connected to an exploration of issues of race, class and gender.²⁴ One striking example of the incorporation of race, class, and gender into the detective genre is the series by African American author Valerie Wilson Wesley.²⁵ In examining her series²⁶ more closely, I will explore how the crime genre can be used as an effective device for discussing the distinct African American experience, including African American women's concerns and a variety of intricate cross-cultural themes. In what follows, I will show that by simultaneously employing and subverting established detective fiction formulas, Wesley manages to adapt the Euro-Americentric genre's conventions to contemporary African American societal questions and concerns.

* * *

The central character in Wesley's detective series is Tamara Hayle, a thirty-something, wise and witty African American woman. She makes her living as a private investigator in Newark, New Jersey, where she has acquired a reputation as "the best P.I. [private investigator] in Essex County" (DGGH 1). She is a divorced mother struggling to make a living for herself and her teenage son Jamal. In *When Death Comes Stealing* – the series' debut novel – Tamara has already been five years in the P.I.-business, and she is said to be

---

relations through a moral vision that does not assume the value of hierarchical order and that does consistently value women's relations to other women." (130-131)
²³ Robin W. Winks, introduction, *Detective Fiction: A Collection of Critical Essays*, ed. Robin W. Winks (Woodstock: Countryman, 1988) 8.
²⁴ See Stephen F. Soitos, *The Blues Detective* (Amherst: U of Massachusetts P, 1996) 17.
²⁵ Valerie Wilson Wesley is a contributing editor of *Essence*, the world's highest circulation Black women's magazine. She is a graduate of Howard University and has earned masters' degrees from Bank Street College of Education and Columbia Graduate School of Journalism. She lives in New Jersey with her husband, screenwriter and playwright Richard Wesley, and their two daughters. (For biographical information see <http://www.vrz.net/bsz/4/wesley.htm> and <http://www.tamarahayle.com>).
²⁶ Six books have been published so far: *When Death Comes Stealing* (=WDCS, 1994), *Devil's Gonna Get Him* (= DGGH, 1995), *Where Evil Sleeps* (=WES, 1996), *No Hiding Place* (=NHP, 1998), *Easier to Kill* (1998), *The Devil Riding* (2000). Almost all Tamara Hayle mysteries were translated into German and published by Diogenes Verlag.

able to handle anything that comes her way, from disappearances and insurance fraud to grand larceny and even homicide. In the series opener, Jamal's father, DeWayne Curtis, calls on his sleuthing ex-wife for help. DeWayne is convinced that someone is systematically murdering all his children from his previous marriages and extramarital affairs, and he wants Tamara to find the murderer before Jamal, Tamara's and DeWayne's son, becomes the next victim.

According to traditional genre conventions, the investigator has to be an emotionally uninvolved outsider. Here, however, Tamara herself is deeply affected by what is going on. It soon becomes clear to both Tamara and the reader that being an outsider would not constitute an advantage in solving the case. Since the murders occurred in Newark's black community, a detective is needed who is not only a professional but also familiar with African American concerns. The novels imply that only someone whose sympathies lie with African Americans will be successful in the quest for truth and knowledge. Tamara relies on her connections in the Black community to get the information she needs for determining motives and checking alibis. Her being African American becomes, as will be shown in detail below, an essential factor for the success of her investigative work. She recognizes the advantages of her own African American-ness as well as what her being Black means to other characters in the series. Issues of race, class, and gender are inextricably interwoven in Wesley's series. Problems resulting from Tamara's ethnicity and sex are first touched on when she reveals information about her time as an officer in Newark's police force. The reader learns that after five years on the beat, she decided (or, to be more precise, was forced) to quit as a police officer. Her main motives for leaving the police are to be found in the roles and identities involuntarily assigned to minorities and women. Her daily experiences as an African American woman in a male-centered profession as well as the officially sanctioned disregard for minority groups in American society made (and, as it becomes obvious in the course of the series, still make) her furious. At the beginning of the series, the reader is made aware of the reasons why Tamara opted to start her own business rather than to stay in the police force. In the opening chapter of *When Death Comes Stealing*, Tamara recounts her achievements in life and reflects that:

> There are three things in this life I cherish: my independence, my son, Jamal, and my peace of mind. [...] In the past few years, I've managed to clear my life of things that aggravate my spirit: I used to be a cop. Some might say I couldn't handle the shit I was supposed to put up with – being black, being a woman – and I guess that's about right. I knew who I was and I wouldn't let them change it. I quit

five years ago and Hayle Investigative Services, Inc., was born. Since then I've changed lots of things. (WDCS 6)

Being Black and being a woman gave Tamara a hard time in the white, male-dominated microcosm of Newark's police force. Although she performed her professional duties extremely well, she was frequently discriminated against on grounds of her race and sex. Wesley's detective series knits tightly together the two contentious discourses of gender and ethnicity. It thus echoes Steve Fenton's observations on parallels between sex discrimination and racial discrimination. In his book *Ethnicity: Racism, Class and Culture*, Fenton points out that "[t]he patterns of gender differentiation frequently take a form similar to ethnic differentiation."[27] Tamara's sobering experiences in the police force are modeled on problems female and non-white cops have to face in reality – a fact that clearly shows the critical potential inherent in recent detective fiction by and about African Americans. Confronted with Tamara's experiences, the reader is made aware of the all-too-present dark side of real policing, as described by Victor Kappeler and others. Kappeler states the obvious when he writes: "Most officers have problems in working with female officers and dislike working with them because they believe women don't have the physical stature to do the job."[28] The policing profession remains a bastion of male chauvinism, and the problems female officers have to cope with in the line of duty are a recurrent topic in contemporary crime and detective fiction. Aimée and David Thulo's Navajo detective Ella Clah, for instance, lives and works as an FBI agent in Los Angeles – a job she later abandons in favor of a more rewarding career as a Navajo Tribal Policewoman. From the very beginning of the series, Ella is characterized as an outsider among her white, male peers. Her problems are very similar to Tamara's. Both minority women know from experience that:

> [G]uys, no matter what P.D. [Police Department] they serve in, tend to resent the presence of women [...] They put on their badges, and that becomes their trademark. They want the world to believe they are the biggest, baddest guys around, and the crooks should all be shaking in their boots. Then they see someone else wearing a badge, only she's prettier to look at, and undoubtedly smells nicer. It sorta smashes the tough-guy image they cherish in their little hearts.[29]

---

[27] Steve Fenton, *Ethnicity: Racism, Class and Culture* 53.
[28] Victor Kappeler, Richard Sluder, and Geoffrey Albert, *Forces of Defiance: Understanding the Dark Side of Policing* (Prospect Heights: Waveland, 1994) 173-174.
[29] Aimée and David Thurlo, *Death Walker* (New York: Tom Doherty, 1996) 15-16.

As a woman (traditionally stereotyped as being weak and unfit for handling tough matters) and as an African American (traditionally stereotyped as being "non-thinking, non-rational, and non-literate"[30] and, therefore, inferior to the white race), police officer Tamara Hayle was (and still is) doubly marginalized. However, in making Tamara a strong, self-confident, independent African American woman, who knows who she is and who stoutly protects her own interests, Wesley subverts the roles conventionally given to women and to members of ethnic groups. She critiques normative perceptions of race and gender, and thus not only participates in an ongoing societal debate about diversity and difference but also in the reversal of role ascription, essential to detective fiction by female and ethnic authors.

In *Sisters in Crime: Feminism and the Crime Novel* Maureen T. Reddy examines recent crime fiction by women. She detects a "countertradition" and an "essential subversiveness"[31] which comments on historical as well as social issues. Wesley's (as well as Aimée and David Thurlo's) series is a case in point. Again, the reader is reminded of the unjust treatment and neglect of minorities in American society. Tamara's former colleagues in the police force are said to have been almost totally ignorant about cases involving African Americans. This naturally fueled Tamara's anger and frustration and speeded her decision to leave the force. Briefing her close friend Basil Dupre on the details of the murder of Terrence, DeWayne's oldest son from a previous marriage, Tamara remarks bitterly:

> You know as well as me how casual cops are when black kids die. Nobody really gives a shit. They'll call Terrence's death the easiest thing they can call it so they can go on to something else. (WDCS 75-76)

Some "lazy cop, tired at the end of the day or late for lunch" (WDCS 34) had opted for "the easy way out" (WDSC 34), proclaimed that Terrence had lived and died a junkie, and simply closed the book on the case. For Tamara this practice is just another instance of "the official incompetence" and "the bullshit so many [white] cops put down when it comes to black folks" (WDCS 34). A talk with Lincoln Storey, Newark's wealthiest Black businessperson and Tamara's prospective client in *Devil's Gonna Get Him*, throws even more light on her reasons for leaving the police:

---

[30] Munt, "A change is gonna come" 85.
[31] Maureen T. Reddy, *Sisters in Crime: Feminism and the Crime Novel* (New York: Continuum, 1988) 2.

"Do you [Tamara] find this line of work [being a P.I.] hard for a woman, a black woman?"
"No harder than being a cop." [...]
"Why did you leave?"
"I got sick of it," I [Tamara] said [...].
"Sick of ..."
"Sick of being called a nigger bitch by my brethren in blue every day of my beat," I said, the old anger surfacing again, coloring the edge of my words. (5)

In addition, while interrogating a white woman in *When Death Comes Stealing*, her irritation at being discriminated on grounds of her African American-ness flashes up again. Although she justly feels offended, she deals professionally with the situation and suppresses her anger:

> I [Tamara] couldn't believe what she'd just said! Who you calling a nigger, white girl? I hadn't heard a white person say that word since I'd left the Department and heard it every day. My reaction was pure reflex: I pushed the anger down to that place inside me where I'd always put it when I'd been on the force. Nigger bitch. Nigger whore. Nigger bastard. Nigger son of a bitch. I'd heard it so much it had lost its meaning. Just another word. I tried to empty my face of any emotion, but she sensed it anyway. (WDCS 86-87)

As a self-confident Black woman, proud of her heritage, Tamara was not willing to tolerate the daily racist and sexist slurs any longer. She handed in her resignation and opted to start her own investigation business with the promising name of Hayle Investigative Services, Inc.

Wesley skillfully integrates African American concerns into her detective plots, her settings and, of course, the depiction of her characters. In doing so, she recasts the hard-boiled genre conventions to suit her non-stereotypical detective. Tamara's office – situated on the corner of Main Street and South Harrison in the area of East Orange – seems to be a recasting of the tough guy's workplace. The building "looks like shit", as Tamara says, and on entering, "a singular odor, somewhere between cabbage and burnt meatloaf, hits you like a fist" (WDCS 61). The headquarters of Hayle Investigative Services consist of a single large room, sparsely furnished and with an "orphan aloe plant" (WDCS 62) on the windowsill. The plant lends some color to the room, which otherwise appears "as dull as bad gravy" (WDCS 62). At first glance, even Tamara herself appears to be an updated, ethnically defined version of the self-confident but alienated 'tough guy' of the American hard-boiled school. However, unlike Philip Marlowe, Chandler's detective and narrator, who lives and works alone, Tamara is part of a larger community. Instead of drawing strength from being isolated (most common among her white and male precursors in the realm of hard-boiled detection), she relies on a tight-knit female network and on her manifold connections in Newark's Black community to make progress in solving her cases. Her primarily female friends support her in her business as well as in private matters. Tamara's bosom friend throughout the series is Annie, from whom she also rents her office space. Tamara and Annie have been close since school days, and Tamara describes their relationship as "get-down-to-the-dirt, nitty-gritty friends like me and Annie" (DGGH 15). Another friend and aide is Wyvetta, the eccentric owner of 'Jan's Beauty Biscuit,' a rather strange shop "specializing in perms, long nails and longer weaves" (WDCS 60). Jan's is Tamara's favorite place for getting information on what is going on in and around Newark, because:

> You can always find out what's going on in East Orange from Wyvetta or her loudmouthed, gold-toothed boyfriend, Earl. All kinds of sisters – schoolteachers, church ladies, women of "questionable repute" – drop into the Biscuit for services, and if you sit long enough with your mouth shut, you're liable to find out anything you need to know about anybody. (WDCS 60-61)

When the need arises, Tamara and her friends barter services. So, Tamara once did a week of surveillance on a relative of Wyvetta in exchange for "a free perm, two make-ups, and a couple of manicures" (WDCS 61). Tamara's phone calls are automatically redirected to Karen, another friend of hers. Karen, "the efficient-sounding sister" (WDCS 63), always takes Tamara's messages, to give the caller the impression that Hayle Investigative Services, Inc., is more than a tiny one-person business.

Chandler's Philip Marlowe and his equals did not have much of a private life. They lived lonely, fragmented lives in the 'mean streets' of Los Angeles's or some other big American city's urban jungle. As Ralph Willett argues in *The Naked City*, a study of urban settings in American crime fiction, Los Angeles appears as "a city of strangers",[32] where community claims and community ties remain weak. The depiction of L.A. enhances the impression that the traditional hard-boiled detective's life as well as his surroundings are without context and identity.[33] Tamara Hayle, on the contrary, does not feel alienated in Newark. The series not only casts light on her good relations with the local community but also on her private life and daily routine. She is the single parent of a teenage son – a role which challenges her at least as much

---

[32] Ralph Willett, *The Naked City* (Manchester: Manchester UP, 1996) 20.
[33] See Willett, *The Naked City* 22.

as her detective work. Jamal's growing-up is given a great deal of attention in the series. His inclusion in the books opens an opportunity for the author to discuss problems young Black men have to face in American society. Jamal's "coming-into-black-manhood changes" (DGGH 18) are accompanied by a complicated, and often painful, search for identity. The intricacies of her son's search for identity and his attempts to create a place for himself in society give Tamara cause for concern. In *Devil's Gonna Get Him*, she reflects on Jamal's recently adopted way of dressing and behaving and criticizes racial prejudice against African American males:

> In the last couple of months, Jamal had adapted a slightly roguish, male teenage style that I wasn't completely comfortable with. Black men carry the weight of other's people's meanness, and I was always afraid that some fool would judge my son by some thug whose mug he'd just seen on the six o'clock news. But my good friend Jake, whom I increasingly turn to for explanations of Jamal's coming-into-black-manhood changes, had assured me that this adaptation of toughness is a natural part of finding his identity. Besides, the real deal is that when it comes to the way America judges the brothers, even a Brooks Brothers suit and Coach briefcase didn't count for shit. More often than not, a black male is viewed as a felon no matter what he puts on, so I should just let the boy dress the way he wanted to. (18-19)

Jake, whom Tamara relies on for insights into Jamal's attitudes and behavior, is described as a "'race man': one of those brothers who will always fight the good fight, a living challenge to every lie that was ever told about black folks – a man in the tradition of Malcolm X, Frederick Douglass, Nelson Mandela" (DGGH 120). However, Valerie Wilson Wesley's view on matters of race, class, and gender is not simplistic. In her series, she does not just invert the conventional detective formula in which white equals good and Black equals bad. Rather than relying on a plain "'positive images' strategy",[34] she presents a multi-faceted picture of society, in which good and evil are not distributed along racial or cultural lines. Anglo-Americans and African Americans alike are cast in the roles of both culprits and victims. Racial hatred and violence are not restricted to white people against Blacks. They are (or at least were) a frequent issue in the Black community as well, which becomes clear when Tamara remembers what her grandmother once told her:

> During one of our talks about what ailed the world, she'd [Tamara's grandmother] told me that once upon a time, if you were darker than a paper bag, you couldn't get into certain 'respectable colored' establishments or marry into certain families. [...] My grandfather was dead by the time I was born, but Grandma still talked bad

---

[34] Munt, "'A change is gonna come'?" 90.

about his people. I remembered their ancient, sepia-colored wedding picture, Grandma's skin the deepest, prettiest brown I'd ever seen against his, the color of cream. His family had been mad because he'd married 'too dark.' (DGGH 44-45)

The issue of skin color is taken up and discussed repeatedly in Wesley's series. The reader learns that Tamara herself was the victim of an abusive mother, who wanted to 'knock her Black off': *"Knocking the black off. That was what she called it when she beat me [Tamara], which was often and without mercy. Knocking the black off, as if she were determined to go to the center of who I was and erase it."* (DGGH 50-51) And later in *Devil's Gonna Get Him* Tamara recognizes with embarrassment that her own thinking and acting is influenced by "the color thing" (133) and that she herself is not free of prejudices:

> You're too dark to be pretty; you must be smart.
>
> I'd grown up during the 1960s, the Black Is Beautiful years, but that voice still fixed itself in the head of kids like me, too loud to be silenced in a decade.
>
> As Daphne Storey rose to meet me and extended her hand, I realized with unexpected shame that from the first moment I had seen her, I had judged her, disliked her because of the color of her skin, and for what I assumed that color had always brought her.
>
> The pretty ones weren't supposed to look like me. They looked like Daphne Storey, with skin the color of cream and hair that cascaded down their backs, the only kind of black woman a 'successful' black man like Lincoln Storey was supposed to want, the closest he could get to a white woman because he'd been told and believed that women who looked like his mother had no value.
>
> If you're light, you're alright. If you're brown, stick around. If you're black, get back. (DGGH 133)

In her detective series, Valerie Wilson Wesley explores issues of cultural interaction, among which race, class, culture, gender, and ethnicity feature prominently. She creates a new image of the hard-boiled detective based on multicultural needs. Tamara investigates from the borderlands of gender as well as race. Being a female private eye gives her "the right to cross borders previously closed, [and] to unfix definitions, [and] to ramble through society with a mobility long considered exclusively masculine".[35] Being an African American opens doors closed to white detectives. Tamara possesses the capacity to bridge cultures. She has access to both cultures, the mainstream's Anglo-American and her inherited African American, and she uses her double knowledge to solve her cases. Occasionally, she voluntarily takes up roles traditionally assigned to minority women. In playing these roles to perfection,

---

[35] Ruby B. Rich, 24.

she outwits her 'masters' and singles out the murderer among the suspects. In *Devil's Gonna Get Him*, she is hired by Lincoln Storey to investigate the relationship between his stepdaughter and a filmmaker, who also happens to be an ex-lover of Tamara. When Storey drops dead at a fundraising party, Tamara continues the investigation in order to protect the sister of a good friend who is accused of the murder. While tailing Brandon Pike, Storey's prospective son-in-law and Tamara's old flame, she muses on her favorite strategy of disguising as a "pleasant young Negress":

> It's easy to follow somebody who doesn't know you from nothing, especially if you're black and a woman. The world takes you for granted then, and you're always somebody's something else – sister-lady ringing up the groceries or sweeping up the floor. I do my best work when people are limited by their own expectations. I smile a lot. Flash my toothiest grin. I've even been known to bend my head slightly and nod a bit to the left. A pleasant young Negress. A dependable, unassuming presence. (DGGH 25)

Tamara uses her race- and gender-based invisibility to her own advantage and thus debunks the stereotype of the stupid black helpmeet. Black investigators, Soitos notes in his study of African American detective fiction, "use their own blackness to mask their true identities as detectives."[36] Disguise and masking, he argues, are essential ingredients in African American detective fiction, which connect the trope of double consciousness to the trickster tradition. Traces of this subtle, yet highly successful approach can be found early on in the development of the genre. Consider, for instance, Rudolph Fisher's *The Conjure-Man Dies* (1932), the first mystery novel written by an African American author featuring African American characters and set in the Black community. In chapter two, Perry Dart, Fisher's "bright, alert, and practical" (14) Harlem detective, is introduced, and the reasons for assigning him to New York's Harlem district are given:

> Of the ten Negro members of Harlem's police force to be promoted from the rank of patrolman to that of detective, Perry Dart was one of the first. As if the city administration had wished to leave no doubt in the public mind as to its intention in the matter, they had chosen, in him, a man who could not have been under any circumstances mistaken for aught but a Negro; or, perhaps, as Dart's intimates insisted, they had chosen him because his generously pigmented skin rendered him invisible in the dark, a conceivably great advantage to a detective who did most of his work at night. (14)

* * *

---

[36] Stephen Soitos, *The Blues Detective* (Amherst: U of Massachusetts P, 1996) 18.

As a Western cultural product, detective fiction had long been considered inadequate for the discussion of cross-cultural and ethnic themes. John G. Cawelti, in a discussion of Arthur William Upfield's detective serial about the half-Aboriginal Napoleon Bonaparte (called Bony), claims that the "angle of vision enforced by the classical detective story is inevitably a limited one, because its basic assumptions are bound to the social and ideological patterns of Western bourgeois democracies of the nineteenth and twentieth centuries." (39) The standard detective formula, the writer argues, "seems to require the importation of certain presuppositions about society, law and morality from the Anglo-American tradition" (39) and thus to prohibit "the expression of deeper and more complex cultural perspectives" (39). While Cawelti's statement holds true for the vast majority of novels written during the 'Golden Age' of detective fiction – the heyday of the genre in Great Britain between the First and Second World War – it cannot be applied to the current state of affairs. Today's mystery writers prove Cawelti wrong. In an attempt to do more than to simply delight their readership with the puzzling aspects of a crime, they include substantial social and cultural information in their detective plots. If the criminal investigator is removed from his or her conventional Euro-American environment, detective fiction – traditionally supposed to be apolitical and restricted to its basic formula – assumes the function of a social document. In these cases, the detective's quest for restoring order "inadvertently turns into an illustration of ethnic friction and cultural confrontation and thus into a comment on the challenges of everyday life in a 'multicultural' society."[37] Authors like Valerie Wilson Wesley do not just make the faces black. Rather, they use established detective conventions to explore issues of African American identity, color consciousness, racism, and sexuality. For them, the mystery form functions as a valuable tool for expressing a social critique of mainstream attitudes towards race, class, and gender.

---

[37] Freese, *The Ethnic Detective* 9-10.

References

BAILEY, FRANKIE Y.
(1991). *Black Characters in Crime and Detective Fiction*. New York: Greenwood Press.

BERGLUND, BRIGITTA
(2000). "Desires and Devices: On Women Detectives in Fiction." In Warren Chernaik, Martin Swales, and Robert Vilain, eds. *The Art of Detective Fiction*. New York: St. Martin's, 138-152.

BROWN, STERLING
(1933). "Negro Character as Seen by White Authors." *The Journal of Negro Education* 2, 179-203.

CAWELTI, JOHN G.
(1977). "Murder in the Outback." *The New Republic* 30 July, 39–41.

COALE, SAMUEL
(2000). *The Mystery of Mysteries. Cultural Differences and Designs*. Bowling Green: Bowling Green UP.

DEANDREA, WILLIAM L.
(1994). *Encyclopedia Mysteriosa: A Comprehensive Guide to the Art of Detection in Print, Film, Radio, and Television*. New York: Prentice Hall.

FISCHER, KATRIN
(2003). *'Time to Tear Down Barriers': Raum, Kultur und 'indianische' Identität im Kriminalroman*. Essen: Die Blaue Eule.

FISHER, RUDOPLH
(1992). *The Conjure-Man Dies: A Mystery Tale of Dark Harlem*. 1932. Ann Arbor: U of Michigan P.

FREESE, PETER
(1992). *The Ethnic Detective: Chester Himes – Harry Kemelman – Tony Hillerman*. Essen: Die Blaue Eule.

GOSSELIN, ADRIENNE JOHNSON (ed.)
(1999). *Multicultural Detective Fiction: Murder from the 'Other' Side*. New York: Garland.

GRUESSER, JOHN CULLEN (ed.)
(1996). *The Unruly Voice: Rediscovering Pauline Elizabeth Hopkins*. Urbana: U of Illinois P.

HEGLAR, CHARLES
(1997). "Rudolph Fisher and the African American Detective." *The Armchair Detective* 30:3, 300-305.

HOPKINS, PAULINE E.
(1996). "Talma Gordon." In Paula L. Woods, ed. *Spooks, Spies and Private Eyes*. Edinburgh: Payback, 2-19.

JABLON, MADELYN AND REHOBOTH BEACH
(1996). "'Making the Faces Black': The African American Detective Novel." In Larry E. Smith and John Rieder, eds. *Changing Representations of Minorities East and West*. Honolulu: U of Hawaii, 26-40.

MATTER-SEIBEL, SABINA
(2001). "'A Medium-boiled P.I.': Interview mit Valerie Wilson Wesley." In Carmen Birkle, Sabina Matter-Seibel, and Patricia Plummer, eds. *Frauen auf der Spur: Kriminalautorinnen aus Deutschland, Großbritannien und den USA*. Tübingen: Stauffenburg Verlag, 115-133.

MULLER, MARCIA
(1977). *Edwin of the Iron Shoes*. New York: McKay.
(1994). *Wolf in the Shadows*. New York: Mysterious.

SOITOS, STEPHEN F.
(1996). *The Blues Detective. A Study of African American Detective Fiction*. Amherst: U of Massachusetts P.

STEIN, THOMAS MICHAEL
(1994). "The Ethnic Vision in Walter Mosley's Crime Fiction." *Amerikastudien – American Studies* 39:2, 197-212.

WESLEY, VALERIE WILSON
(1995). *Devil's Gonna Get Him*. New York: HarperCollins.
(1998). *No Hiding Place*. New York: HarperCollins.
(1994). *When Death Comes Stealing*. New York: HarperCollins.
(1996). *Where Evil Sleeps*. New York: HarperCollins.

WILLEN, MARGARET M.
(1997). "Saying Ourselves: Women of Color Writing Detective Fiction." *Clues: A Journal of Detection* 18:2 (Fall/Winter 1997), 43-57.

WILLET, RALPH
(1996). *The Naked City: Urban Crime Fiction in the USA*. Manchester: Manchester UP.

WILLIAMS, JOHN A. AND CHARLES F. HARRIS (eds.)
(1970). *Amistad 1*. New York: Random House.

WINKS, ROBIN (ed.)
(1988). *Detective Fiction: A Collection of Critical Essays*. Woodstock: Countryman.

WOODS, PAULA L. (ed.)
(1996). *Spooks, Spies & Private Eyes: An Anthology of Black Mystery, Crime, and Suspense Fiction of the 20th Century*. Edinburgh: Payback.

African Popular Theatre in Diasporas: Racism and Identity

EMELDA NGUFOR SAMBA
Yaoundé, Cameroon
SEBASTIAN BERG
Chemnitz, Germany

> *When we come to see things differently, to perceive the natural and the social worlds through different lenses, we pursue avenues for re-experiencing the conventional or the taken for granted.* (Landon E. Beyer 2000: 144)

Introduction

In this paper we attempt a discussion on the adaptability of African popular theatre (APT) in a European setting. Our illustration is a popular theatre workshop we conducted in 2002 on *Racism and Identity* at the University of Chemnitz in Germany. The theatre workshop was part of the activities in celebration of the *Afrika in Chemnitz* weeks that were organised within the English Department. The paper describes in detail the workshop process and provides a glimpse of the immediate transformation in the performers' and audiences' sensitivity of racism and identity.

Popular theatre is an inside-out method of development that creates forums for socially disadvantaged and marginalised groups to identify their problems, analyse them and seek solutions to them. Popular theatre, which is in essence participatory, is deeply rooted in Paulo Freire's *Pedagogy of the Oppressed* and *Pedagogy of Hope* that propound a teaching for oppressed people in search for their liberation. The former emphasises collective action that could lead to positive social and attitudinal changes among oppressed groups on the one hand and their oppressors on the other. The latter offers hope and dream as the key to understanding human existence, and the struggle needed to improve it. Freire (1992, 1999: 9), maintains that as an ontological need,

> hope needs practice in order to become historical concreteness...Hope as it happens is so important for our existence, individual and social, that we must take every care not to experience it in a mistaken form, and thereby allow it to slip into hopelessness and despair.

In Freire's pedagogy, the hope to induce social change is the driving force that motivates marginalised people to engage in political processes expressed in ideological and pedagogical struggles. Augusto Boal's *Theatre of the Oppressed* takes off from Freire's pedagogies as the starting point for a theatrical expression that makes use of improvisational tools as opposed to rote learning of lines, which is characteristic of mainstream theatre. The affinity between Freire's pedagogy and Boal's theatrical forms lies in their participatory approach in problematisation. In both cases, the masses, whom Frantz Fanon refers to as the "wretched of the earth", and Boal as "spec-actors" collectively investigate the sources of their problems, seek and propose solutions to them. While Freire's pedagogy is limited to dialogical learning, Boal extends Freire's dialogics to improvisational theatre that creates room for all possibilities to be examined in a play situation. This method of collective play-creation has a number of advantages for the performers. Primarily, the ideas or thematic content of the plays created come from the people themselves and the plays are performed in the people's own language(s). Because the masses are involved in critical intervention about their reality, they cease to be objects of that reality and emerge as subjects capable of designing their history. Additionally, the artistic devices spec-actors employ in communicating messages of social change are reflective of their cultural repertoire. More so, the active participation of the spec-actors at almost all levels of play-production helps to build in them a sense of responsibility and ownership of the entire process. The participatory nature of this kind of theatre also heightens the level of community commitment in affecting attitudinal and practical changes during the play-creation process and long after the project is over. This brings us to the relationship between Freire's liberating pedagogy and Boal's theatre of the oppressed on the one hand, and African Popular Theatre on the other.

African Popular Theatre borrows generously from Traditional African theatrical forms and Boal's dramatic aesthetics. Traditional African theatre is immediate, lively and deals with issues that are relevant to the community. It is a participatory activity that engages the community at the levels of creation, improvisation, and performance. Courtyards constitute the stage, and the natural environment provides a natural backdrop for performances. The entire community are at one and the same time actors/actresses and the audience. Their intervention takes the form of ululation, hand clapping, singing, dancing and sometimes direct confrontation with the main performers. The story lines of the performances revolve around daily events in the community or mythical and legendary heroes. Traditional African theatre therefore lends itself to a people's sense of themselves as communities in processes of self-identification, self-assertion, popular mobilisation, and cultural action for change. Often it highlights the relationship between cultural expressions and a people's overall socio-economic structure, and expresses strong traditional values and attitudes that validate these structures (Mlama 1991).

African popular theatre is an aesthetic experience that is tied to social and cultural change. Its dramatic form provides a popular medium of entertainment and instruction, which is sufficiently indigenous to appeal to audience needs for an African aesthetic. Songs, dance, mime, and story-telling constitute the main forms of communication. Their inclusion in theatre performances enhances community participation, validate the culture of the exploited majority, and help interpret changing socio-economic mores. Popular theatre therefore provides a forum for oppressed groups to collectively seek ways of transforming negative personal and group experiences into forward-looking strategies for a better living. As an art form, it moves both performers and audiences to new ways of thinking and of doing things, that is, it helps to shape their consciousness, informs them and thus radically changes their perception of life, their very existence as human beings.

There is hardly any fixed methodology for African Popular Theatre. Different practitioners have adopted different approaches depending on the situation 'on the ground'. In some cases, theatre practitioners have taken tailored-cut plays to people on themes they esteem important to them. In an attempt to make the plays content and culture effective, adjustments are made to the plays and members of the community are integrated into the performance in the final stage of the production. This gives a semblance of community participation whereas in reality there is an imposition of expert ideas, culture, language and theatrical devices on the people with the intention of impacting changes in their lives. This approach of popular theatre makes people objects rather than subjects of change. In theatre that is truly popular, the community generates plays that reflect its realities, that is, the people speak to themselves through dramatic images that are real and relevant to them. For such plays to capture perspectives and insights into the people's existence, there is need for a methodology that enhances a critical analysis of what makes the people what they are. Hansel Ndumbe Eyoh's methodological approach for popular theatre (fig.1) (1986:143) is not the ultimate but a guideline to a methodology, which is flexible and adaptable to any given situation.

```
┌─────────────────────────────────────────────────────┐
│                    APPROACH                         │
│                       ↓                             │
│                    PROBLEMS                         │
│                       ↓                             │
│   ANALYSIS FOR PURPOSES OF CONSCIENTIZATION THROUGH │
│       BETTER UNDERSTANDING OF DEEPER REALITY        │
│                       ↓                             │
│           USE OF IMPROVISATION TO ACHIEVE THIS      │
│                       ↓                             │
│               EFFORTS OF MOBILIZATION               │
│                       ↓                             │
│                POSSIBILITY OF ACTION                │
└─────────────────────────────────────────────────────┘
```

African Popular Theatre, Racism and Identity

When Anne Schröder first informed us of her intention of inviting Emelda Ngufor Samba to conduct an African Popular Theatre workshop in the English Department of the University of Chemnitz, we marvelled at such a possibility. African popular theatre should naturally take place in Africa among Africans with African worldviews. It has often been geared towards having a deeper insight into those limit situations that have kept some marginalised groups such as women, children, the rural and urban poor in perpetual poverty and in a state of political impotence. In cases where popular theatre workshops had been sponsored by international or non-governmental organisations, the priority had been to provide practical community needs like roads, health centres, medication, and pipe-borne water. In other cases, the focus had been on awareness-creation and education for attitudinal changes.

What issues could be raised and discussed in depth in a workshop in Europe among Europeans that would be pertinent to Africans? Who would constitute the workshop participants and what interests would they have in African affairs? Would they be conversant with African cultures and would they seek to valorise them? We toiled with these questions for some time, wondering how to seek the intersection point between what is African in popular theatre and how such a theatre could be adapted to a European situation. The flexibility of the popular theatre methodology and its adaptability to diverse geographical locations and social contexts partially resolved the problem. The workshop theme — *Racism and Identity* — a subject matter that is relevant to all people irrespective of "race", nationality and social class lifted the last iota of uncertainty off our minds.

Racism and identity was a welcome theme for an African Popular Theatre workshop with students who had experienced racial discrimination in foreign lands and with nationals who apparently had never given a thought to the impact discriminatory practices had on foreigners, or who could hardly perceive their attitudes as discriminatory against foreigners. Working with students of various nationalities and cultural backgrounds provided a rich repertoire on which the process was based and the story line built.

Racism and Identity

In the social sciences, racism is a contested term. There is no single or generally accepted definition covering all its aspects. There is not even unanimity about where to look for it – in the minds of individual people, in patterns of collective attitudes and behaviour, or in social and political institutions[1][2]. Those debates on racism that share the presupposition that it is a phenomenon linked to social and political developments, concentrate on three key questions:

- Is racism (just) an ideology or (also) a structure?
- What functions does it have in society?
- Is there a new "cultural" racism?

It is not our intention here to comprehensively discuss the various theories on racism but to consider some possible questions and problems that are related to "identity" and that were raised in the theatre workshop, especially the history and the changes of racism as a concept.

Racism as an ideology, i.e. as a set of ideas or as a belief system, is closely linked to European expansion and the rise of trans-national trade since the early modern period. Thus, modern racism is qualitatively different from medieval ideas about both imagined and real "others" (cf. Miles 1989). This does not mean that the imagery was not taken over from these medieval concepts of moors, barbarians, heathens, etc. (cf. Malik 1996: 38-70). What was new, was the systematisation of their physical and phenotypic differences

---

[1] It is important, in this context, that institutions are not only the structural features of a society, like, for example, government, church, trade unions, but also less material ones, like family, marriage, religiosity, communities, neighbourhoods, "subcultural" and generational networks.

[2] Informative collections of the various positions and theories provide (at least for the Anglo-American context) Rex & Mason 1986 and Bulmer & Solomos 1999.

into "racial" categories and the belief that these were decisive for a human's character. These fixed traits could not be changed through either baptism or education. Difference became absolute, culminating in theories of polygenesis[3] and questions whether people who were not European were human at all. There is an ongoing debate about whether these ideas were prior to modern transatlantic racism (and thus making it possible) or posterior to it (developed in order to legitimise it) (cf. Hund 1999: 33). It can be argued that slavery acted as a catalyst systematising various stereotyped and prejudiced attitudes and transforming them into a structure. This structure then became responsible for giving public life in multi-ethnic societies a particular shape, influencing or even creating its institutions[4].

Structures in societies do not emerge by accident. They are formed in order to fulfil particular functions. In the case of racism, three main functions can be identified:

- The ideological legitimisation of slavery and colonialism, which means the economic exploitation and social oppression of non-European people.
- The fragmentation of exploited and oppressed groups into different "races" in order to stabilise structures of dominance.
- The provision of personal feelings of superiority and of possibilities to use "racially" defined groups as scapegoats.

Arguably, the use of "racial" categories became less frequent in the second half of the twentieth century. This is due to the experience of Nazism, the development of molecular biology (proving that genetic variation within a "race" is much wider than between "races"), anti-colonial liberation struggles as well as the civil rights movements in North America and Western Europe. Nowadays, the belief in the superiority of one "race" over another has become rare (though it certainly still exists — as was shown in the debate triggered off by the publication of the study *The Belle Curve* in the early 1990s, when two academics interpreted different IQ test results for white and black Americans as proof of their different capabilities as *"racial" groups* [cf. Malik 1996: 206-208]).

---

[3] This is the idea that the human "races" might have different origins.
[4] The most drastic example, of course, is the "peculiar institution" (as slavery was called in the Southern states of the USA) itself. There are countless others: segregated armed forces; colonial bureaucracies staffed (in the lower ranks) with middle-class colonial people; unofficial families of white plantation owners, their female slaves, and common children; the prohibition of "mixed-race" marriages; "colour bars" in public places; "vouchers" for non-European employees; the invention of "guest workers".

It seems, however, that "culture" has replaced "race" as a marker of clear-cut distinctions between imagined groups of people. The problem with "culture" is the complexity of the concept on the one hand and the almost synonymous use with concepts like "ethnicity", "nation", and "religion" on the other. Understood in the latter way, "culture" provides a foundation for distinctions as stable and clear-cut as those based on "race". There might be more emphasis on the incompatibility of cultures than on the superiority of one over the other. The case of Islam, however, reveals a close link between its assumed incompatibility with western cultural traditions and its supposed inferiority and backwardness. Like biological racism, the claim of cultural incompatibility is used as a tool to separate groups of people from each other — protecting old-established citizens from new migrants, rich societies from poorer ones, and fragmenting people with arguably common or similar interests. Therefore the ideological source of racism might have changed (that is why numerous social scientists speak of "cultural racism" these days [Goldberg 1999]) as might the structural imprints it leaves in state institutions (which segregate less on the basis of skin colour than on that of legal status), but the social and political functions are still the same.

In Europe, identities to a high degree are formed by these structures (and were so over generations). This, however, is not necessarily obvious to people who live in predominantly white and supposedly mono-cultural societies (whose "official" political discourses emphasise "equality" and "meritocracy"). Therefore, explicit reflections on the historical lineage and the changes of racism can illuminate the ways our heads work. So at an early stage in the workshop these stages and variants of racism were thoroughly discussed (see below). Additionally, comparison with other people's identities can shed light on the many traces and scars racism leaves in different minds. Traces and scars of racism and identity emerged quite distinctively in the workshop since the group of participants consisted of students from Germany as well as from several African countries — that is, people who had rather divergent experiences with, and of, racism. Such exchanges gave new insights into the intricacies and the extent of racism in society. The workshop was able to contribute to an increase in sensitivity towards these issues. It could not, of course, directly confront the racist structures as they have become inscribed into social and political institutions. Central to our thinking therefore, was a basic concern for the transformative personal experiences of the workshop participants during the play-creation process and a certain level of attitudinal change among the audiences who watched the final product — the play.

Workshop Report

a. Objectives of the Workshop

The workshop had been conditioned by a need to bring together people who had experienced racism in diverse forms and were willing to share these experiences with others. It was hoped that by speaking to themselves through drama, those affected by racial differences would come to a better understanding of the cause and effect nexus of racism and identity, and collectively seek ways of changing attitudes towards migrant and other minority groups. The workshop was going to function as an arena for sections of the population for whom there was no structured forum to carry out discussions on hypersensitive topics like racism and identity. Opened to the public, it was hoped that the workshop would rally people from different nationalities, "races", professions, and social classes. Because racism and identity are phenomena common in every society, the entire community was going to be the beneficiaries of the project.

b. Participants: Background and Interests

Eleven university students, one trainee teacher, a university lecturer and one high school leaver constituted the workshop team. Most of the students were of the English Department of the University of Chemnitz who took up the course as an elective. Some of the students had lived in other continents like America and Africa where they had come in contact with racism and identity in its raw form. Others, who had plans of visiting or studying in Africa had come to the workshop with an open mind, eager to learn more about a continent about which they knew very little. For others, it was more a question of experiencing African Popular Theatre than gaining insight into racism and identity as one of the participants attested:

> Before the workshop, I surely was looking for African dances, music and other ways of doing theatre. When we met the first time, it was how it always was with workshops; many new and different people who are quite open and very interesting for me to observe...and there were even some African people who were twice as interesting to me because I suffer from a lack of foreign contact. (Antje Schmidt, workshop participant)

The African students participated in the workshop on the basis of their identity. They had all suffered the effects of discriminatory practices abroad because of their skin colour and saw the workshop situation as the appropriate forum to express their frustration and exasperation with the way foreigners, especially black Africans, were treated in Germany. The workshop apparently satisfied the diverse needs of the various participants in a way personal to each of them.

c. The Workshop Process

The methodological approach of the Chemnitz African Popular Theatre Workshop was a hybrid of traditional African theatrical approaches and Western dramatic forms. The play emerged from a process of theatre games, elaborate discussions on racism and identity, problem identification and analysis, and scenario creation. The games created a relaxed atmosphere for critical reflection and improvisation. Emphasis was laid on the training of the body and voice of the participants to communicate messages in the most effective way.

Problem Identification and Analysis: Participatory Research

The theatre workshop followed the participatory research approach of collective data collection. Information was derived from participants' experiences or observations of racism and identity. Every piece of information was given a critical analysis before being retained or discarded. From the experiences narrated, it became clear that racist attitudes could be overt or subtle and at times pass unnoticed by individuals, national and international organisations. In isolation these attitudes could be branded as personal inclinations against individuals. But when victims of racist prejudices narrated these experiences, they opened up new avenues for perceiving and analysing them as exemplified by one participant's revelation:

> Our theme racism and identity was nothing new to me but during the workshop, I became aware that I never really thought that intensively about it or even experienced racism in a realistic and personal way.

This affirms David Kerr's (1994:15) assertion that conflicts always exist in the society and popular theatre plays the 'significant part in bringing latent contradictions in people's sphere of vision'.

Considering the multi-faceted nature of Racism and Identity as seen above, it was impossible to discuss every one of them elaborately. Predictably, the participants, who were predominantly students, found interest in discriminatory practices against students in foreign countries. Such discriminatory practices were not directed to them as students, but as a subgroup within the larger group of migrants whom nationals considered inferior or superior, and backward or more civilised. There were two sides of the story. On the one hand, there were problems African students faced in non-African countries. On the other hand there were experiences of European students in mainly black African countries. The latter were significantly issues of identity as the problems indicate:

- Children running behind them and singing songs that described their skin colour and the shape of their noses.
- Adults stopping them along the street ever so often to ask for money.

For the Africans, it was more a question of racial prejudice propagated by the belief of superiority of some "races" over others. Another issue that emerged from the workshop was nationals' anger against foreigners for usurping some of their social benefits such as child allowances, jobs, and free education at the university level. These prejudices manifested in the following ways:

- African students refused jobs because of their skin colour.
- Africans offered menial jobs only.
- African students isolated on the University campus.
- Africans receiving beatings from skinheads.
- Negative preconceptions Europeans have of all Africans as cheats, thieves and drug traffickers/addicts.

At the initial stages of the problem analysis, participants attempted to justify their reactions to certain situations. For example, the African participants did not regard the act of singing children running behind Europeans as abusive. To them, it was an innocent expression of children's bewilderment at the existence of a different kind of human being. This is explicated by a common song that has been translated into many African languages. The Cameroon Pidgin version goes thus:

> *Since my mother born me,*
> *a never see this kind one.*
> *Whiteman, whiteman, whiteman,*
> *Whiteman with e long nose.*[5]

Europeans who had lived this experience saw it differently. Each time they heard this song or similar ones, they were reminded of their difference and felt unaccepted in the society. The songs therefore were a manifestation of prejudices against non-Africans.

---

[5] Standard English translation: Ever since I was born, I have never seen anything like this. White man, white man, white man, white man with a long nose.

To the African participants, prejudices against them were more significant for they considered them both individual and institutional. Wars, poverty, political turmoil and inadequate educational set-ups for certain fields of study had been their reason for migrating to other countries. For a great majority of the students, studying abroad would create more opportunities for better jobs when they returned home. Considering the fact that the target audience was multiracial and hence multicultural, the participants reached a general consensus to present racism and identity as it could manifest in any part of the world.

Play-creation

Performers in African popular theatre are often neither professionals nor amateurs. They are community members who have probably never received any formal training in acting. Without getting into the depths of actor training, the performers went through a series of exercises necessary for relaxation, concentration and imagination. This included breathing exercises, relaxation of all the body muscles, and voice training through singing and dancing. Some participants of the Chemnitz workshop suffered from stage fright. To overcome this, they went through mirror exercises, hot seats and eye contact. These proved rewarding especially for the narrator who was constantly in direct communication with the audiences and the rest of the participants who needed a relaxed environment suitable for reflection and improvisation.

At different levels of the play-creation process, participants worked in pairs and in groups, creating scenes with racist undertones. Each group chose a sculptor who instructed group members on the postures to take and the facial expressions to maintain that would best communicate the moods and inner selves of the characters they were impersonating. Satisfied with the still pictures, the sculptors instructed the performers to move in ways and directions of their choices in order to advance the development of the stories. Both instructions and their observance took place through non-verbal communication. Each scenario was opened to criticisms and there was an attempt to juxtapose what the sculptor and the performers attempted to create and what the rest of the participants deciphered from the still and moving pictures. From the discussions, it became clear that personal experiences on discriminatory practices against minority groups and migrants provided the foundation for the various scenes. The narratives had been documented in still pictures and later on transformed into moving pictures that told the stories of many who had suffered social and class prejudices. The participants eventually wove the scenes together to create a story which they judged was cohesive, captivating and capable of bringing a positive change in people's attitudes towards foreigners, minority groups, and those they considered inferior.

To reach out to a great number of the audiences, the participants agreed to use mime as the main communication medium. English and German were the preferred languages when spoken languages became of utmost necessity. German would be used because the play would be performed to a predominantly German audience and English, firstly because it is the most widely spoken language and secondly because the workshop was organised within the department of English.

The Play/Performance

The play begins with a narrator who announces that what will happen on stage is a true story, her own story. She tells the audience to watch and listen keenly as she narrates her experiences as a university student in a foreign country. She invites the audience to reflect on her experiences as something that could happen to anybody abroad.

The story opens at a train station. A student has just arrived in a foreign country where she is to begin her university education. Luggage in hand, she marvels at the beauty and sophistication of the buildings at the train station. Everything looks different and beautiful. She takes out a piece of paper from her bag and moves towards a couple standing near by. She would like to know the direction to the university. The couple move away with a look of detest on their faces. She looks around and notices two women and a man talking to each other. She moves close to them to ask for directions. One of the women turns and walks away keeping a safe distance between her and the foreigner. The others, though they have not moved, ignore her completely. The couple then moves towards the man and woman and cautions them against associating with foreigners, who, generally are thieves, drug traffickers and drug addicts. Taking every precaution to avoid contamination from the foreign student, they all move away from her. Frustrated, she looks round for someone else who could help her, but there is none. She moves from one section of the stage to the other shouting out the question, 'Kann niemand mir helfen?' ('Can no one help me?') In the absence of help coming from any quarter, she picks up her luggage and walks off stage.

In the next scene, the performers create still pictures. The pictures capture images of racial discrimination that manifest as oppression, domination, and authoritarianism. In pairs, the performers create pictures of citizens maltreating foreigners in diverse work situations. Emotions of suffering, frustration, fear, and humiliation are what characterise the facial expressions and body postures of the foreigners. In contrast, the citizens re-present dominance, affluence and superiority. The foreign student is taking a tour of the university town and comes in contact with these outrageous pictures. She is shocked at the intense painful emotions the pictures convey. In the shops, at train stations, and along the streets are pictures of foreigners condoning discriminatory practices from citizens. She moves through the pictures in silence, looking at each intensely and wondering if it is possible for any human being to experience such pains and still live a psychologically normal life. From back stage comes the song '*Why? Why? Why should things be like this? Why?*' which is an echo of the student's innermost thoughts. She moves with the rhythm of the song and stops at each picture to examine the postures and facial expressions of the oppressors and the oppressed. The further she moves into the town, the more deplorable she finds the exposition of the relationship between foreigners and citizens. The last picture is so terrifying that she staggers off stage in shock.

The narrator returns on stage with the same emotion as the student. She looks intently at the audiences and addresses them directly. She describes the feelings she had for the citizens of that country because of the way they treated foreigners like her. She hated them and could do anything to avenge the maltreatment she and other foreigners were made to suffer. But she was still to have a taste of overt discrimination and invites the audiences to experience it with her. She goes off stage.

The next scene is a mime. Citizens of the country are found in different places carrying out their daily activities. The foreign student moves from one group to the other to integrate in the society but is rejected. First, she moves to a bar where two ladies are drinking. The third chair by them is empty. As she moves to occupy the chair, one of the ladies places her bag on it to prevent her from sitting. She removes the handbag from the chair, hands it over to the lady, but as she is about to occupy the seat, the lady pulls the chair away. She stumbles, loses her balance and tips backwards. When later she gains her balance, she walks away in confusion.

She moves to a shop to buy a drink. At first, the shopkeeper refuses to attend to her. He simply ignores her. When she insists, he gives her the drink but refuses to collect the money from her hand. In anger, she throws the money on the table and marches off. At the university, she has the worst experience. When she walks into the classroom for the first time, everyone stops what they are doing to stare at her as if to ask what a foreigner is doing at the university. As she moves to occupy a seat, the other students all move away and isolate. Some go to the extent of asking her what she was doing there. They tell her she is in the wrong place. She must have mistaken the University for some place of work. There is however one sympathetic student among the lot. She moves over and occupies a seat next to the foreign student. She engages her in a dialogue and this cheers her up. Her final encounter is with a police officer. He takes her passport, gives her a suspicious look, examines the passport critically and hands it back to her with a look of disgust.

The student has come to the end of her self. She cannot take the hatred and discrimination any longer. For the first time in the play, she breaks down. Addressing the audience as if they constituted her tormentors, she tells them that she hates them with the kind of burning passion that would only subside when she must have avenged herself for all the discriminatory practices against her and other foreigners. She promises hell to all foreigners who will ever find themselves in her country. She decides to withdraw into a life of seclusion. She moves over to a chair, sits down with her hands folded and her head bowed. Her posture paints the picture of a lonely and unhappy young lady in need of friendship. At this point, the narrator comes on stage and tries to talk to the student. She remains incommunicado in spite of the narrator's great efforts. Having failed to bring the student back to her original enthusiasm, the narrator turns to the audience and addresses them directly:

> See what you have done to her. Do you realise it could be any of you being treated that way? You all gaze at me as if to say you are not guilty. If you were in the same situation, would you have treated the student differently? Would you have treated **ME** differently?

There is a loud cry of '*yes!!!*' from the audience. This is the beginning of audience involvement in the performance. The narrator invites them to demonstrate how they could have acted differently. The performers who played the role of the citizens go into the audience and select volunteers to take up their roles. The narrator turns to the student and pleads with her to make another attempt at socialising with the citizens. She argues that some people could be different. They could be more welcoming and accommodating than others. She further cautions her that it is impossible to live a life of isolation especially in a foreign country. Finally convinced, the student moves over to the new performers or spec-actors who have taken up the places of the original actors/actresses. The new set of performers treats her with respect and interacts freely with her. The student brightens up each time she meets a group of cheerful citizens. As the play rounds off, she moves to the centre of the stage and all the performers join her in a 'trust game'. She is at the centre of a circle with her eyes closed. As she sways from left to right, forward and backward, the performers give her a gentle push from one angle to the other. At the background are words of encouragement to people all over the world to bring an end to discrimination, to trust one another and to show love to people no matter their race, nationality, social class and gender. At the end of the game, the actors dance to the tune of *'kwesim kwe'* a victory song from the Northwest Province of Cameroon. The audiences are invited to join in the singing and dancing. This dance brings the play to an end.

Conclusion: Implications and Complications

The play was performed on the occasion of the African Evening, the final party of the 'Afrika in Chemnitz' weeks, celebrating the end of the activities. Africans, other non-Germans and Germans constituted the audience. The relevance of the play's theme to people of all nationalities accounted for the large number of spec-actors who rallied to watch it. The ideological implication of racism and the negative image it captures makes some scholars and politicians desist from using the term. This does not, however, cancel the reality of racial prejudices in all societies today. The theatre event played the significant role of bringing to the spectator's field of vision existing cases of open and ferocious racism directed at ethnic minorities and those considered as socially inferior. One of the participants confirmed by indicating that,

> Although I had claimed myself cultural sensitive, that is open-minded, without people from Africa, it is possible to fall prey to prejudices. The workshop helped me to overcome this ignorance. I enjoyed the dancing and chanting a lot. I find it great that I can learn and practise songs from Africa. For me this shows that in our everyday life, there are so many cultural treasures in our community and proactive potentials that lie undiscovered. (Frithiof Svenson, workshop participant)

A change in negative attitudes was one of the main objectives of the African Popular Theatre workshop. Seeking alternative ways of doing things and of perceiving difficult life situations constituted an important agenda of the workshop which was rooted in Boal's theatre of the alternative. The alternative proposed in the play was a fair treatment of migrants, and other minority groups. The play could not have influenced institutions, as already suggested in section B, but it definitely made a difference in the lives of the workshop participants as one of them asserts:

> Well, I do not think that (the play) did change something. Certainly, in this room, there were certainly no racists otherwise they would not have been there, and from just one performance people do not just change in my opinion. All in all, I think the participants learnt the most out of it.
>
> I very much like the idea of learning things through theatre. It is a different learning, and I guess, longer lasting since those changes in thoughts are produced by oneself and not through someone telling you something. (Susanne Rantzsch, workshop participant)

African popular theatre aims at creating awareness among people of things they would like to know about. Through the process of democratic learning, participants came to know and perceive old things in new ways they never thought possible. Racism and identity are concepts that are common in political and academic discourse though they are sometimes dismissed as far-fetched and non-existent.

The Chemnitz workshop provided two levels of interest to the workshop participants. Their main interest lay in discovering the nature and content of African popular theatre. Like the facilitator, some of the participants had wondered how a theatre that was uniquely African could be transposed to Europe. To some of the non-African participants, the workshop opened up avenues for learning more about African cultures through a direct contact with Africans.

> I really liked the workshop. It was different from all the things I did before, but I don't really mean the acting itself. I learned very much about myself. I did not really think that I had so many prejudices, well, better put it this way, I did not recognise being ignorant in a certain way. I learned many things about Africa, of course this was very good since I am planning to go there. (Susanne Rantzsch, workshop participant)

And another participant pointed out:

> The discussions we had were quite interesting although I did not understand everything: that was a pity for me because I wanted to know what everybody had to say. Sometimes there were just too many words and I thought of moving, acting, dancing and getting to know each other in a more playful way without words but with feelings. (Antje Schmidt, workshop participant)

All in all, the African Popular Theatre workshop in Chemnitz gave its participants the opportunity to learn about aspects of their own identity and personality they had not known or had ignored before. For the audience, the play gave some impetus to further think and feel about daily situations which they undoubtedly had witnessed but where they probably had not intervened. Put together in succession and in an exaggerated way, racist acts inadvertently triggered sensations of self-defence and self-judgement on negative attitudes towards minority groups among the audience. Maybe in this European, academic context, the purpose of African Popular Theatre was less strategic (empowering) but didactic (raising consciousness and sensitivity) in a positive sense.

References

BEYER, E. LANDON
    (2000). *The Arts, Popular Culture and Social Change*. Studies in the Postmodern Theory of Education, Vol.142. New York: Peter Lang.
BOAL, AUGUSTO
    (1979, 2000). *Theatre of the Oppressed*. New Edition, Trans. Charles A. Maria-Odilia Leal McBride and Emily Fryer, London: Pluto Press.
BULMER, MARTIN AND JOHN SOLOMOS (eds.)
    (1999). *Racism*. Oxford: OUP.
EYOH, HANSEL NDUMBE
    (1986). *Hammocks to Bridges: Report of the Workshop on Theatre for Integrated Rural Development; Kumba, Cameroon* 1-16 December 1984. Yaounde: Bet &Co.
FANON, FRANTZ
    (1963). *The Wretched of the Earth*. Translated from the French by Constance Farrington. New York: Grove Press.
FREIRE, PAULO
    (1970, 2001). *Pedagogy of the Oppressed:* 30th Anniversary Edition, Trans. Myra Bergman Ramos. New York: Continuum.
    (1992, 1999). *Pedagogy of Hope: Reliving Pedagogy of the Oppressed*. With Notes by Ana Maria Araujo Freire, Trans. Robert R. Barr. New York: Continuum.
GOLDBERG, DAVID THEO
    (1999). "The Semantics of Race" in: Bulmer & Solomos, 362-377.
HUND, WULF D.
    (1999). *Rassismus. Die soziale Konstruktion natürlicher Ungleichheit*. Münster: Westfälisches Dampfboot.
KERR, DAVID
    (1995). *African Popular Theatre: from Pre-colonial Times to the Present Day*. London; James Kurrey.
MALIK, KENAN
    (1996). *The Meaning of Race. Race, History and Culture in Western Society*. Basingstoke: Macmillan.
MILES, ROBERT
    (1989). *Racism*. London: Routledge.

MLAMA, PENINA MUHANDO
(1991). *Culture and Development: The Popular Theatre Approach in Africa.* Sweden: SIDA.

REX, JOHN AND DAVID MASON (eds.)
(1986). *Theories of Race and Ethnic Relations.* Cambridge: CUP.

Contributors

JOYCE ASHUNTANTANG ABUNAW received her Ph.D. in English from the Graduate School and University Center, City University of New York. Scriptwriter and co-producer of the Film *Potent Secrets*, Joyce A. Abunaw is also a well known actress and personality in Cameroon. She has recently published a Comprehensive Bibliography of Anglophone Cameroon literature (primary texts and selected criticism) and is now working on a volume dealing with postcoloniality and the dissemination of Anglophone Cameroon literature. Joyce A. Abunaw is presently an Assistant Professor of English at the University of Connecticut at Storrs.

JIGAL BEEZ is an Anthropologist who studied, worked and did research in Tanzania and Uganda. He has published articles on various aspects of East Africa including comics. Since 2000, he has been a member of the collaborative research programme *Local Agency in Africa in the Context of Global Influences* at the University of Bayreuth, Germany.

SEBASTIAN BERG received his Dr. phil. in British Studies from Chemnitz University of Technology, Germany, where he now holds a lecturer post. Before, he has taught at the Universities of Oldenburg and Bielefeld, as well as at Manchester Metropolitan University. Sebastian Berg has written a book on anti-racism in the British Labour Party and articles on racism, migration, postcolonialism, British politics, and concepts of Social/Cultural Studies. Presently, he compares how the "intellectual lefts" in Britain and the USA have reacted to political changes since 1989.

KERSTIN BOLZT is a lecturer at the Institute for African Studies at the University of Bayreuth and received her MA in British Studies at the University of Passau, Germany. Presently, Kerstin Bolzt is working on her Ph.D. project on gender roles in the areas of literature, film and music of contemporary Zimbabwe.

BOLANG BUTAKE was born in Yaoundé, Cameroon. After her secondary and high school education, she learned German at the Goethe Institute in Yaoundé. She currently studies business management at the Chemnitz University of Technology, Germany. Bolang Butake has written several poems and has been actively involved in the organisation of the *Afrika in Chemnitz* series of events from 2001 to 2004.

BOLE BUTAKE is a professor of African Literature and Performing Arts at the University of Yaounde I in Cameroon. He is also one of Cameroon's most popular playwrights. Many of his theatre plays as well as poems and short stories have been published. In addition, Bole Butake has worked as a critic and theatre director. He has also carried out many workshops throughout Cameroon using theatre as a technique for development working on various issues, especially on the living conditions of African women, women's empowerment and women's rights.

BIRGIT ENGLERT is a lecturer at the Department of African Studies in Vienna where she is currently writing her doctoral thesis. Her publications include a monograph and articles on land reform and land right issues in Zimbabwe and Tanzania as well as contributions to Swahili-Studies. She is the managing editor of the Africanist journal *Stichproben – Wiener Zeitschrift für kritische Afrikastudien/Vienna Journal of African Studies.*

KATRIN FISCHER teaches American Cultural Studies at Chemnitz University of Technology, Germany. She received her Dr. phil. in American Studies from the University of Paderborn, Germany, and has published *"Time to Tear Down Barriers": Raum, Kultur und 'indianische' Identität im Kriminalroman* (2003) as well as articles on American literature and teaching English as a foreign language. Her compilation of English-German Shakespeare quotations, *Reclams Lexikon der Shakespeare-Zitate*, was published in 2002. Currently, she works on a book project about Germans in American Indian captivity.

FLORIAN HETZE received his Dipl. Soz. from the Freie Universität Berlin with his diploma on "Body, Consciousness and Movement. About the Language of Rhythm in Music and Dance of Africa". He is engaged in a long time research about the formation of acoustic human civilization as opposed to spatial i.e. Western culture. He runs the Shava record label specialised in African music and manages African musicians. His publications in non-scientific media point at cultural and musical aspects of Bantu Africa. He is a director of the Institute for Rhythm Research, Berlin.

VIRGINIA MUKWESHA received her degree in Sociology at the University of Zimbabwe in Harare. She has done field work on the situation of women in rural areas of Zimbabwe and is specialised in cultural politics, Shona traditions and problems of development. She also works as modern traditional musician and her work is known in Zimbabwe as well as in the Western world music market. Her publications are song lyrics about social and cultural problems in Africa with intense consideration of women's rights. She is a director of the Institute for Rhythm Research, Berlin.

EMELDA NGUFOR SAMBA holds a doctorate in African Theatre and Drama from the University of Bayreuth, Germany. She works as a high school teacher and part-time lecturer of Performing Arts in the Department of Arts and Archaeology at the University of Yaounde I, Cameroon. In addition, she is a Theatre-for-Development practitioner in Cameroon and has conducted several workshops with children on environmental education and with village groups on women's empowerment. She is one of the artistic directors of The National Association of Theatre Troupes in Cameroon, and the founder and coordinator of Goodwill Theatre, a theatre troupe that fights for the rights and social integration of disabled people in Cameroon. Emelda Ngufor Samba is also one of the coordinators of People Theatre, a group that organizes and conducts Theatre-for-Development workshops with self-help groups.

ANNE SCHRÖDER received her Dr. phil. in English Linguistics from the University of Freiburg, Germany. Before taking up her present post as a senior lecturer at Halle University, Germany, she worked as a lecturer at Chemnitz University of Technology. Her publications include a volume on Cameroon Pidgin English, some articles on the same topic as well as on Camfranglais. She presently works on a contrastive study of tense and aspect marking in English, German and Cameroon Pidgin English and on a project on patterns of language change in English word-formation. Anne Schröder has organised the *Afrika in Chemnitz* series of events from 2001 to 2004.

HANS-GEORG WOLF is an associate professor in the English Department at the University of Hong Kong and coordinator of the program in Language and Communication. He has published a book on *English in Cameroon* (2001) and one on *The Folk Model of the 'Internal Self' in Light of the Contemporary View of Metaphor – the Self as Subject and Object* (1994). His research interests include sociolinguistics, cognitive linguistics, varieties of English, corpus linguistics and pragmatics. Particularly, he focuses on the application of methods developed in cognitive linguistics/cognitive anthropology and corpus linguistics to the study of second language varieties of English, and is presently working on a joint book-project for Mouton de Gruyter's Cognitive Linguistics Series.

EVELYN WLADARSCH is a senior lecturer at the University of Heidelberg, Germany, where she also received her Dr. des. phil. in Ethnology. She has worked in Burkina Faso and gave several presentations on medical anthropology and time anthropology.

Hartmut Zinser
Ethnologie: Forschung und Wissenschaft
Mythos des Mutterrechts
Um ein Nachwort ergänzte Neuauflage.
Im Anhang: Rezensionen der 1. Auflage
Was ist das Mutterrecht? In welchen Ländern und in welchen historischen Epochen hat es ein Mutterrecht oder eine Gynäkokratie gegeben, wie sahen oder sehen die gesellschaftlichen Verhältnisse und besonders die Geschlechterbeziehungen unter ihm aus?
Die vorliegende Arbeit bedient sich dennoch nicht der psychoanalytischen Methode in der Darstellung ihres Gegenstandes. Sie wählt die Form des Plädoyers, in dem die Argumente für und wider, auch solche, die sich der Symptomanalyse verdanken, dem Urteil des Lesers ausgesetzt und die Urteilsgründe zusammen mit den Interessen und Bedürfnissen, die in ihr wirksam sind, zur Diskussion gestellt werden.
Bd. 1, 1997, 100 S., 15,90 €, br.,
ISBN 3-8258-2554-X

Günther Schlee
Identities on the Move
Clanship and pastoralism in Northern Kenya (second edition 1994, first published in 1989). This is a title distributed by LIT Verlag. The book was first published by Manchester University Press in 1989. The distributed version is part of the second edition published by GIDEON S. WERE PRESS, Nairobi, Kenya in 1994.
Clans are normally thought of as contained within ethnic groups. In the Horn of Africa the pastoral Rendille, Gabbra, Sakuye and some Somalis of northern Kenya and southern Ethiopia have many clans in common. As a result the clans are not always smaller or less important than the ethnic groups. How such inter-ethnic relationships came about is the subject of this study many go back beyond ethnic divisions to over 400 years ago. The book also examines the uses to which they are put, for instance in managing herds.
Oral history is combined with cultural comparison and the analysis of social structure. The many original texts are themselves of linguistic interest. Blending synchronic and diachronic perspectives, the book synthesises historical ethnology in the Continental tradition with social anthropology. Historically it overturns some established ideas about how the Horn was settled. Anthropologically it shows how relations may exceed the bounds of the ethnic group as the conventional unit of study. It will be of interest to anthropologists, sociologists and social geographers or planners concerned with pastoral development.
Bd. 2, 1994, 288 S., 24,90 €, br.,
ISBN 3-8258-4800-0

Wim van Binsbergen
Intercultural Encounters
African and anthropological lessons towards a philosophy of interculturality
This book brings together fifteen essays investigating aspects of interculturality. Like its author, it operates at the borderline between social anthropology and intercultural philosophy. It seeks to make a contribution to intercultural philosophy, by formulating with great precision and painful honesty the lessons deriving from extensive intercultural experiences as an anthropologist. Its culminating section presents an intercultural philosophy revolving on the tenet 'cultures do not exist'. The kaleidoscopic nature of intercultural experiences is reflected in the diversity of these texts. Many belong to a field that could be described as "meta-anthropology", others are more clearly philosophical; occasionally they spill over into belles lettres, ancient history, and comparative cultural and religious studies. The ethnographic specifics supporting the arguments are diverse, deriving from various African situations in which the author has conducted participatory field research (Tunisia, Zambia, Botswana, and South Africa).
Bd. 4, 2003, 616 S., 40,90 €, br.,
ISBN 3-8258-6783-8

LIT Verlag Münster – Berlin – Hamburg – London – Wien
Grevener Str./Fresnostr. 2 48159 Münster
Tel.: 0251 – 23 50 91 – Fax: 0251 – 23 19 72
e-Mail: vertrieb@lit-verlag.de – http://www.lit-verlag.de

Afrikanische Studien

Gabriele Altheimer; Veit Dietrich Hopf; Bernhard Weimer (Hg.)
Botswana
Vom Land der Betschuanen zum Frontstaat. Wirtschaft, Gesellschaft, Kultur
Bd. 1, 2. Aufl., 1997, 350 S., 19,90 €, br.,
ISBN 3-88660-511-6

Stefan Brüne; Joachim Betz; Winrich Kühne (eds.)
Africa and Europe: Relations of Two Continents in Transition
Bd. 2, 1994, 272 S., 19,90 €, br.,
ISBN 3-89473-714-x

Michael Bollig; Doris Bünnagel (Hg.)
Der zentralafrikanische Regenwald
Ökologie, Geschichte, Gesellschaft, Wirtschaft
Bd. 3, 1993, 248 S., 17,90 €, br.,
ISBN 3-89473-577-5

Werner Biermann
Wachuurizi Na Halasa
Händler und Handelskapital in der wirtschaftlichen Entwicklung Ostafrikas (900 bis 1890)
Bd. 5, 1993, 328 S., 30,90 €, br.,
ISBN 3-89473-712-3

Ulrich van der Heyden; Achim von Oppen (Hg.)
Tanzania: Koloniale Vergangenheit und neuer Aufbruch
Bd. 7, 1996, 160 S., 15,90 €, br.,
ISBN 3-8258-2146-3

Werner Biermann
Tanganyika Railways – Carrier of Colonialism
An Account of Economic Indicators and Social Fragments
Bd. 9, 1996, 150 S., 19,90 €, br.,
ISBN 3-8258-2524-8

E. Adriaan B. van Rouveroy van Nieuwaal; Werner Zips (eds.)
Sovereignty, Legitimacy, and Power in West African Societies
Perspectives from Legal Anthropology
Bd. 10, 1998, 264 S., 19,90 €, br.,
ISBN 3-8258-3036-5

Beat Sottas; Thomas Hammer; Lilo Roost Vischer; Anne Mayor (Hrsg./éd.)
Werkschau Afrikastudien – Le forum suisse des africanistes
Bd. 11, 1997, 392 S., 24,90 €, br.,
ISBN 3-8258-3506-5

Hans van den Breemer; Bernhard Venema (eds.)
Towards Negotiated Co-management of Natural Resources in Africa
Bd. 12, 1999, 368 S., 25,90 €, br.,
ISBN 3-8258-3948-6

Lilo Roost Vischer; Anne Mayor; Dag Henrichsen (Hrsg./éd.)
Brücken und Grenzen – Passages et frontières
Werkschau Afrikastudien 2 – Le forum suisse des africanistes 2
Bd. 13, 1999, 480 S., 25,90 €, br.,
ISBN 3-8258-4398-x

Fred Krüger; Georgia Rakelmann; Petra Schierholz (Hg.)
Botswana – Alltagswelten im Umbruch
Facettes of a Changing Society
Bd. 14, 2000, 224 S., 15,90 €, br.,
ISBN 3-8258-4671-7

Deutsch-Madagassische Gesellschaft e. V. (Hg.)
Madagascar: Perspectives de Développement
Croissance de la Population et Croissance Economique contre Sauvegarde de la Nature
Bd. 15, 2000, 344 S., 20,90 €, br.,
ISBN 3-8258-4807-8

LIT Verlag Münster – Berlin – Hamburg – London – Wien
Grevener Str./Fresnostr. 2 48159 Münster
Tel.: 0251 – 23 50 91 – Fax: 0251 – 23 19 72
e-Mail: vertrieb@lit-verlag.de – http://www.lit-verlag.de

Joe L. P. Lugalla; Colleta G. Kibassa
Urban Life and Street Children's Health
Children's Accounts of Urban Hardships and Violence in Tanzania
The authors examine the dynamics of urban life and street children's health in the era of globalization and structural adjustments in Tanzania. They discuss the factors that push children out of their homes, how the children survive in streets, the hardships and violence they endure and how this affects their health. They argue that the impact of the legacy of colonial policies and some post-colonial development policies, the negative consequences of uncontrolled process of globalization, the impact of structural adjustments and the HIV/AIDS epidemic are simultaneously intensifying the situation of poverty in Tanzania. These processes are not only destroying families and communities that have for many years acted as safety nets for children in need, but are also manufacturing poor, helpless and powerless children most of whom resort to street life.
Bd. 16, 2003, 176 S., 20,90 €, br., ISBN 3-8258-6690-4

Christoph Haferburg; Jürgen Oßenbrügge (Eds.)
Ambiguous Restructurings of Post-Apartheid Cape Town
The Spatial Form of Socio-Political Change
What will tomorrow's Cape Town look like? This volume reflects a variety of aspects of urban development and restructuring efforts in Cape Town in the last years. A focus lies on the question if the "apartheid city" is reproducing itself. This leads to an evaluation whether current policies really counter societal imbalances. The essays presented here illuminate possible pathways towards the urban futures unfolding in a South African city in transition.
Contributors: Jürgen Oßenbrügge, Patrick Bond, Vanessa Watson, Christoph Haferburg, Steven Robins, Marie Huchzermeyer, Antje Nahnsen, Edgar Pieters
Bd. 17, 2003, 200 S., 20,90 €, br., ISBN 3-8258-6699-8

Eva-Maria Bruchhaus (Ed.)
Hot Spot Horn of Africa
Between Integration and Disintegration
The volume includes most of the contributions to a meeting on recently completed or ongoing research projects concerning the "small" Horn of Africa, that is Ethiopia, Eritrea and Somalia, held in Hamburg in May 2002, as well as a few complementary articles. Contributions are widely diversified, as the Hamburg meeting had gathered young scholars from German universities working on extremely different themes. The subjects range widely from Agro-Anthropology to Political Science, with Sociology and Social Anthropology enjoying the strongest coverage.
Bd. 19, 2003, 208 S., 19,90 €, br., ISBN 3-8258-6835-4

Politics and Economics in Africa
Series Editors: Robert Kappel and Ulf Engel
(Universität Leipzig)

Jedrzej Georg Frynas
Oil in Nigeria
Conflict and Litigation between Oil Companies and Village Communities
Bd. 1, 2000, 288 S., 25,90 €, br., ISBN 3-8258-3921-4

Ulf Engel
Die Afrikapolitik der Bundesrepublik Deutschland 1949 – 1999
Rollen und Identitäten
Gibt es angesichts der Vielschichtigkeit der afrikapolitischen Beziehungen Bonns eine übergreifende Klammer für die Interpretation der westdeutschen Afrikapolitik? Auf der Basis einer als "empirischer Konstruktivismus" bezeichneten Wissenschaftsmethode

werden in dieser Arbeit vier Interpretationsdimensionen bemüht: Rollen, Normen, der Prozeß der Normenaneignung und das Verhältnis von Identität und Paradigmenwechsel. Dabei steht die Frage im Vordergrund, wie sich afrikapolitische Identitäten konstituieren, reproduzieren oder verändern. Einem Überblickskapitel zu den dominanten politischen Paradigmen der Bonner Afrikapolitik folgen Fallstudien zur Anwendung der Hallstein-Doktrin gegenüber Tanzania (1964–65), zur Beteiligung der Bundesrepublik an der UN-Sicherheitsratsinitiative 435 zur Lösung der Namibiafrage (1973–83), zur im Rahmen der Europäischen Politischen Zusammenarbeit betriebenen Sanktionspolitik gegenüber Südafrika (1985/86) sowie zur Politik in Zentral- und Westafrika unter den Vorzeichen regionaler französischer Hegemonie, mit besonderer Berücksichtigung von Togo (1956–67 bzw. 1991–94).
Bd. 2, 2001, 344 S., 25,90 €, br.,
ISBN 3-8258-4709-8

Barbara Praetorius
Power for the People
Die unvollendete Reform der Stromwirtschaft in Südafrika nach der Apartheid
Bd. 3, 2000, 312 S., 25,90 €, br.,
ISBN 3-8258-4772-1

Ulf Engel; Robert Kappel (Eds.)
Germany's Africa Policy Revisited
Interests, images and incrementalism
Although Germany has been a major international player in Africa ever since its readmission to international politics after 1955, suprisingly little has been written about this topic – and even less reliable knowledge has been established. "Germany's Africa policy revisited" firstly poses the need for a review of Germany's relations with the African continent over the past decades. Secondly it presents a challenge to fill in some of the factual gaps which characterize the state of research so far. Thirdly, it calls for scrutiny of some of the theoretical and methodological undercurrents of this past research. The authors that collaborated on this exercise represent a fair mix of academics and practitioners. Their interest and personal involvement in the subject is longstanding. With contributions by Friederike Diaby-Pentzlin, Ulf Engel, Ernst Hillebrand, Rolf Hofmeier, Robert Kappel, Volkmar Köhler, Reinhart Kössler, Stefan Mair, Henning Melber, Andreas Mehler, Peter Molt, Volker Vinnai, and Jürgen H. Wolff.
Bd. 4, 2002, 224 S., 20,90 €, br.,
ISBN 3-8258-5985-1

Schriften der Vereinigung von Afrikanisten in Deutschland (VAD e. V.)

Klaus von Freyhold; Rainer Tetzlaff (Hrsg.)
unter Mitarbeit von Regina Wegemund
Die "afrikanische Krise" und die Krise der Entwicklungspolitik
Bd. 12, 1991, 320 S., 17,90 €, br.,
ISBN 3-89473-080-3

Rolf Hofmeier; Rainer Tetzlaff; Regina Wegemund (Hrsg.)
Afrika – Überleben in einer ökologisch gefährdeten Umwelt
Ergebnisse der Jahrestagung 1991
Bd. 14, 1992, 350 S., 19,90 €, br.,
ISBN 3-89473-074-9

Anna Maria Brandstetter; Gerhard Grohs; Dieter Neubert (Hg.)
Afrika hilft sich selbst
Prozesse und Institutionen der Selbstorganisation
Bd. 15, 1994, 512 S., 30,90 €, br.,
ISBN 3-89473-698-4

Peter Meyns (Hrsg.)
Staat und Gesellschaft in Afrika
Erosions- und Reformprozesse.
Jahrestagung der VAD vom 28.–30. April 1995 in Duisburg
Bd. 16, 1996, 552 S., 35,90 €, br.,
ISBN 3-8258-2461-6

LIT Verlag Münster – Berlin – Hamburg – London – Wien
Grevener Str./Fresnostr. 2 48159 Münster
Tel.: 0251 – 23 50 91 – Fax: 0251 – 23 19 72
e-Mail: vertrieb@lit-verlag.de – http://www.lit-verlag.de

Heike Schmidt; Albert Wirz (Hg.)
Afrika und das Andere
Alterität und Innovation
Afrika und das Andere. Alterität und Innovation. Mit diesem thematischen Schwerpunkt knüpfte die gemeinsame Fachtagung von Afrikanistentag und VAD 1996 an die Diskussion um die Möglichkeiten der kulturellen und sozialen Differenz an, welche im Zeichen von Postkolonialismus und Globalisierung neue Dringlichkeit erreicht haben. Jede Gesellschaft, jede Zeit imaginiert sich ihr Anderes und entwickelt eigene Formen des Umgangs mit diesem Anderen. Wie aber sind afrikanische Gesellschaften in Vergangenheit und Gegenwart mit dem Problem der Alterität umgegangen? Zusätzliche Sprengkraft erhält die Fragestellung, wenn man sich vergewissert, daß der rationale Umgang mit dem Anderen in der Form von Neuem ein Wesensmerkmal der Moderne ist. Sollten afrikanische Gesellschaften in wichtigen Bereichen des gesellschaftlichen Lebens vielleicht moderner sein als die europäischen? Der Sammelband legt Zeugnis ab vom Stand der aktuellen Diskussion, wie er in der 1996er Tagung zum Ausdruck kam. Es melden sich Literaturwissenschaftler und Ethnologen, Soziologen, Agrarwissenschaftler, Religionswissenschaftler, Politologen und Historiker, Theoretiker und Praktiker.
Bd. 17, 1998, 408 S., 30,90 €, br.,
ISBN 3-8258-3395-x

Hans Peter Hahn; Gerd Spittler (Hg.)
Afrika und die Globalisierung
Aus dem Inhalt:
Entwicklung, Wirtschaft und Migration. Organisationskultur und interkulturelles Management in Afrika, *Erika Dettmar;* Cultural Environment, *Olukunle Iyanda;* Wer ist dein Ndugu? Verwandtschaftsbeziehungen in einer tansanischen Fabrik, *Gundula Fischer;* Konsum, Bedürfnisse und materielle Kultur, *Hans P. Hahn und Gerd Spittler;* Kleidung, Eleganz und Macht in Zentralafrika, *Anna-Maria Brandstetter;* Das nubische Lehmhaus in der Savanne Kordofans, *Gerhard Hesse;* Mais-Insima und Milch – Ausdruck von Freiheit und Modernität. Konsumvorlieben in kultursoziologischer Interpretation, *Sabine Tröger;* Zur Ethnologie des Krieges, *Trutz von Trotha;* Genocidal Civil Wars and the Construction of Mythical-Histories: the View from the Great Lakes Region of Africa, *René Lemarchand;* Afrikanische Kriegsherren – Überlegungen zur Entstehung von Gewaltmärkten im präkolonialen und postkolonialen Afrika, *Michael Bollig;* Krieg und Kriegserfahrung im Luwero-Dreieck, Uganda, 1981-1986, *Frank Schubert;* Vom Krieg zum Frieden im Norden von Mali, *Georg Klute*
Bd. 18, 2000, 528 S., 30,90 €, br.,
ISBN 3-8258-4363-7

Schweizerische Afrikastudien – Etudes africaines suisses
herausgegeben von der Schweizerischen Afrika-Gesellschaft (SAG)/édité par la Société suisse d'études africaines (SSEA)

Lilo Roost Vischer; Anne Mayor; Dag Henrichsen (Hrsg./éd.)
Brücken und Grenzen – Passages et frontières
Werkschau Afrikastudien 2 – Le forum suisse des africanistes 2
Bd. 2, 1999, 480 S., 25,90 €, br.,
ISBN 3-8258-4398-x

Yvan Droz; Anne Mayor; Lilo Roost Vischer (Hrsg./éd.)
Partenariats Nord-Sud/Forschungspartnerschaften
Werkschau Afrikastudien 3 – Le forum suisse des africanistes 3
Bd. 3, 2001, 392 S., 30,90 €, br.,
ISBN 3-8258-5688-7

Jürg Schneider; Lilo Roost Vischer; Didier Péclard (Hg./éds.)
Werkschau Afrikastudien 4 – Le forum suisse des africanistes 4
Bd. 4, 2003, 344 S., 24,90 €, br.,
ISBN 3-8258-7208-4

LIT Verlag Münster – Berlin – Hamburg – London – Wien
Grevener Str./Fresnostr. 2 48159 Münster
Tel.: 0251 – 23 50 91 – Fax: 0251 – 23 19 72
e-Mail: vertrieb@lit-verlag.de – http://www.lit-verlag.de